MW01534179

MANJAMPATTI PASSAGE

Boarding School Adventures
in the Hills of South India

by

Charles A. Franklin

MANJAMPATTI PASSAGE

Boarding School Adventures
in the Hills of South India

By Charles A. Franklin

Copyright © 2023 by Charles A. Franklin

All rights reserved.

No part of this publication may be reproduced, distributed, or transmitted in any form or by any means, including photocopying, recording, or other electronic or mechanical methods, without the prior written permission of the publisher, except as permitted by U.S. copyright law.

For privacy reasons, some names may have been omitted. The persons depicted in this book are real people. The events depicted in this book are real events. Some people and events may have been mixed together, and some of the sequencing of events may have been different than the actual occurrence for dramatic effect or because memory fails.

Book Cover Illustration by Bruce Peck

Color Illustrations by Charles A. Franklin

Photographs by Robert Coleman and the Eucy Staff

Second edition, May, 2023

To Bibbi
True Friend, Gentle Soul

Reviews for Manjampatti Passage

Reviews on Amazon from the United States
***** *5.0 out of 5 stars* **Great read!**

 I enjoyed this book and its insight into a time and place that no longer exists. Descriptions of the school and its history were accurate and tales of life in a boarding school were true. While girls were not allowed nearly the freedom the boys had, we did have our own adventures (which shall remain secret). Thanks for the memories, Charlie!
 -Michele Ivy Davis

***** *5.0 out of 5 stars* **Lifelong influence of growing up in a unique missionary boarding school in South India**

 If you're an alum of the school, Charlie's vivid recollection of so many details and the individuals in the student, staff, and Indian communities he names will bring your own memories flooding in. If you're not, you'll gain real insight into what that experience was like and what a powerful influence it had and continues to have on all who have lived, studied, and worked there.
 -Mike

***** *5.0 out of 5 stars* **A must read for anyone interested in boarding school life**

 If you attended Kodai School as I did, you will not want to miss reading this book. And if you are merely interested in what boarding school life was like, you will get a vivid picture from this well written, very readable book. I felt like I was riding the train and hiking the trails right along with the author.
 -Ashley D.

***** *5.0 out of 5 stars* **Beautifully written adventures**

 An amazing and sympathetic coming-of-age book set in the mountains of Southern India. The book evoked many memories of the adventures of our classmates at Kodaikanal, a boarding school. Wonderful descriptions of hiking down the ghats through numerous trials.
 -Susan P. Martin

***** *5.0 out of 5 stars* **Great coming of age adventure**

 A missionary boarding school in South India located in the rough terrain of the Palni Hills, surrounded by jungles, nature preserves,

and rugged peaks. The book focuses on the author's adolescent angst, which culminates in his competing to climb the most mountains around the school, thus gaining self-confidence and the respect of his peers.
-Antoinette S.

***** *5.0 out of 5 stars* **Manjapatti Passage**

The evocations in this book struck chords deep in my heart, it took me back to memories of times lived long ago when there was innocence about everything in life. The characters and the beautiful settings are so pristine and pure. The camaraderie and complicity that only youth can achieve. Enjoyable, easy reading; cute illustrations and photos
-barry

***** *5.0 out of 5 stars* **Honest and engagingly written memoir of a gentler time**

Manjampatti Passage is a colourful and well written coming of age memoir. The writer does a great job of describing his growing up in a less complicated time, but makes careful observations of those times from his present state of wisdom. I enjoyed it thoroughly and recommend it highly. The reader will not be disappointed.
-Chellie Dickinson Reviewed in Canada

***** *5.0 out of 5 stars* **An evocative biography of an American boy growing up in a hill station in India.**

This is an evocative memoir about the life of a boarding school boy in a very special place; - the beautiful hill station of Kodaikanal, South India. It brought back many happy memories of my own experiences as a boy. It is easy to read and has some lovely drawings by the author.
-jonmal Reviewed in the United Kingdom

Reviews on Facebook

Just finished MANJAMPATTI PASSAGE.... read it without stopping... laughed a lot... cried a little.... felt the excitement, the anxiety, the fears, the freedom... and all the 'wonder' that goes into an experience at Kodai School.... either as student, teacher, or family member. I got the relive many wonderful memories of Bibi (Bob) Coleman... one of my all-time favorite students!!
-Bob Granner

Awesome! I LOVE IT! The people and places are meaningful to me, but beyond that, there is a story which has universal appeal. Well done! I would give it TEN stars, not five.
-Bob Edwards

Reviews from eMails

Charlie's memoir "Manjampatti Passage" is an honorable tribute for the memory of our high school class of 1966 classmate Bob or Bibbi Coleman. Bob was a loyal, decent friend and Charlie speaks to his worthy characteristics as a high schooler, including Bob's commitment to precision and to friendship. But Charlie doesn't write only about Bob. He tells about his own passage through life, and he does so with sensitivity, humor, and humility. Even if we can't imagine being sent to a boarding school, this time in Kodaikanal, South India, for the umpteenth time, and having to make friends and fit into a new school over and over, we will learn from Charlie how to endure graciously.
-Joe Rittmann

Reading your book Manjampatti Passage with its nostalgic depiction of your years in Kodai, delighted me.
The excursion to Manjampatti with your companions sharing curious experiences and risks, the frustrated trip to Assam and the parting of friends to follow diverging paths through life, were all endearing. I was fascinated by Bibbi, he is a character that will always stay with me.
-Emma Rau

I have just started reading your book and I am loving it. Are you planning on publishing? It certainly is of that quality...
-Clarice Poirier

Table of Contents

Illustrations

Lake View – 1995 - Color Etching by Bruce Peck......   Cover

***

Foreword

Although set in India, and even though India provides the colors and backdrop to the events that occur, this is not a story about India. It is a story set in a boarding school for expatriates. There are boarding schools all over the world that offer a similar range of experiences, a blend of nature and nurture, of climate and culture, which provide structure and discipline, mentoring and guidance with morality and purpose in beautiful bucolic settings.

This is a story about one such community, Kodaikanal School, of boys and girls and dedicated teachers brought together from a variety of backgrounds and cultures to engage in the process of growing up as moral world citizens. It is the story of a community that nurtures positive growth and development as exemplified by my best friend, Bob Coleman (Bibbi). It is the story of one boy's passage through this community: mine.

Nevertheless, being in India in the first half of the 1960's was unique, and the culture of India does play a major role in this narrative. India's rich cuisine and colonial past are referenced in many of the tales included here.

A number of terms used in the stories might be unfamiliar to the uninitiated, and since I set out to write these tales for my school community, I may not have provided needed interpretations for others. Words, like 'chappals' (flip-flop sandals), 'dhobi' (laundry), 'yenna' (for 'what's up' – literally 'what' in Tamil), 'Gurkha' (security guards recruited from the North Indian Gurkha tribe), 'wallah' (vendor), 'pukka' (genuine), crop up a number of times. Our local slang, such as 'budge' for 'bazaar', 'dish' for 'dispensary' also appears. There are surely other terms whose meanings should become clear through context.

Additionally, a reader should bear in mind that, in its remote setting, Kodaikanal, along with most of South India, was largely spared the upheavals caused by two World Wars and post-Raj Partition of India, and so Kodaikanal School existed relatively peacefully for the sixty-two years since its founding in 1901 until my arrival in 1963. As such the Kodai of this tale can be considered a temporal oasis, mainly unaffected by world affairs.

Soon after my departure in 1966, however, things began to change. In the late '60's India began to restrict visas for foreigners, especially missionaries, and Kodai School began to recruit a wider, more diverse range of students, including Indians and students from other nationalities, many of whom are seeking a pathway to universities around the world. The student body mix of mostly American and Canadian expatriates of my story was significantly altered. Today's students are computer-literate, Google-wise, and plugged in to social media.

Other circumstances caused changes as well: a religious cult invaded one of Kodai's off-campus compounds, taking it over for a number of years; a thermometer factory polluted the lake with mercury, and the population more than doubled. In short, the world and its cares intruded.

The Kodaikanal depicted in this book no longer exists. Kodai School, now known as Kodaikanal International School, still endeavors to turn out moral world citizens, a goal that hasn't changed.

Acknowledgements

Without the encouragement and active participation of a number of people, this book would never have come into existence.

Bob Coleman, known as Bibbi, my high-school roommate, mentor, and lifelong friend, had often remarked in our conversations and reminiscences that we should write down some of the stories that we had lived during our time at Kodai. When he died suddenly after a tragic bicycle accident just before the start of the COVID pandemic, I began to set down some of our adventures.

Mary Coleman Lowry, Bibbi's older sister, found out that I had written and circulated the story about Skinny Dipping in Kodai Lake when a classmate of mine forwarded it to her. She insisted that I allow her to read the rest of the stories, and offered to edit them. Reading a raw narrative and ferreting out typos, grammatical errors, repetitious passages and inconsistencies are tedious tasks. Mary worked selflessly on every page of the original manuscript, and gave me constructive suggestions of how to improve my stories. She came to terms with my descriptions of 'bodily functions' which she found a bit too graphic for her sensibilities. It is due to her tireless attention to detail that this tale is at all readable.

After an early draft, Mary asked me if I would like to borrow the cache of more than one hundred letters that Bibbi had written to his parents from Kodai, especially the ones dealing with the years we shared there. I was, of course, thrilled to have the opportunity to consult this original source, so I said 'Yes!' As I went through them, I found many passages that confirmed my original narrative, but I also found cases in which my memory had failed. Additionally, I found passages that pointed out important episodes that I had omitted. So I embarked on a major revision, correcting details, adjusting time frames, adding episodes. The result is the current iteration of this story, for which I must acknowledge Bibbi himself, and thank his parents, Margaret and William Coleman, albeit posthumously, for saving these letters for more than half a century.

Mary was also instrumental in introducing me to Helen Kline, my content editor, who has guided me through the process of bringing the book into line with literary norms and critiquing the readability and flow of my story, courageously telling me what worked... and what didn't. Helen was Mary's roommate and classmate at Kodai. Helen went on to enjoy two careers: One teaching English as a second language, an occupation that I also followed for a number of years; and one as a professional editor in New York, Minneapolis and Vancouver, where she now lives. Our shared backgrounds and her professional experience make her a natural to work with me on this project.

Paul Heusinkveld came to the Kodai Reunion at Camp Kirchenwald in September of 2017 having just published his Kodai Memoirs in **Elephant Baseball**. He needed a place to stay at the camp, and I had an extra top bunk in the room I had rented. My brother, Johnny, and Bibbi were my other two roommates. He was enthusiastic about the writing process and after several conversations about our backgrounds; he encouraged me to write down my experiences. He declared that everyone has a tale to tell and a book they could write. I didn't think about those words for more than three years, but when I began to write **Manjampatti Passage**, they came back to me. When I later told him I was writing a book, he was enthusiastic and encouraged me heartily.

I worked with Bob Edwards from March to August of 2021 to organize the Celebration of Life for Bibbi. We went over the program and wrote anecdotes to deliver at the event and recruited others to participate. Bob praised my writing and shared the beginnings of his narrative about his life in India, which I look forward to reading when it is complete. As I began accumulating more and more stories, and my anecdote about a hike became a book, Bob helped me with names and background that I had forgotten and gave me constant feedback and encouragement. He is the 'piano checker' in the story of Bibbi's study habits.

John Coleman, Bibbi's brother, reminded me of Bibbi's encounter with an elephant, expanding on some of the details I had learned from Bibbi, and Tim Lomperis, John's classmate who had been with them on the expedition, read my account and declared it essentially accurate, and filled in even more of the particulars of the account.

Lyn Krause was also instrumental in getting some of the details straight and reminding me of episodes that otherwise might have been left out, and reminding me, unnecessarily, of the qualities of a Diplomatic Passport.

Emmy Riber reminded me of some of the details of our drive, which should have been etched in my heart, such as that the flower I gave her was a white orchid, and that I had scaled a rock face to get it for her (and to show off).

Narain Mahtani listened to me read the story about stealing the Communist flag, and the one about becoming lifeguards and suggested some details that I had left out.

Several members of my immediate family read through the manuscript and gave me gentle feedback and suggestions which helped to build some of the stories into more readable shape.

My son, Sebastian, lent me his technical expertise to boost me up the learning curve of self-publishing technology and marketing, which my generation is not prepared for. He also made important suggestions about the more effective sequencing of narrative elements.

My niece, Lisa Sylvester, an Editor for the University of Southern California, gave me valuable input on fonts and graphics.

There are many others who have given me valuable feedback. Thank you. You know who you are.

1. A School in the Hills

Prologue   *Bibbi and I set out on our final, nostalgic walk around Kodai Lake on a brilliant Saturday morning in early May. At 7,000 feet, the mountain air was fresh and clean, and scented with eucalyptus. The May sunshine had softened the morning, so we wore shorts and T-shirts, with chappals (flip-flops) on our feet.*

With the pressure of final exams or choosing universities behind us, the fact that we would soon embark on a journey that would send us to strange cities eight thousand miles away and nearly five thousand miles apart was the only cloud on our horizon. Rather than let the mood turn somber, we joked and bantered about all the times and adventures we had shared since my arrival at Kodai almost exactly three years before.

"Do you remember when you helped me and Johnny carry our stuff down to Wissy?" I asked. "Of all the kids at Kodai, why did you have to be the one passing the office? Why couldn't it have been one of the girls? Maybe then I would have been able to get a girlfriend!"

"Nah!" he replied, laughing. "She'd've run away screaming and just left you standing there with your trunk and duffle bag. Anyway, she wouldn't've been able to take you down to Wissy."

"Yeah, I s'pose you're right... about the 'not being able to take us down to Wissy', not the screaming, I mean."

"And anyway," he said, "she never would have joined you for all the crazy adventures we had. And if you'da been stuck with her, you'd've skipped Tope, Mount Perumal and Manjampatti, just like Kris and Lyn."

"I dunno," I countered, "plenty of girls made it to Tope and Mount Perumal... with chaperones."

"Yeah, but not to Manjampatti, and not from there up to the Caves!"

"Yeah, that was a pretty awesome trek, wasn't it?" I replied. "Remember Linwood falling in the stream and soaking his bible and the toilet paper?"

Bibbi laughed. "I think about that hike all the time. It really was the greatest hike! So many things happened."

As we had often over the past few months, we went back and forth, recalling details and funny events, sometimes with just a word or a phrase, which had occurred on that trail. The events seemed to take on magical qualities, the pleasant memories infused with golden light, the hardships standing out more starkly, and overcoming them more heroic.

Now it was all behind us, and our distant futures waited to open up to us...

Another Country   I arrived in Kodaikanal, Madras State, India in the latter half of May of 1963 after an epic journey nearly halfway around the globe. I was 15 years old, and traveling with my brother, Johnny, who had just turned 14.

We were happily leaving behind our year at Andrew Lewis High School in Salem, Virginia, where we had landed ostensibly to patch together a full school year before our father's next assignment. The real reason we had left our father at his post in Tegucigalpa, Honduras, was because our mother had finally become fed up with his philandering and was leaving him. However, I didn't find this out till years later.

Andrew Lewis High School was a typical Southern, small-college-town institution. Johnny and I were clear outsiders and treated as such. I was beat up in P.E. class by one of the resident bullies, and the P.E. teacher's solution was to offer me the opportunity to don boxing gloves and have a fair fight that he would referee. I declined, and from then on was labeled a chicken. As a result of this experience and others like it, both Johnny and I were relieved when our father's new assignment was posted, and we learned that we would be going to India.

Our mother drove us from Salem, Virginia to Washington, D.C. where we boarded a short flight to New York as unaccompanied minors. As we neared Dulles Airport, Mother lit the last cigarette I would ever see her smoke. All my life she had smoked Chesterfields. I always enjoyed the smell of the first puff when she lit up. She quit cold-turkey soon after that, on her fifty-third birthday. She would join us in India in a month or so, she said, after she had made all the necessary preparations.

Dad had spent Christmas with us in Salem while he was negotiating his next posting with the State Department, and he and Mom had patched things up over the holidays, thank goodness. Otherwise, we would have been stuck in Andrew Lewis High School for at least another year.

The hop from D.C. to New York International took about an hour from gate to gate. In New York, the stewardess from our plane walked us through to the international terminal where we transferred to Pan American World Airways flight 002, the east-bound round-the-world flight. She turned us over to the gate attendant who told us where to wait until it would be time to board our flight. We had about two hours to wait, and nothing to do but sit there, reading the comic books we had brought with us. There were few, if any, restaurants or food stalls in airports, and none in the International Departure lounge, in 1963. Our mother had sent sandwiches with us, which we ate and washed down with water from a drinking fountain located outside the restrooms.

When the time came, another gate attendant came over and checked our tickets and walked us through a doorway and then through the latest modern contraption we had ever seen in all our travels. It was called a "jetway", and it took us directly from the building out to the waiting DC-8. Up till then we had always boarded a plane by climbing a gangway from the tarmac.

When we reached London about seven hours later, most of the passengers deplaned, and a few new ones boarded. In those days, airplanes were rarely full, and we were able to stretch out on two or three seats from time to time, but sleeping wasn't easy: mostly fitful or intermittent napping. We played card games and read comic books a lot. There were some magazines on the plane for passengers, and I read all the jokes in both copies of _Reader's Digest_ I found.

There were several flight crew changes along the way. Our stewardesses from Frankfurt to Tehran were the best, and I remember developing quite a crush on one of them. She seemed to enjoy chatting with us, and brought us apples and other snacks from the first class cabin. In the sixties, air travel was reaching its golden age, and stewardesses were young and good-looking. There weren't any stewards.

We weren't supposed to disembark at any of the stops, but in Teheran, our friendly stewardess took us off the plane with her and walked with us around the terminal. We used some of our travel money to buy a bag of pistachios. It was the only time we left the plane. In due time, she walked us back to the gate and gave us each a hug before sending us through.

For both Johnny and me the flight was a time for reflection. The days since we found out where we were going and leading up to our departure had been filled with frantic preparations. The boarding school we were heading to had sent us an extensive list of items we would need to bring as they were not readily available in India. There were items like rain ponchos, hiking boots, sleeping bags, canteens and backpacks that spoke to the resident activities that we would be expected to join in. There was a list of more domestic items such as sheets, towels, pillows and pillowcases and something called a dhobi bag. From our time in Rangoon, Mother knew that this was a laundry bag. There was an extensive list of clothing we should bring. There was a list of optional items, such as tape players, musical instruments, tennis racquets, and so on. We each got a new footlocker and duffle bag. Our last few days in Salem were a jumble of final exams, doctors' visits, shots and shopping trips.

In contrast to the 'lavish' lifestyle we enjoyed when we were overseas, life in the States was always a time for scrimping. There were no housing allowances, hardship allowances, school allowances, servant staff allowances or other perks that came with overseas assignments. Dad's basic salary was all that we got. So my mother was a genius at saving money and stretching every dollar. She sewed our dhobi bags from an old sheet, and Johnny and I personalized them by embroidering our names on them. She bought one fat pillow for the two of us, which she divided into two skinny ones. She used the rest of the old sheet to make us pillowcases. Every shopping trip was a bargain hunt, looking for the best possible deals on every item on the school lists.

We were on our way to our seventh country since we were born in South America and the eighth school in my K-12 career, Johnny's sixth. The schools we attended were a patchwork of the Good, the Mediocre and the Ugly.

I had attended Mrs. Quinn's Kindergarten in Rangoon, and subsequently moved on to first grade in Mrs. Kirkham's one-room schoolhouse for English-speaking children. My memories of these schools are spotty, but I think they were both positive experiences. I remember making paper lanterns for Light Festival in kindergarten, learning to use dull scissors and edible glue on colored paper. My favorite "teacher" in first grade was Mrs. Kirkham's daughter, Helena, a fourth-grade girl who taught me reading from a second grade primer, while Mrs. Kirkham was busy with second or third graders.

My second, third and fourth grades were at a public elementary school in Herndon, Virginia. The kids treated us like weirdos, and I guess we were. We wore hand-me-down Sears and Roebuck clothes with patches on our knees and elbows, and spoke with "proper" accents as opposed to the local drawl. It took us quite a while to acclimate and develop tenuous friendships which could disappear the moment we said or did something considered 'foreign'. I wasn't any good at most of the sports, so I was relegated to the nerds. The classes were mostly boring, covering things I already knew, so I didn't apply myself (as confirmed by teacher comments on all of my report cards).

I spent my fifth grade at École Saint Joseph in Jerusalem. All classes were in French, except for English class and, possibly, math. The Catholic nuns running the school were very strict, and were generous with their rulers on the knuckles of misbehavers. I loved the school and did very well, finishing first in my English course and third in my French course. The only significant drawback was the bathroom. In 1957, in the heart of Jerusalem, the privy was basically an outhouse in a courtyard with a reeking open pit beneath a wooden plank with holes in it. It was so disgusting to me that I developed a habit of holding my bowels until I got home, only going pee when I absolutely had to.

For some reason, Dad decided that Johnny and I should be sent away to boarding school for my sixth grade and Johnny's fifth grade. I think the justification was that since I was entering Middle School, my courses needed to line up with an American curriculum. My older brother and sister were attending the American Community School in Beirut for that reason. Why Johnny was subjected to heading off to a boarding school even though he was not yet in Middle School is a mystery, although he and I had always been treated as a single person even though he is nearly two years younger than me. In any event, we were packed off to the Friends Boys School in Ramallah, Jordan (now part of the West Bank).

Here I endured the worst school year of my life. Johnny and I were the only two Americans in the Middle School Boys barracks, where we were bullied and sexually accosted frequently. It may have been simply because we were the 'outsiders', but it felt more personal than that. We were the only non-Arab foreigners there. There were boys from Egypt, Syria and Lebanon, as well as Jordanians. Our skin was fairer than most of the boys in the barracks, and we were less assertive, making us interesting prey, I suppose. Being younger, Johnny probably had it worse than I did and made him the butt of many mean comments and nasty looks.

Although we boarded at the Friends Boys School, we didn't study there. Each morning we had to walk with Norman, Amy and Vernon, the children of the American principal of the Friends Boys School, Mr. Smuck, across the town of Ramallah to the Friends Girls School, where we were tutored by a Mrs. Khatib, supposedly in a curriculum that was more attuned to American standards. This detail was not lost on our predatory barracks-mates, and we were often teased about attending the girls' school.

I don't think that Mrs. Khatib was a credentialed teacher, more of a caretaker. The School Principal would stop by at intervals to tell her what she should be teaching us. We studied Arabic and learned to cross-stitch and spent minimal time on English and math.

We were elated, therefore, when, at the end of that year, our parents informed us that we would be leaving Israel to Dad's new posting in Tegucigalpa, Honduras.

I attended seventh and eighth grades at the American School in Tegucigalpa. Due to the mismatch of the school calendars, we arrived in

Honduras with six weeks left in the school year. I was supposed to join in the last month of sixth grade to get acclimated before starting seventh grade.

After my experience in Ramallah, I didn't want anything to do with school, so I began feigning sickness. I would warm a thermometer over a lightbulb when Mother wasn't looking and claim to have a headache. This went on for more than a month. Mother fed me aspirins and took me to see doctors and specialists until one of them found something wrong with my blood counts: Ironically, it seems I am allergic to aspirin.

I think Dad understood that my underlying problem had more to do with depression than illness, and so one day he asked me if I would like to have a horse! From that point on, I loved my time in Honduras. Sugarfoot, a three-year-old mountain pony joined the family. I regained my health and confidence, and (through no fault of the American School), had a thoroughly wonderful time.

I supposedly started ninth grade during my last year in Tegucigalpa, but the American School only went through eighth grade, and offered correspondence courses for ninth and tenth grades. Self-managed schoolwork was not my specialty. There was talk of sending me off to a boarding school in New England, (Middlesex was mentioned, but quickly discarded when it was determined that the State Department would only cover part of the cost), but Mother said that she would take "the boys", meaning me and Johnny, to the States. So we were pulled out of school, again in the middle of a semester, and carted off to Salem, Virginia for a miserable time.

As we flew east on our flight to Southeast Asia, Johnny and I ruminated on these experiences in education. Although we had both hated the Friends Boys School and Andrew Lewis High School, we had differing opinions about our other schools. Johnny had not been as happy in Tegucigalpa as I had, but had had a happier time than I did in Herndon. We were both anxious about what lay ahead for us in India. We were especially concerned about being stuck in another boarding school. We had never really discussed our experience in Ramallah, but I knew that he had been groped in the communal shower, as had I, and been subjected to jokes and cutting comments. He was smaller and younger than I, but I had been too worried about my own treatment to offer him any support through his. Would our new school again put us in this kind of peril? All we could do was hope for the best.

Welcome to India   Our round-the-world flight stopped in London, Frankfurt, Istanbul, Tehran, and finally, for us, in New Delhi, where we landed at around 5:30 in the morning.   There were no jetways in Delhi 1963, so we exited the plane down a gangway some distance from the terminal.   The temperature as the sun rose on that late-May morning was already over 90 degrees Fahrenheit and the air was thick with smog and smells.

After some thirty hours in air conditioning, and eating only coach-class airline food, the heat and miasma struck me like a fist, and I was suddenly assaulted with an urge that had me charging down the gangway and running to find the nearest bathroom.

I Charge Down the Gangway

A smiling policeman in wide khaki shorts over spindly brown legs kindly pointed the way when he connected my incoherent groans to the look on my face. I burst into the indicated room and into the nearest stall.

I was confronted with two stained porcelain footprints, one on either side of a porcelain fixture around a hole in the floor. There was a fair amount of residue in the bowl of the fixture, and several scummy brown stains on the walls where occupants had apparently cleaned messy fingers. The smell was overpowering, but so was my urge, so I planted my feet, dropped my pants, and squatted in immense relief, trying not to release until I was all the way down.

Local Toilet

Squatting there, allowing my own smell to quell the stench of the place, I looked around me. There was a leaky water faucet in the wall on my right with a small green bucket below it, and no toilet paper.

Such was my welcome to India.

I cleaned myself up as well as I could, awkwardly splashing water while squatting, trying not to get my pants too wet. Fortunately, I was wearing blue-jeans, so the water stains weren't that visible. There wasn't any soap or towels, so I rinsed my hands as thoroughly as I could, pouring water from the bucket over them into the bowl. I rinsed the bucket out and poured some more clean water over my hands, flapped them dry, and hoped for the best.

When I was able to leave the restroom and continue into Customs, we were met by an American Embassy person who introduced himself as an old acquaintance of our father's. He was short and balding with a trim mustache, dressed in a light tan suit with a conservative necktie. He assisted us through Customs and the transfer to the Indian Airlines flight that would take us onward to Madras via Hyderabad, where our father, the recently installed American Consul General, would meet us.

Dad's embassy friend laughed when I told him about my bathroom adventure.

"You were shown to the facilities for locals," he chuckled. "You have to request western facilities. They have sit-down toilets and toilet paper, along with sinks for handwashing and an attendant you should tip. However, they were farther away. Whoever showed you to the Indian side must have had a good laugh."

Ha, ha. Very funny, I thought. But I wouldn't have known to tip the attendant and didn't have any local money anyway.

After a short stop in Hyderabad, where the head of the American consular section met our Indian Airlines DC-4 to greet us and gave us a basket of fruit to carry to our dad, we landed in Madras at around noon. Dad was there to pick us up and walk us through the local formalities. We were loaded into the official Consul General's car with flags flying from the posts on the hood and whisked through the crowded streets to the official residence. Somehow our arrival and Dad's trip to pick us up had been designated "official consular business", which allowed the chauffer to fly the flags.

We had three days to recover from jet lag at the Consul General's residence (our new vacation home), Agnur, at Number 7, Pycroft Garden Road in Madras. Agnur was a beautiful colonial era high-walled villa with a carport and a large open great room with ten-foot-high ceilings and whirring fans. We were given a sumptuous late lunch, consisting of mulligatawny soup followed by roast beef with mashed potatoes and salad, and taken to our shared air-conditioned bedroom suite where we were allowed to shower and sleep off our jetlag. It took two full days for me to adjust to Indian Standard Time so that I was able to rise at a normal morning hour after sleeping through the night. I spent my waking hours exploring the grounds and reading the novels I had brought with me to read on the plane.

There were four servants in the house who lived in the servants' quarters off the kitchen. Joseph was the head bearer and Das was the second boy. Joakim was the cook, and there was a sweeper woman who took care of all the "untouchable" jobs. Outside there were two gardeners, Krishnan, the chauffer, and Ram Singh, the Gurkha night watchman.

After just one full normal day, Dad and the Consulate driver, Krishnan, drove us southwestwards across Madras State (Tamilnadu, in current nomenclature), this time without the flags flying. We stopped in Trichinopoly (Tiruchirappalli in Tamil), at around two or three in the afternoon, and visited the Sri Ranganathaswamy Temple and the Rock Fort Temple, before checking in to a guest house where we spent the night. Krishnan slept in the car.

Following breakfast in the morning, we continued our journey. We drove for about two and a half hours to the city of Madurai, where Dad wanted us to see the Meenakshi Temple. He had heard about it from many of his colleagues when they heard he was taking us to Kodai, and declared it a must-see monument. We toured the temple in bare feet, which we had learned to do at the Shwedagon Pagoda in Burma. The foot-polished stone walkways were velvety soft and cool as long as they were in the shade. After an hour, though, Johnny and I had had enough, so we returned to the car and continued on to the Western Ghats, and the small Hill Station of Kodaikanal.

With no radio in the car, Dad decided that this would be a good time to give us a history lesson about the school he was sending us to. He was quite proud of himself for having studied up on all the alternatives and selecting the school he thought would be best for us. He had reviewed the American School in New Delhi, which he deemed hot and dusty, but it had a reputation for poor behavior among the students, including drug use and promiscuity. After my experience at the Delhi Airport with the heat and smog, I was thankful that he had discarded that option.

Woodstock School, in the Himalayan foothills near the hill-station town of Mussoorie, was another one he looked at, but found that it would take quite a trek to get us there, and didn't offer any advantage over

Kodai, where we were now headed. Besides, Woodstock would have been outside of his consular district, so he would be unlikely to visit us there.

The Ghat Road

"A hill station," he told us, "is an invention from the time of the British Raj; a place where westerners can retreat to, to escape the oppressive heat of the hot dry season on the plains. "More than a hundred years ago," he told us, "American missionaries in South India began to explore the Palani Hills around the city of Madurai where they had their headquarters in search of cooler climate to establish a sanitarium for their members who came down with malaria or dysentery, or other tropical illnesses that nowadays are prevented by all the shots you had before you came. They learned that the British had established Hill Stations to which they retreated during the searing months of April, May and June.

"They discovered the village of Kodaikanal and found that their children thrived in the cooler weather. The idea of a year-round school in the heights would be a healthy option and give them a place to retreat from the heat from time to time.

"The idea was kicked around for more than fifty years," he went on, "but finally, at the turn of the century, they found a candidate for headmistress and established the school in a local hotel 1901. Later they bought the hotel and some land around it, where you are going to study now.

"At first everything had to be carried by coolies up a stony winding path called a Coolie Ghat. Ladies would be carried up in palanquins, and gentlemen would walk up or ride mules. Eventually the British engineered a properly graded road, which, though much longer, allowed motor vehicles to climb the hill. That's the road we'll be driving up today. It's still called a Ghat Road."

As we were traveling in May, we were in the very middle of the hot season, and only the air conditioning in the car was keeping us comfortable. I was glad that we were headed for a cooler place, and I hoped that the climate would be similar to that of Tegucigalpa, Honduras. At ten degrees north latitude, Kodai was closer to the equator than Tegucigalpa by about four degrees, but it was also about 4,000 feet higher.

The total population of 'Kodai' (our shortened version of Kodaikanal) in the 1960's was somewhere in the range of twelve to fifteen thousand people. That's just my best guess, as the statistics are not readily available, but it was a very small place. Kodai life followed the rhythms of a typical rural village, which well suited the School's schedule. People would rise early to begin their day's labors, taking advantage of the daylight. Many homes and even some businesses had no electricity or running water in those days. The School was probably the biggest entity, as well as the largest employer, in the town, and everyone knew where it was.   Krishnan paused a few times to ask for instructions, and we soon arrived at the main gate.

Arriving at Kodai School   Our arrival in Kodai was unremarked since the School had completed the scholastic year a week or two earlier and summer break activities were in full swing. Also, it was a Saturday. May is the hottest month on the plains, and many of the students and their parents were enjoying the relative cool of the surrounding mountains. The school was sponsoring concerts, plays and rummage sales put on by staff and parents to raise funds that subsidized the tuition of deserving students and worthy school activities.

We went with Dad into the school office, where we were checked in and basic arrangements were made. The school Bursar, Mr. Leonard, who received us, told Dad that the school recommended a monthly allowance of ten rupees per student, but that the maximum allowable was twenty rupees. Dad went with the higher number (after a bit of lobbying from us). Twenty rupees was the equivalent of about four U.S. dollars in 1963, making each rupee worth less than 25 cents, so even that amount seemed insufficient to us. But then, Dad explained that twenty rupees a month was more than many working people in India made.

Once the financial dealings were done, we were shown into Mr. Cassidy's office. He was the school Counselor, and one of the few Americans working on campus that day. The rest of the staff, he said, were off enjoying the ongoing activities that were winding up. He and Mr. Leonard were only in the office because they had been told that we would be arriving.

Mr. Cassidy was a thin, bespectacled balding man with a large Adam's apple, a goofy smile, and a weak chin. I would have cast him as Ichabod Crane in a play about the headless horseman. He asked Dad for our report cards from our last schools and looked them over. He wasn't very impressed, I don't think, as our grade averages had always been shaky. Moving from school to school every few years was not conducive to maintaining good grades.

He took some notes and consulted some charts, and then wrote out schedule cards for each of us. I was going to be taking Biology even though I had failed the Science course at Andrew Lewis, so I would be with the tenth-grade group for all of my classes.

"I'm sorry I don't have a map of the campus to give you," he said, "but I'm sure the other students will help you find your way around."

With registration formalities out of the way, we were free to go settle ourselves in to the dormitory.

Parents were not allowed into the dormitories since school was technically back in session, so Dad left us with our footlockers and duffle by the main office and headed off with Krishnan to the nearby Carlton Hotel where he would spend the night.

"I'll pick you up here at the Flag Green over there at around six o'clock for dinner at the Carlton. See you in a couple of hours." He waved and walked off to where Krishnan was waiting at the car.

Johnny and I were then escorted down to Wissahickon Dormitory (Wissy) by a passing student that the bursar collared.

"Hoy, you, sar," Mr. Leonard called to the student, in his clipped Indian accent. "Oh, Bob, be a good chap and show these Franklin boys down to Wissy. They've just arrived."

The kid was about our age, and gave us a wide, welcoming smile. "Hi! My name is Bob, but everyone calls me 'Bibbi'," he said. "Here, I'll help you with your gear."

He was taller than me, lanky and wiry. He was dressed in shorts and T-shirt with flip-flops on his feet. He had a messy shock of brown hair, and large, dark-rimmed glasses. The eyes behind the glasses were grey or blue, depending on the light.

"Hi. I'm Charlie, and this is my brother, Johnny," I replied.

"What grades are you in?" he asked.

"I'm in tenth and Johnny is in ninth," I replied. "What about you?"

"I'm in tenth, too. Where are you guys from?" There it was, again. The question that was so hard to answer.

Luckily, Johnny spoke up before I could start my complicated answer and said simply "We're from the States. What about you?"

"I'm from the States too, but I was born here and have lived here most of my life. My folks came to India a long time ago. We get back to the States once in a while," he answered. "We'd better get going."

Bibbi shouldered our duffle bags, and Johnny and I lifted our footlockers for the walk down to the dormitory.

As we walked along, Bibbi began telling us about Kodai, pointing out the various offices and dormitories that we passed on our way down the hill to Wissy.

"Over there, that building is the Library. All the main campus high-school boarders go there for Study Hall every weeknight from seven to nine. You do your homework or read if you're all caught up. And you can use the time to write your weekly letter to your parents. If you get any demerits, you serve time there between nine and ten." He went on, "That building is the Quad, where we have most of our classes. That's the back of the gym, and these are the piano practice rooms… and that's Phelps Hall where the younger boys room."

Our New Friend, Bibbi

"Wait a second," I interrupted. "What's 'a demerit'?"

"Oh," he replied, "it's a bad mark given for breaking rules. One demerit costs you a half hour of detention. You get them for swearing, skipping class, missing study hall or lights out, throwing food in the cafeteria, you know, anything that breaks the rules."

We saw the lake through a stand of eucalyptus trees, and he pointed out the Boat House, which was doing brisk business with all the high season tourists. A number of boats that I recognized as punts from our time in Burma, flat-bottomed square-tipped craft, were scattered across the water, each with two or three people wielding oars with varying degrees of skill.

A covered walkway took us down a long hill towards the lake. There were steps down unevenly spaced every three to four feet or so, so that one had to watch to meet each one in stride. I kept awkwardly craning my neck to see over my footlocker and adjusting the length of my strides at each step, but Bibbi seemed to take them all in stride, never looking down. The buildings to either side of the walkway were made of native stone and had red tile roofs.

"You'll get used to these steps," he said, noticing my struggles. "We go up and down them at least four times a day. We think that the workers who built them were drinking toddy on the job."

"What's toddy?" I asked.

"Palm liquor. It's illegal here, but they get it somehow," he laughed.

When we got to the bottom of the walkway, we turned right into an open hallway with doors on one side and a central courtyard on the other. Bibbi took us to meet the Housemother of Wissy, Mrs. Daisy Gibbs.

We walked across a grassy space to the far end of the building and set our trunks and duffle bags on top of a two-foot tall wall that lined a walkway. Bibbi knocked on a glass-paneled door, which was presently opened.

Mrs. Gibbs was a straight-backed, elderly lady straight out of a Victorian novel. She was stout, with a large figure, and was dressed in a purple dress that came to her mid-calf and buttoned up the front. She wore support hose on what could be seen of her legs. She had on a ruffled high-necked white blouse and her hair was piled on top of her head. Her face was weathered, and she had a ready smile as she welcomed us to her cottage, which was attached to one end of the 'W' that formed the dormitory. She spoke with fruity English-accented vowels and used very proper language. (I later discovered that when she got agitated or angry with "her boys", her voice would rise into a shrill falsetto.)

"Hello, Robert. Thank you. Who have you brought me here? Hello, boys. My name is Mrs. Gibbs. You must be the Franklin boys. Is that right?"

"Yes, Ma'am," I replied, trying to imitate her smile.

After consulting her list, she gave us our room numbers.

"Charles, you'll be in Room Four. You'll be with Steve for now, but it might change. I'm waiting for some requests from upper classmen. You're in tenth grade, aren't you? He's in eleventh, but that should be alright if he doesn't request someone else. Most of the other tenth-graders are paired up. He's not there right now, but you may leave your things on the empty cot. And John, you'll be in Room Eight with Robert here. He's your same age, even though he's in tenth grade. Welcome to Wissy. Let me know if you need anything. I am usually here. Robert can show you to your rooms, thank you, Robert."

Daisy Gibbs Makes Her Points

And she turned to go, seemingly in a hurry to return to whatever she had been doing when we knocked. Bibbi cleared his throat. "Mrs.

Gibbs, I think they'll need some toilet paper," he said. I wouldn't have known to ask, assuming that it would be available in the bathroom.

"Oh, dear," she replied, "how thoughtless of me! I'll be right back," and she swung around back into her cottage, to emerge in a moment with two rolls of Premier Toilet Tissue which she handed, one to each of us.

"Use this wisely, boys," she said. "You can get some more in a couple of weeks."

Based on our experiences at the boarding school in Ramallah when we were ten and eleven years old, Johnny and I had trepidations about our pending circumstances at Kodai. We stood looking at each other, realizing that we would be in separate rooms with strangers for roommates, at least in my case. I thought that Johnny was lucky. Bibbi seemed to be warm and friendly. I could only hope that my roommate and our reception by the rest of the kids in the dorm would be as friendly.

A Tour of Wissy and Kodai School Bibbi must have sensed our nervousness and seemed to go out of his way to put us at ease.

"Follow me. You guys are lucky. I know your roommate, Charlie, and he's both a good guy, quiet, and like... friendly," he ventured. "He's been here for a few years, so he'll be able to help you settle in."

He led us to our assigned rooms, first to mine, which was in the middle of the left leg of the 'W', and then to his and Johnny's which was in the base of the 'W'. We were relieved that we would each have only one roommate.

There were two beds and two armoires in each room. The other students had already been in, and Bibbi pointed out which bed I would get, and which armoire to store my things in, before heading off to show Johnny his room.

The bunk he pointed to was visible as soon as the door to Room 4 was opened. "That's the open bunk in here. I guess Steve already put his sheets on the other one and took the left-hand closet. You can lock your side with a padlock if you want to, but most kids don't. Just keep any valuables or private stuff, especially your toilet paper, locked in your footlockers under your bed." The room was about eight by twelve feet, with two cots lined against the longer walls. The floor was the same polished concrete as the hallway, and the walls were whitewashed cement. The ceilings were about eight feet high, and there was a small window in the back wall opposite the door. Even in the warmth of the May day, there was a chill coming off the floor and the walls.

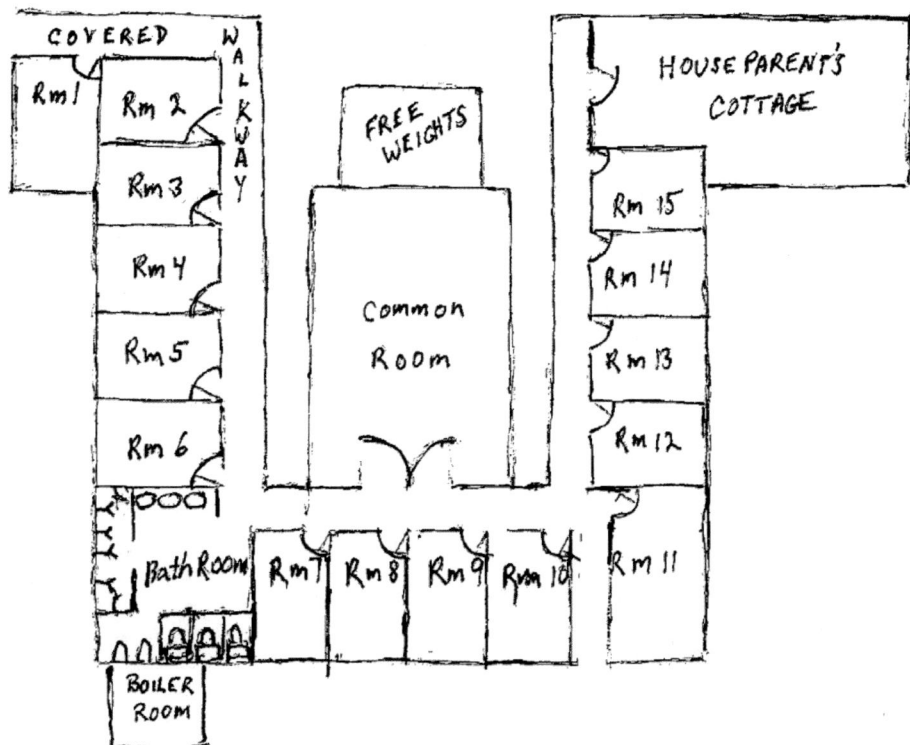

Wissahickon (Wissy) - High School Boys Dorm

I inspected the bunk Bibbi had pointed out to me. It was basically a frame of two-by-fours attached to four four-by-four posts painted with forest-green glossy paint. There were wide canvas straps, or rather one long strap, looped round and round and stretched over the frame in both directions, with the straps on the top side woven under and over each other creating a tight woven grid. On top of this, there was a striped canvas mattress bag about four inches thick, filled with a substance I later discovered was coir fibers, that is, the coarse fibers harvested from pounded coconut husks, which was held in place by about twelve buttons on each side of the mattress. (I often awoke mornings with a button shaped indentation somewhere on my body.) The whole thing seemed fairly sturdy but didn't look very comfortable.

It wasn't till my junior year that I was shown (again by Bibbi) that it was possible to untie the canvas straps and tighten them in order to counteract the normal loosening and stretching that occurred over time that caused the mattress to sag at the middle. This also had the salutary effect of tightening the whole frame, which, when paired with a little bit of ghee in the cracks, reduced or eliminated many squeaks and creaks.

When we had dropped off and stowed our gear, Bibbi took us on a quick tour of Wissy. The rooms were the outer legs and bottom of a squared "W". Room 1 was at the tip of left end of the W, and was the only room whose door didn't face toward the center of the W. The Housemother's cottage formed the tip of the right end. The rooms opened onto a covered concrete walkway lined with a stone wall about two feet tall. The center leg of the W was a large common room with a ping pong table in the center, and ringed by mismatched sofas and chairs. There was a large fireplace at the top end of the common room leg.

The fireplace was bracketed by doors out onto a covered patio occupied by an array of body-building weights and benches. The lake was visible straight ahead.

"This is where we have our dorm meetings. We have them once a week. I think Peter Hoffman or John Aung-Thwin is gonna be president this year. They are seniors, and it's almost always a senior. Mrs. Gibbs sets the agenda and runs most of the meeting, though," Bibbi informed us. "She only leaves after she runs her agenda, and then we can take care of our own business. That's when you'll be initiated.

"All new students will have to go through initiation here. Um, don't worry, though, it's not that bad, hah, hah," he laughed, seeing our worried looks. "You have to swear to obey Wissy rules and obey upper classmen when they give you orders. And then they stamp you on your butt with a rubber stamp. You get a certificate, and that's it."

CERTIFICATE OF NATURALIZATION

This certifies that *Charles A. Franklin* has undergone the traditional course of naturalization. He now enjoys all the privileges of a full citizen of WISSAHICKON.

naturalized in (place) *Wissy Social Room*

On the *Butt*, at *8:44* ..... June *24*, 19 3.

(Seal)

Certificate of Initiation

In due course, a couple of weeks later, we were duly inducted along with the rest of the ninth graders and new students.

"The bathroom is over this way," he led us back through the common room and into the hallway. "It can get pretty busy after P.E. and before canteen. And seniors can be touchy about lower classmen getting in their way, so you want to wait till they're out of the way if you can."

The bathroom was a large room at the base of the left leg of the W with three stalls containing, I was relieved to see, Western toilets with overhead flush tanks, and two urinals along one wall, an open shower area with six shower heads along the back, and five sinks along the third wall.

Bibbi was full of information and advice for us. He let us know that the boiler that supplied hot water for showers was only lit on Wednesday and Saturday afternoons, so everyone could shower between four and six until the hot water ran out. Otherwise, you could have a cold shower whenever you wanted. As underclassmen we were expected to let seniors and juniors shower first on hot water days, so we often got only lukewarm showers.

The toilet paper that Mrs. Gibbs had given us was all we would get for two weeks, so we needed to ration it out accordingly or buy a roll in the market. The weekly dorm meetings were held in the common room on Monday nights. Wake-up was at six thirty; breakfast was at seven; and classes started at eight. Lunch was from noon to 1; classes ended at three; teatime was at four followed by P.E. at four-thirty. Supper was at six, followed by study hall from seven to nine. Lights out was at ten. Of course, all of this information flowed over us without sticking, but with experience over the next couple of weeks and many repetitions, they became the rhythm of our lives.

The orientation tour over, Bibbi asked us if we wanted to go around to Bendy Field. "Do you want to go watch the staff versus student baseball game? It was supposed to start earlier, but it got delayed and should be starting soon. The students usually cream the staff, but this year the staff team has a couple of really good players. Almost everyone is going to be there. I'll introduce you to some of the other kids and to some of the staff," he promised.

With nothing else to do until it was time to meet our dad at the Carlton Hotel for supper, Johnny and I went along with Bibbi across the campus to the sports fields, while he pointed out the places on campus that would soon become so familiar to us: the Quad, the cafeteria, the flag green, the chapel, the girls' dorm (Kennedy); crossing the entire hill upon which the campus perched. We had to cross Carlton Road to get to

Bendy Field, where the games were taking place, and Bibbi pointed out the hotel where we would be going to have dinner with Dad.

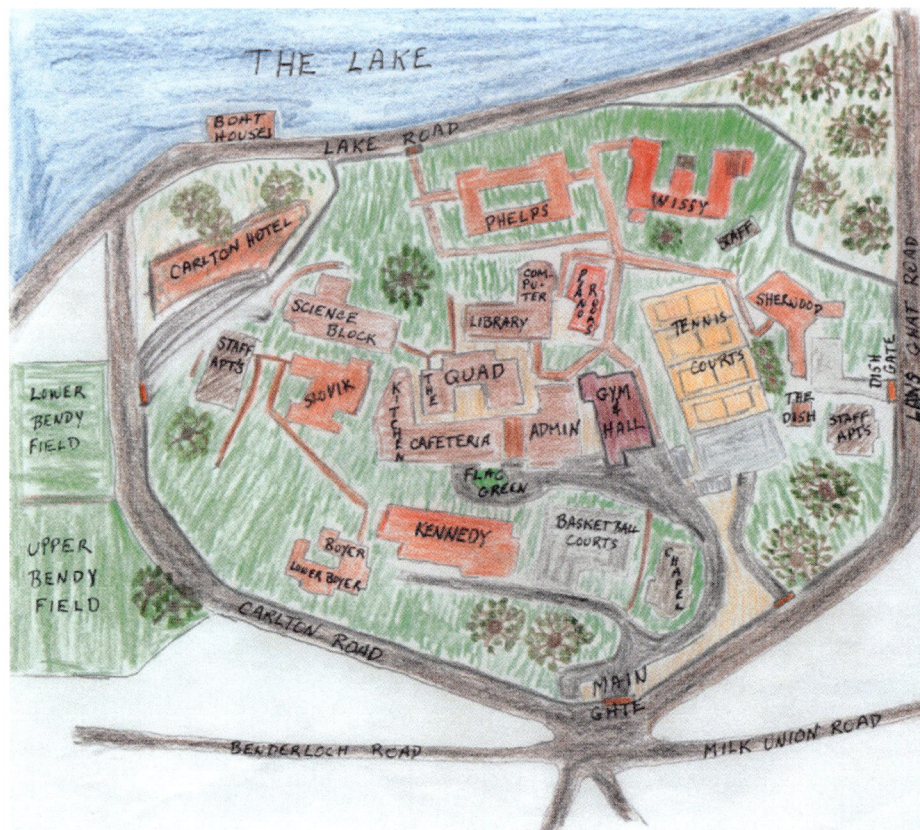

Map of Kodai School Campus

Local residents and tourists, mostly Indian, were lining the wall along the side of Carlton Road overlooking the field. The majority of those gathered were men wearing white dhotis, and there were a few women wearing brightly colored saris. A few of the men wore western suits, and there were a couple of policemen in wide khaki shorts and shoulder belts over khaki shirts.

Bendy Field, overlooking the lake, is divided into two levels; Upper Bendy, which has a large field for soccer and football surrounded by an oval track; and Lower Bendy, which has a softball diamond and other track and field venues for long jump, high jump, pole vault and so on. The parents and staff were playing softball on Lower Bendy, so we walked to the edge of Upper Bendy where a lot of the students were gathered, to watch. As we approached, Bibbi was greeted with enthusiasm, and he began introducing us around.

Very few of the names I was given stuck with me for long, and I would take several more days to learn them. Kris Riber, a tall, blond kid with a broad and friendly face, and Lyn Krause, also tall and blond with pink cheeks (and the principal's son), were in tenth grade with us. There were several girls as well, but as I was then very shy with girls, I couldn't now tell you who they were. Bibbi also made a point of introducing me to his sister, Mary, who was starting her senior year, and John, his brother, who had just graduated.

Bibbi had great admiration for John and introduced us to him with great courtesy. "This is my big brother, John. He just graduated and is on his way back to the States to go to college."

John was a tall, well-groomed person with neat, sandy-colored hair and clothes that one and only time when I met him. He gave us a friendly grin and shook our hands before turning back to the boy he had been talking to.

Bibbi later would often tell us about some of the things John had done or heard about at Kodai. John Coleman soon became a legendary figure in my mind. The image of him on the bluff over Lower Bendy, neatly dressed and combed stayed in my mind as I listened to Bibbi's stories about him, no matter how incongruous the image was to the thrust of the story.

I suspect that some of the exploits Bibbi attributed to John may have been undertaken by classmates or may have been handed down and exaggerated from previous classes' tales and legends. Some stories dealt with clandestine meetings with girls, staging panty-raids on the girl's dormitory and running their panties up the flag pole on the flag green; breaking in to various locked spaces, and so forth.

That said, Bibbi and I replicated a number of the escapades attributed to John that Bibbi recounted, so maybe they were all true. Though innocent enough for the most part, they were often daring, and could have ended in tragedy and a black eye for the School. That didn't bother us at the time, but looking back… What were we thinking?!

The baseball game on Lower Bendy Field ended as the sun was dipping toward dusk. Johnny and I were supposed to meet our dad by the Flag Green, so we returned to campus across Carlton Road and up through the Bendy gate. Bibbi stayed with his friends at the field, busily chatting with Kris and Lyn as we left. He waved and said he would see us later at Wissy.

A Parting Gift   Dad and Krishnan were already at the Flag Green when we arrived. We had made a couple of false turns on our way back through the campus and had to retrace our steps, which made us a little late. The drive took us right back to where we had been, except now we drove into the Carlton driveway.

The Carlton was a relic of the British Raj, with an elegant portico and high ceilings and white-gloved attendants. We were shown into the dining room with linen-draped tables and more attendants. It was early for dinner, and only one other table was occupied, so we chose a table by a window overlooking the lake.

Dinner was a fixed menu, starting with a bowl of consommé, followed by a fish course and then a meat course with sorbet between courses, and ending with stewed prunes. It wasn't my favorite meal, but it was good and filling.

"Well, boys," said dad, "Enjoy your last feast. I don't think you'll be getting this kind of food at School. School kitchens are not famous for their food." He chuckled. "By the way, I stopped in the bazaar this afternoon and set up an account for you at Hamidia's Sundries. You can't go wild, but you can get soap and toothpaste there, and an occasional snack or chocolate bar."

"Wow, thanks, Dad!" I said.

"Yes, but don't go around bragging about it at School. I don't think many of the other boys have accounts there, and I don't know if the School has any policy about it. Sometimes it's better not to ask," he said.

I decided that I would find out how to get to Hamidia's the next chance I had to see what the shop carried. Bibbi would show me how to get there, I hoped.

Dinner and last goodbyes over, Dad left us back at the Flag Green before eight o'clock. He would be leaving for Madras at first light. It was dark, and there weren't many lights on campus. The covered walkways had dim bulbs every forty feet or so, but the buildings were dark in the cafeteria, Quad, and Library. Thanks to Bibbi's tour earlier, though, Johnny and I found our way down the hill to the dormitory.

The common room was lit, and there were boys playing ping pong, and others sitting around chatting. Bibbi was there, and welcomed us in. We soon got over any shyness we felt and joined in conversations, although many of the topics involved places and people that we didn't know. The atmosphere was friendly and convivial. There was a discernible hierarchy, with upper classmen at the top, but no bullying or coercion such as we had felt at our last boarding school.

By around nine-thirty, everyone started drifting off to their rooms to get ready for bed. Lights out was at ten, and the next day, Sunday, we would all dress up and go to church after breakfast. I went to my room and met Steve, my eleventh-grade roommate. He was a tall kid with sharp features and a serious demeanor. He greeted me with a slight air of superiority, possibly not happy with being paired with a lower classman. He nevertheless helped me settle in, letting me know where to keep my stuff, and warning me to stay in my side of the room. He then went with me to the bathroom to brush our teeth.

Soon enough, the gong for lights out was struck, and I slipped into my lumpy, hay-filled cot, and settled in for my first night at Kodai.

I didn't realize that first night, how deeply I would be influenced by Kodai, or how closely my life would be tied to the people and places I would discover over the next three years. Up to now, most memories and experiences were fleeting, easily sloughed off by moving to a new country. I had left people and places behind with regrets, but those were soon dissipated and overlaid with new experiences, new people, new places. We had left our family dog, Tito, behind in Argentina when I was four; more recently, we had left another family dog, Poli, behind in Honduras, which we all regretted, but somehow accepted. I had left my beloved horse, Sugarfoot, in Honduras as well. To this day I don't know how I recovered from that blow, but I know that my immersion in Kodai helped.

Lying there, that first night, with the chill mountain air creeping into my bed with me, along with the discomfort of altitude sickness, I couldn't help feeling somewhat adrift and afraid. Once more, for now the eighth time, I was faced with new circumstances that I would have to deal with. I would have to build new friendships, get used to new routines, adapt to a different climate, different food, different accents.

By nature, I am an optimist. I have always faced a change as an opportunity more than as a threat. There had been times in my life when I looked forward to changes, as when we left Ramallah and moved to Honduras. There my optimism had been reinforced by my joyful adventures with my horse, Sugarfoot. I had looked forward to going to Salem, Virginia, with Mom, but had been disappointed. I found myself hoping that Kodai would somehow be like Honduras; that I would find the joy I had experienced while riding around the countryside on horseback.

However, in the darkness of that strange room, with the strange new smells and sounds carried by the thin mountain air, my fears began to rise up around me in the gloom. Only the generous welcome that Bibbi had offered me and Johnny that first day nourished a small flicker of hope, that I clung to, and I fell sound asleep.

2. Dorm Life

Learning the Ropes I awoke at dawn to the sound of the same gong that had signaled lights out. Steve was already up and on his way out the door in his underwear with his towel and a toothbrush. His bed was already made. I quickly took off my pajamas and put on my underwear, grabbed my towel, my bar of soap and my toothbrush and followed his example.

There were already several boys in the bathroom, and I was relieved to see that Bibbi was among them. He was standing to one side with his towel over his shoulder waiting for one of the sinks or urinals to open up. However, when one did, he looked around and waited for another boy who had just come in to take it.

"It's all yours, Bernie," he said to the boy.

He saw me looking at him with a confused expression, wondering why he had let the other kid get ahead of him. He smiled and said, in a low voice, "You have to let the upperclassmen go first."

"Why?" I asked.

"That's just the way it is," he replied. "It's tradition, I guess. You'll be happy next year when we're upperclassmen... especially when we get to have showers first with hot water."

"Okay… but how do I know who's an upperclassman? I don't know most of these guys yet. That guy you let go ahead is shorter than you, so just letting tall people go first won't work," I noted.

"Yeah, I get that, but you'll know who's who in a few days. There, that sink is open, go ahead." Bibbi said.

Thanking him, I stepped up to the sink and turned on the hot water tap. I stood waiting for the water to warm up to wash my face, but Bibbi poked me. "There's no hot water at this hour. You have to use cold."

"Oh," I remembered what he had told us on our tour, "there's only hot water on Wednesday and Saturday."

"Right," he agreed, "and it's only hot in the afternoons."

I splashed the freezing water on my face and soaped quickly. Rinsing was almost painful, but it felt really bracing, and I liked it. I splashed some water on my hair and smoothed it down with my fingers before brushing my teeth.

Bibbi had found another sink and was working through his morning routine. I moved over to an empty urinal after checking that no one else seemed to be heading for it. The brand on the urinal said 'Shanks'. "You're welcome!" I thought, as I relieved myself.

As I was finishing, Bibbi came and stood in front of the urinal next to me. "I'll wait for you to go up to breakfast if you hurry," he said.

"Great!" I exclaimed, thankful that I wouldn't be on my own. "I'll get dressed and be out in two minutes!"

I hurried back to my room, and arrived to find Steve putting on his shoes. I hurriedly grabbed a shirt and threw a pair of jeans on my bed as I stuffed my arms into the sleeves.

"Wow, you look like you're in a hurry," observed Steve.

"Yeah, I'm going to head up to breakfast with Bibbi, and I don't want to make him wait," I replied.

"Okay, but don't forget to make your bed and straighten up your closet before you go. If our room is messy, Gibbsy will give us both demerits, not just you. She usually checks our rooms while we're at breakfast. I'll be really pissed off if I get a demerit because of you." Steve gave me a hard look.

In reality, I hadn't been thinking about making my bed before heading up, thinking that I could put it off till later, but I said, "Oh, yeah, I was going to."

By the time I finished dressing, making my bed and straightening up my closet, Bibbi was sitting on the wall in front of my door.

"Sorry," I said. "I didn't realize I was going to have to make my bed and hide my pajamas before heading up."

"Oh, yeah," he laughed. "Even though it's Sunday, Mrs. Gibbs will prob'ly check our rooms, especially since it's kinda the first day, and she can catch a lot of the new kids. She might not give out demerits yet, only warnings, but you never know. Me, I make my bed while I'm still in it, sorta. If you ease out of it and smooth the blankets and sheets as you go, all you've gotta do is tuck in the sides. You'll learn."

"Yeah," I said. "Seems like I've got a lot to learn… make my bed, straighten up, bow to upperclassmen… I better stick close to you for a while so I don't put my foot in it."

"Yeah, don't worry," he smiled. "I'll keep you out of trouble."

"Are we waiting for Johnny?" I asked. Since Johnny was Bibbi's roommate, I figured he would join us.

"Nah," Bibbi replied, "he said he's not hungry and wanted to stay in bed a while more." He sounded a little disappointed.

"Yeah," I joked, "he likes his beauty sleep."

"He's a funny guy. He stayed up after lights out reading a comic book under his covers. And he leaves his underwear and his shoes in the middle of the floor."

"Tell me about it. I've been sharing rooms with him for years." I replied. "He can be annoying."

We were moving down the hallway past the other rooms toward the covered walkway leading up to the center of the campus. Bibbi started to trot.

"Are we late?" I asked.

"No," said Bibbi, "it's just easier to run up these stairs. If you walk, you catch every stair with the same foot, but if you run up, you can catch most of them with alternating feet. Here, watch me." He jogged toward the first riser and leapt from step to step with long, loping strides. He stopped about four steps up and told me to try it.

I jogged forward, imitating his technique, and found that I was indeed able to meet each riser with alternating feet. However, after the third or fourth step I found myself gasping for breath.

"All right! Let's go!" he cried, and set off again.

I tried to keep up, but found that after a few more strides I had to stop to catch my breath. Bibbi looked back and waved me to come on, but I held up my hand and panted. He came back down to where I was leaning against a post.

"I guess you're not used to the altitude yet. In a couple of days you'll be able to fly up these steps," he said. "We'll walk up the rest of the way."

"Thank you," I panted, and we continued at a slower pace up the walkway. He was right; by walking we caught every step with the same foot so that only one leg was doing the lifting. As we walked up, several of the other guys from the dorm ran by us. I could tell that Bibbi was eager to get to breakfast, and tried to hurry. By the time we reached the Quad I was panting.

"I really need to get used to this altitude!" I exclaimed, glad to have an excuse for my weakness.

In the dining room we found seats at a table with Kris and a boy Bibbi introduced as 'Hammo'. I later learned that his real name was Bob Hammond. Local staff wearing white uniforms and caps brought a plate of pancakes for us to share out. There was a bowl of molasses Bibbi called jaggery syrup and a bowl of thick cream and another of oily peanut butter to top them with.

"I love pancakes!" Bibbi exclaimed, pulling two from the stack onto his plate. He proceeded to slather one of them with peanut butter, put the other one on top and spoon molasses over them. He topped the creation with a generous dollop of cream and dug in.

I took two pancakes in my turn, but I just put molasses on mine. Kris and 'Hammo' mimicked Bibbi loading up their pancakes.

I was quite satisfied with my breakfast, but when Bibbi was done with his, he flagged down one of the staff and said "Hey, Jackie, are there any more pancakes?"

"I will check," replied the man Bibbi called Jackie, and went off. He returned a few minutes later with a plate with three pancakes on it.

Bibbi looked at us to see how we were reacting to the gift.

"I'm good," I said. "You guys can have them."

'Hammo' also said he had had enough.

Kris grinned at Bibbi. "One each, and I'll flip you for the extra one," he declared.

"You're on!" said Bibbi, pulling a coin out of his pocket. "Heads or tails?"

"Heads I win, tails you lose!" said Kris

"Yeah, right! Here, Charlie, you flip the coin and I'll call it in the air." Bibbi handed me the coin.

I flicked the coin and it whirred up into the air. Bibbi called 'heads' when it reached its zenith. I caught it in my palm and covered it with my other hand.

"Heads it is!" I declared when I looked.

Bibbi and Kris divvied up the pancakes accordingly. But, while Bibbi was waiting for Kris to use the peanut butter, my brother Johnny walked up to the table.

"They told me that all the pancakes had been given out!" Johnny lamented. "They're just going to give me some toast."

"That's what you get for sleeping in," I said. "You're lucky they're going to give you anything."

Johnny made a wry face. "I would still be sleeping in if Mrs. Gibbs hadn't come and stormed into our room. She didn't even knock! She just barged in and told me I should be at breakfast and that she was giving me a warning for having a messy room. And now I don't even get any breakfast?"

"No, here, Johnny, you can have one of my pancakes," said Bibbi, sliding one of his two back on to the empty platter.

When Bibbi and Kris had finished their extra pancakes, we left Johnny topping off his breakfast with some dry toast the staff brought him and headed back down to the dorm. At the top of the stairs, Bibbi again showed me how one could take the steps in stride by loping down them with long strides. It was physically easier than going up, but way more scary as one built up momentum. Bibbi seemed to float down the hill, while I felt like I was bouncing from step to step. Kris and Hammo watched the lesson for a couple of minutes, and then loped off down to the dorm.

We had about an hour before we had to get ready for church, so we went to the common room and joined the round robin ping pong match in progress by calling out "winners!" The table was being held by John Aung Thwin, who seemed to be beating all comers. When my turn came, he was still holding forth, but I thought I gave him a decent run before he put me away with a series of wicked smashes.

After the games we wiped down with a damp washcloth in the bathroom and got dressed for church. The service took on a shape that was familiar to me, with hymns and readings and a sermon by the Reverend Reble. Bibbi was in the choir, so I sat with 'Hammo', who made hilarious comments all through the service, and Johnny, who seemed to sleep through most of it.

There were still some parents around, so lunch was sparsely attended, as dorm kids took every opportunity they could to have lunch off campus and with their parents. Bibbi and Johnny and I sat at a table and chatted with a cheerful black girl named Carolyn Morgan. I noted that she and Bibbi seemed to get along very well.

"Kennedy night is in two weeks," Carolyn told us. "Are you guys going to go?" Although she included us in the question, she was looking at Bibbi.

"Yes, of course!" Bibbi answered, again including us.

"What's Kennedy night?" Johnny asked.

"Oh, Kennedy is the girls' dorm, and guys are never allowed to go there except on Kennedy Night," Bibbi replied. "They usually have cool refreshments and snacks."

"Yes, and there'll be dancing as well," said Carolyn, emphatically, still looking at Bibbi. I thought he blushed.

When lunch was over, we said goodbye to Carolyn and headed back down to Wissy.

A Lazy Sunday   Sunday afternoons, Bibbi told me, were 'free time'. On the more conservative compounds, where kids of parents in stricter denominations lived, there was often time set aside for reflection and prayer. At Wissy, however, it was a good time to catch up with school work and reading. Since school had not yet started, and there was no work to catch up on, he suggested that we go down to the boat house and rent a punt, but that first he wanted to stop by the gym where the house parents of the 'Loch-enders' were having a rummage sale. Loch End was the compound of the Missouri Synod Lutherans, who were very conservative. Bibbi was hoping to find a decent pair of basketball sneakers to replace the ones he had inherited from his brother John.

The rummage sale featured items that had been left behind by graduating seniors and others who had left the school over the break. It had been going on for the last two days, so the pickings were slim: only three tables of items. The only pair of basketball shoes on display was too small for Bibbi and was missing its laces, so he struck out. I, on the other hand, picked up a decent pocket knife and a dented canteen with its canvass cover and belt-loop in good shape. It had a large top that could double as a little drinking cup. The knife cost me one rupee and the canteen cost two. Bibbi found a bag of marbles that included an 'aggie' and a 'steelie' that he bought for eight annas.

We pocketed the knife and the marbles, and I hung the canteen on my belt, and headed off down to the boat house.

The Boat House was bustling with students and parents getting in their last paddle of the season. We got one of the last punts, which must have been from their back-up fleet. Its paint was peeling in places, and the dampness of the floor deck spoke of a slow leak somewhere. The attendant saw our appraising looks and lowered the fee from eight annas to six, claiming it was a 'final weekend special' just for Kodai students. We gave him 35 p., (about seven cents) which was as close as we could come to 6 annas in new currency. He handed us oars once we had paid and positioned ourselves on the benches. We paddled out of the dimness of the depths of the Boat House into the bright afternoon sunlight.

For the next two hours or so we paddled around greeting other paddlers we passed and exchanging life stories. Bibbi had been born right here in Kodai at Van Allen Hospital during the 'season', in May of 1949.

"Wow!" I remarked. "That makes you one month younger than Johnny. How come you're already a tenth-grader?"

"I got moved ahead a half year when Kodai changed its school year. Some kids stayed back, but some of us got moved forward. It had to do with how your grades were. I guess mine were good enough," he replied.

Punting Shirtless on Kodai Lake

We learned that we were both the third child in our families, each with an older brother followed by an older sister. I had a younger brother, though, while he did not. He and his older siblings were closer in age than I was with mine, but we agreed that being the third child was an important similarity.

He told me about his life on the plains during long vacation; about riding his bike all over; about his few trips back to the States; and about his travels around Kodai. He marveled at my varied upbringing and all the countries I'd lived in. He was particularly interested in my stay in Jerusalem and travels through the Holy Land to places he had been told about all his life, such as Jericho, Bethlehem, the Jordan River, the Red Sea and the Dead Sea (which included a trek to the caves where the Dead Sea Scrolls were discovered).

We took off our shirts and basked in the warm afternoon sunshine, dipping our hands and forearms into the cool waters of the lake from time to time, or hanging our legs over the gunwales to dip our toes in the lake. As we talked, the punt drifted slowly around. From time to time we had to row to get ourselves out of some reeds in the shallows or to avoid other punts that were drifting around as well.

We found that we enjoyed each other's company, and could speak freely about our likes and dislikes, concerns and joys without feeling judged. I felt much relieved that I had a person that I could relate to in this new environment, whom I felt I could rely on to be of some help and support in rough times. I had had several promising friendships through the years and travels of my life, but this beginning felt special. I just had no idea of how special it was to become.

As we had floated around, clouds had begun to bump up over the hills around the lake, and Bibbi suggested that it was time to head in before it rained. We picked up our oars and joined the other punts that had made the same observation. Playfully, we began to race with several other punts manned by students and found ourselves vying for position with another craft with upperclassmen at the oars. To Bibbi's great delight, we were able to beat them to the Boat House, although I felt totally winded by the time we drifted up to the dock.

The slow leak in the bottom of the punt had allowed about an inch or two of water to accumulate on the flat bottom, and our shirts were soaked. We wrung them out and put them on anyway for the walk back to our dorm.

We entered campus through the Phelps gate and made our way to Wissy.

"It's almost Tea Time," Bibbi observed. "I hope Mrs. Henderson made cinnamon rolls. I could sure use some right now after all that strain!"

"Tea Time?" I asked.

"Yeah," said Bibbi. "We get high tea at four o'clock. This is India and the British ruled here, so it's a tradition. Besides, Mrs. Henderson is Scottish and it's part of their tradition, too. Usually it's just a roll or a biscuit, or maybe a piece of fruit, but since it's a new term, maybe we'll get lucky with cinnamon rolls. They're really great."

Guys at the dorm were mostly just hanging around. Some were sitting on the walls outside their rooms; Casey DeJong and Mike Aung Thwin were lifting weights on the porch. There was a raucous ping-pong game going on in the common room, with three players at each end of the table alternating shots. Sam Turner was playing his guitar out on the grass. Bibbi and I left our shirts drying on the wall outside my room and headed for the bathroom.

"After Tea Time let's come back down and listen to some music on your tape recorder. What do you have?" suggested Bibbi.

"I've got The Three D's; Peter, Paul and Mary; Gordon Lightfoot; Chubby Checker; Elvis; Joan Baez; The Highwaymen… a whole bunch of stuff. I've got some Bob Dylan, too," I replied.

"I love Peter, Paul and Mary!" Bibbi exclaimed.

"I've got their whole album and two Joan Baez albums on my tapes," I bragged.

"We won't have time to listen to all of that before supper," said Bibbi, "and after supper we have to get ready for vespers. Most parents have left, but there will still be some of them at the church, so we can't skip out. We'll have to listen to more of your collection next week."

"Tea Time, vespers… what other surprises are you going to spring on me?" I asked. "Next you'll be telling me that there's a midnight bed check!"

Bibbi laughed. "You'll get used to the schedule in a couple of weeks. No midnight bed checks, but the lights-out-monitor makes sure you're in your room after he sounds the gong."

We joined Hammo, Kris and Johnny for Tea Time, and we all came back to my room to listen to music. Unfortunately, my roommate, Steve, was there and not in the mood for music and putting up with underclassmen, so we took my tape recorder to Bibbi and Johnny's room and listened there. Johnny's bed was unmade, and I sensed a bit of disappointment in Bibbi, but we ranged ourselves around, Johnny and me on his unmade bed and Bibbi, Kris and Hammo on Bibbi's and played Peter, Paul and Mary at good volume.

We stayed together as a group through supper and vespers, after which Johnny went back to his room and the rest of us went to the common room to hang out with some of the other guys. Mrs. Gibbs came by to announce that the first dorm meeting would take place on Monday evening this week instead of Tuesday because she wanted to make some announcements about room changes that had been requested.

I went to my room shortly after 9:30 to get ready for bed. My first day of dorm life had been pretty busy, and I was tired but pleased. I felt that I was fitting in fairly well, and was happy that Bibbi had seemed to be happy to hang out with me most of the day, or rather, that he had allowed me to hang out with him.

Steve was in the room when I got there sitting up on his bed and reading a book. He barely acknowledged my entrance, and responded to my tentative "Hi" with a grunt. I didn't know him well enough to feel slighted, but I wished that I had a roommate that was more communicative. Maybe it was better than someone who was quarrelsome, or too talkative, or messy. Maybe his attitude was normal for an upperclassman rooming with an underclassman. I would have to watch and see how things went before I made a final judgement. I put on my pajamas and grabbed my toothbrush, and headed to the bathroom. Tomorrow was the first day of classes, and I would have a whole lot more to learn about Kodai and its culture.

Roommates The semester unfolded quickly after that first day, and looking back I was struck by how gently that first Sunday had passed. Many of the events passed in a blur, but there were a number of salient events that made my first semester at Kodai memorable.

The first of these events was a grave disappointment to me, disappointment which was only mitigated by events nearly six months later.

On Monday night we filed into the common room at Wissy for our first dorm meeting. Everyone was talking about their first day of classes and the teachers they had met. Bibbi and I had the same classes, along with all the other tenth graders, and were comparing notes on which teachers we were going to like or hate. The room was quite noisy.

Suddenly a hush seemed to spread across the room from the back towards the front, so we all looked up and saw Mrs. Gibbs walking in. She smiled and raised her walking stick in salute.

"Welcome, boys! I'm glad to see you all here on time. We have a number of items on the agenda, and I'd like to get through them quickly, please." Her authoritative English accent and careful grooming gave her immediate control over the room.

The agenda she referred to included electing dorm officers who would run the meetings, lights-out and wake-up monitors, and going over the rules that we would live by while housed here, of which she had an exhaustive list. Afterwards, she said, she would go over some proposed room changes that should take place the following Saturday morning.

We elected Peter Hoffman as Dorm President and John Aung Thwin as vice president. I think that Hal Oliver was elected Wake-up monitor, and Bernie Plock, the boy Bibbi had let go ahead of him to the sink, became Lights-out monitor.

Once elected, Peter took over the meeting, although it was Mrs. Gibbs' show. She went over rules about timeliness, cleanliness (bed-making and closets), respect (to her), etiquette, visitors (no girls!), her office hours, dhobi day procedures, privacy (hers and ours), and many others. I was hopeful that these extensive rules would prevent the type of bullying Johnny and I had suffered at the Friend's Boys School in Ramallah.

When the rules had been explained, John Aung Thwin announced that there would be a special short meeting for freshmen and newcomers after the end of Mrs. Gibbs discussion of room assignments to go over any questions and to explain about the hierarchy of grade levels. As newcomers, both Johnny and I would attend, but I felt that with Bibbi's help, I already knew much of what was to be discussed.

Then Mrs. Gibbs took the floor and flourished a sheet of paper. "I have received requests from several boys to change some of the room assignments. This will also affect some of you who have not made requests, since you will either have new roommates or will have to move into another room. I am sorry that we have to do this, but with so many turnovers, not everyone made their roommate preferences clear at the end of last term. So, here goes."

I think that there were four changes that had been requested, which affected eight of the fifteen rooms. One of the first ones was welcome.

"Steven Cook and David Morris have asked to be moved together. Steve will move into David's room, room 9 and Douglass Seaton will move in with Charles Franklin in room 4."

Two more pairings involving seniors followed. And then, like a blow from a hammer, Mrs. Gibbs announced, "Robert Hammond and Robert Coleman will be sharing room 13, and David Martin will be moving to room 8 with John Franklin."

"What...???" I stammered, looking at Bibbi. I would have given anything to be able to room with Bibbi. I actually felt somehow betrayed and jealous. It suddenly occurred to me that I had known Bibbi for little more than two days and was already feeling as though we were best friends.

"Yeah," said Bibbi, with an embarrassed chuckle. It seemed that he, too, shared the feeling that we should have talked about it. "Hammo and I talked about rooming together at the end of last semester and I agreed to, but apparently Mrs. Gibbs forgot until Hammo reminded her."

"Jeez, why didn't you tell me?" I complained

"Well, Hammo just reminded me about it last night and told me he had reminded Mrs. Gibbs after her announcement Sunday night, but he wasn't sure she had put us on the list," he replied.

I attempted to hide my disappointment and asked, "Okay, so who is this Douglass Seaton that I'm getting stuck with?"

"He's a ninth-grader. He's been at Kodai for a few years. That's him over there with Tim and Phil." He pointed to a group of three boys that I didn't know.

"Which one is he?" I asked, looking at three boys I had barely noticed before.

"He's the one in the middle. Phil is the tall one, the brother of Sam who's in our class, and the other one is Tim." He was looking at me so they wouldn't guess that we were talking about them.

"Oh, you mean Sam who was playing guitar yesterday afternoon? And who is Johnny's new roommate?" I wanted to know.

"He's a newer kid. I think that's him over there... See? He's talking to Johnny." I looked where he was pointing.

Still feeling hurt, I said, "Well, I guess I better go over and meet my new roommate," and headed across the room towards Douglass.

I introduced myself and we shook hands. His handshake was soft. He was shorter than me by six or more inches, and seemed timid, but friendly enough. I thought to myself that rooming with him had to be better than rooming with "Sullen Steve".

The Swallows Are Back　　The following weekend I got better acquainted with two more of Bibbi's circle of friends: Bob Rushton and

Linwood Delong. Bibbi, Linwood and Bob had their own bikes and liked to peddle around. They kept them locked in a rack behind the dorm. At breakfast on Saturday morning, Bibbi told me that he, Linwood and Bob were going to ride out to Pillar Rocks, and asked if I would like to join them.

"I really would, but I don't have a bike," I lamented.

"That's not a problem if you have eight annas," said Bibbi. "You can rent one for half a day. We want to be back by lunchtime anyway."

We left Wissy and went out the Dish gate after breakfast, with Bibbi, Linwood and Bob walking their bikes to a bike shop where I rented a sad looking, beat-up bicycle with slightly off-center handlebars and only one speed for eight annas. Not being a good cyclist to begin with, the challenges of keeping up with the others on that old bike were even greater, and I found myself falling behind a lot of the time. I was beginning to acclimate to the altitude, so I didn't get quite as winded by the exertion as I had on my first few days, but I was still pretty gassed. Fortunately we didn't have to peddle up any steep hills, but getting up to Upper Lake Road and the Observatory was tough enough.

We made the nearly seven mile ride out in about forty minutes, arriving before ten in the morning. We locked and left our bikes near the Observation Point and hiked in to the rock formations. Bibbi said that there was a chimney he liked to climb, and took us into a crevice in the side of one of the pillars. It was eerie inside, and as our eyes grew used to the dimmer light, I saw that the crevice did indeed extend upwards into the rock, and there looked to be multiple cracks and projections that would serve as hand- and foot-holds.

I had always prided myself in my ability to climb trees, so this looked like a piece of cake to me.

"Wow!" I said. "That looks like a fun climb!"

"Yeah," Bibbi responded. "I love to climb it. You get a little dirty, but most of it brushes off. You gotta be careful about tearing your clothes, though. Some of the edges are pretty sharp. And if you're the one on top, don't even think of falling or sliding down!"

As the new kid, I got the honor of going first if I wanted, which I did. I was to be followed by Linwood, Bob and finally Bibbi. I looked up for potential handholds and footholds, and picked my starting place. When I was about five feet up, Linwood started up. As I went up, the light from the crack began to fade as it narrowed, but there was still enough light to make out where to place my feet and hands. I was about twenty feet up the chimney when Bibbi finally started up.

As I got higher, I began to notice a half-familiar pungent smell that I couldn't quite place. As I went a little higher, I thought I heard rustlings, but attributed the sounds to the three boys climbing behind me. I reached for a new handhold which seemed to crumble as I grasped it and suddenly there was a loud flapping and twittering as a bird flushed out of the cleft I had been reaching toward. I was so startled that I almost lost my footing, and shouted out an unintelligible sound that might have been a swear word.

"The swallows are back!" shouted Bibbi from below when he heard the flapping. "I was hoping they would be. They weren't here last time I came."

I was still shaking from my fright and hanging tightly to the wall. From above me, there came a chorus of twitters and flutters, and suddenly there were birds all around us flying right at our faces.

"We better head back down!" I shouted down. "I think they're protecting their nests. It smells like a chicken coop up here! I *knew* I had smelled that smell before." I began to work my way back down.

Reluctantly, Bibbi agreed after both Linwood and Bob agreed with me. The way down was a quite a bit more difficult than the way up, because now there were angry swallows darting around us. I was unable to use my eyes as I kept my head ducked away from flapping wings, feeling my way from hold to hold. Additionally, with people below me, I had to wait for them to move before I could.

Soon enough, though, we were all back down and had exited the crevice not too much worse for the wear. We were dirty, though I was the dirtiest of all with stains on my shirt that didn't brush off. I was also the stinkiest, with the smell of bird poop in my hair and clothes. There was a trickling stream nearby, and I took off my shirt and soaked it to wash out some of the guano that was clinging to it and rinsed my head and hands.

As we walked back to the bikes we each recounted the adventure from our own perspective, and when we were done, I said, "I think you could've warned me about the swallows, Bibbi."

"I didn't know they would be there!" he professed. "The last two times we came out here the chimney was empty. It's been a year since they were here."

"Yeah, well, duh!" I replied. "It's their nesting period now. The rest of the year they're out and about."

"Yeah, you're right, now that I think about it," Bibbi agreed. "I think there's a song about swallows returning every year to the same place. Anyway, it was a cool adventure. I'm glad we came."

The ride back to campus was easier than the way out since it was mostly level or downhill, and with my damp shirt, I kept fairly cool all the way even though it was a warm morning in June.

Kennedy Night　　　　The following Saturday night was Kennedy Night. It was a rare opportunity for us to get a look inside the girls' dorm, and we were all gung ho to attend. In Kennedy dorm, however, there was only one way in and all the rooms fronted on a central courtyard, and as long as doors were kept open, nothing untoward could occur without being observed.

"Is there a 'Wissy Night'?" I asked Bibbi.

"Yeah, but it was put off till next semester. Mrs. Gibbs said she would need help supervising since you can't see all the rooms from the common room where we'll be having a dance. Also, I think the dorm president last semester forgot to schedule it," he explained.

We walked over from Wissy after supper. We had showered in the afternoon, and were wearing our cleanest clothes. Bibbi had even found time to visit Muthu, the barber, for a haircut. We were heading over as a class group: Bibbi, Kris, Hammo, Phil Koszarek, Stan Bissel, Sam Turner and I. Linwood had declined on the grounds that he had to study, which we thought was a bit lame, since we all had the same classes. We were all excited, but Bibbi seemed especially eager.

The girls had decorated their dorm with streamers and welcomed us to the central courtyard. They were all wearing skirts and colorful shirts and blouses and dress shoes. They had all fixed their hair up prettily and many were even wearing makeup.

We milled around the courtyard as a group. Lyn Krause joined us, as did a couple of our classmates from other compounds such as Loch End and the Lutheran compound. For a while the boys huddled in class groups. Seniors and juniors seemed more at ease, and were soon mixing with the girls who had mainly stayed around the edges, close to the doors of their rooms. Carolyn came over and told us that we needed to move around and that we could peek into a couple of the rooms if their owners would let us. She led Bibbi off to show him her room.

When everyone was gathered, Sam, who had agreed to be the disc jockey for the event, started the record player and put on some lively music. Refreshments were brought out and put on a table outside the housemother's apartment. Soon enough, there were a number of couples dancing and the party began.

Bibbi, Kris, Lyn and Stan seemed much at ease, and were soon chatting away and dancing with multiple girls. Sam was busy with the music, and always seemed to have girls around him giving him suggestions of what to play next. Hammo, Phil and I stood to one side together taking in the scene and chatting about this and that. Maureen Aung Thwin, who had been dancing with Kris and Lyn came over and scolded us for being such party poopers.

"Come on, you guys!" she chided us. "It's a party! Have fun!"

Thus encouraged, we broke up and went to talk to girls. I soon saw Hammo dancing with someone and Phil was talking to a pretty girl I didn't know. I actually didn't know most of the girls other than the ones in our class, and most of them were busy talking or dancing. I was feeling very alone and left out, which I knew was my own fault. My own brother, Johnny was dancing with his new roommate's sister Sue Martin. I was thinking about sneaking out back to the dorm when a cute girl came up and asked me if I would like to dance with her.

Surprised, I said "Sure!", and led her to the floor.

She told me her name was Margie Graham, and she was in Doug Seaton's class. He had told her that I was his roommate. We danced through two fast dances but stopped when a slow dance came up and stood talking for a few more minutes. She was, it seemed, interested in finding out about my brother Johnny, who was still dancing with Sue Martin. Nevertheless, she rescued my evening and made me glad that I had come.

I did get up my courage to dance with a couple more girls in my class and talk to a few more, so I didn't feel like a total outcast by the end of the evening when we were told it was time to leave. Bibbi had been mostly monopolized by Carolyn and seemed to have stars in his eyes on the way back to Wissy. Kris and Lyn were comparing notes on the girls they had danced with and spoken to. Stan had had a good time with Layla Nykirk, an upper classman. Hammo and Phil seemed happy, but didn't speak about anyone special.

Roommate Issues   The rhythms of life at Kodai and the dorm began to become more familiar to me. Weekends, afternoons and evenings were 'Dorm Life'. We built up strong and lasting relationships with our fellow 'dormies'. We shared goodies that we received in 'Care Packages' from home. We borrowed clothes and money from each other. We studied and did schoolwork together, prepping each other for tests and reading each other's term papers to make suggestions for improvement. And we talked: about girls, about plans, and food, always about food.

We also bartered when we needed to raise money. Bibbi was a master at it. He needed money to pay off some 'debts' that his brother John had left behind. John owed to Dawson 1.50 rupees and another vendor about 2 rupees. He had left Bibbi a 'rumble' knife, and Bibbi bartered it for 15 rupees plus a smaller knife.

Bibbi and I had now both moved in with our new roommates, me with Douglass Seaton and Bibbi with Robert 'Hammo' Hammond. We were in the period of adjustment, getting used to our new roommates' habits. Doug liked to talk after lights out, while I preferred to drift off. Hammo was a noisy sleeper, and complained about Bibbi's early rising. We both had issues, but were both better off than before the switch. I approached the idea of rooming together with Bibbi.

"We should be roommates at some point," I posited. "We spend a lot of our time in each other's' rooms anyway, and we're always studying for something or other at the same time."

"Yeah, well, I agree, but I think Kris and I are going to be roommates next semester. We've been talking about it ever since I was promoted to this class. But maybe after that…"

"Yeah, I was just thinking," I said, hiding my disappointment, "it's just hard rooming with a ninth-grader who has all different classes from mine."

"I know what you mean," he said. "I've been in that situation, too. When I got moved to this class my roommate was suddenly a year behind me and our classes didn't line up. I've had probably ten different roommates over the years, and I can tell you this: The key is to work to get along with him. Some guys are harder to deal with than others. One of my roommates was a kind of bully and tried to take over all the space in the room. I had to work hard on that one, but I made a point of getting along with him and not giving in to him either. I think it's good to have different roommates. It makes you a more tolerant person and you learn how to get along with anyone."

"Well," I replied, "it sure would be great to room with you at some point. I hope that I won't have to room with Doug forever. He's nice enough, but he's just a kid."

"Yeah, talk to Mrs. Gibbs about finding a classmate to room with for next semester. She might have some ideas, and there might be other kids asking, too."

First Time to Tope   The fourth of July was on a Thursday, so the school had declared a holiday on Friday so that we could have a three-day weekend. Bibbi was very eager to go on an overnight hike to Tope. I'll let him tell the tale as he told it to his parents in his weekly letter home. My additions to the tale are in brackets or at the end:

July 4, '63

I didn't get a very good letter sent this week-end so I guess I'll send a slightly better one now.

This week-end, July 4th with Friday off, I'm going to Tope (at the bottom of the Coolee Ghat). We're staying overnight so it ought to be fun. Mr. Shaw, Kris Riber, Phil Koszarek, Bob Hammond, Lyn Krause, Charles Franklin and I will be going. I'll tell you all about it in my next letter. I'm taking my sleeping bag and 5 rupees worth of food (we get that much from the dining room for the five meals we miss.)

This Thursday night there will be fireworks and a movie so I'm glad we aren't leaving until Friday morning.

I really haven't been doing much these week-ends except a little boating on the lake. In the next letter you send could you say that I shouldn't lend my bike out because people ask me if they can borrow it and I don't have any reason not to let them. I've been using my bike for going to the budge and on little jaunts (Pillar Rocks). I got my new clothes but I don't have any name tags for them. Could you send me some or tell me what I can do? Thanks for the letter you sent me. I also got one from Mr. Hamm. He's traveling in Europe now.

For my Biology term paper I am planning to do something about the development of the reptile family. [Charlie's doing his on sharks, and his dad is sending him magazine articles from the Consulate's library. He's lucky!] *I've also got a report in Biology which I am planning to do on the topic of atomic energy used in medicine. The extra reading for English is due Monday and so I've got a lot of work to do over the week-end and not much time to do it in.*

Everything is going fine here but the weather is getting a little wet and rainy (just what you need).

***

I went and forgot to send this letter when I wrote it. It's now the 7th and we are back from Tope. It was gobs of fun! We started out early (six in the morning) and got down at 9:00. We took our own food. I had bread, peanut butter and jam, sardines, crackers and oranges. Oh ya, water too. I've got the worst sunburn, my poor back is sore.

There are a whole lot of rock slides down there and it sure was a lot of fun going down them. The hiking was terrible on the plains. It was cloudy, but it sure was sweltery. The swimming was the best part of the whole deal.

It was terrible sleeping on a 30 degree angle, under a big rock with a pool of water 15 feet beneath you. Every fifteen minutes I woke up to find that I had slipped two feet towards the water. [None of us fell in, but one time I woke up because my feet were over the edge.]

Finally, after 3:00 in the morning we left the protection of the rock and went to one that was not so slanted. Finally I slept (yea!)

The next morning we went down stream and had a shower under a falls. It was cool fun. We stuck around until about 1:00 and then left for the 5 mile hike to Periaculum on the plains. It was hot, but it wasn't too bad. We had something to eat at Periaculum, which I was glad of.

We got a bus out of Periaculum for the petrol bunker [where we] *got a* [another] *bus (5:30) up to Kodai. We got up* [to Kodai] *at 8:30 and I went to bed right away. Boy, that sleep sure was cool!*

[Oh, I forgot to tell you,] *Charlie bought a jack fruit* [at the petrol bunker] *for 8 annas and* [only] *ate a quarter of it and gave the rest away* [to the rest of us]. *As I said before, we sure had gobs of fun!!!!*

We might be going boating this afternoon (if we can borrow some money). I can't think of anything else to say, so I'll sign off for now. I'll write another letter soon.

Lots of love, Bob

As one of my first hikes at Kodai, this one had been a real eye-opener for me. Hiking down the Coolie Ghat had been an experience all by itself. Seeing the trail twist back and forth all the way down to nearly six thousand feet below, appearing and disappearing depending on the terrain, and then realizing that we were going to have to negotiate it was shocking enough. But then Bibbi would lead us down cut-offs from time to time, which were very steep and treacherous. I was glad I had good hiking boots, but I still turned my ankle more than once on the stony ground.

The gradual increase in the temperature of the day, due both to the time of day and to the lower elevations we were reaching was daunting. We started out at six into the chilly mountain air at around sixty degrees Fahrenheit, and by nine o'clock, when we reached Tope; the temperature was already in the nineties. We were all wearing our jackets and sweaters tied around our waists by then.

The rock slides in the stream were awesome and fun, but (and Bibbi left this out of his letter) we were doing it in the nude, and they weren't all terribly smooth. The ones with moss and algae growing in them were okay, but we did end up with some painful skid marks on our butts, backs and arms.

I was greatly relieved the following day when I realized that we weren't going to be going back up the way we had come, but rather out to a road where we would catch rides back up to Kodai. This fact was kept from me for a good while just to see how I would react. Once they let the cat out of the bag, they said that I had seemed game enough to hike back up in spite of my sore and swollen ankle, which made me feel good.

We were well into 'Hiking Season' now. Bibbi signed us up for hikes on a regular basis, intent on earning the coveted 'Tahr Pin'. We went on a chaperoned hike to Palar Dam, about ten miles down and ten miles back. We couldn't stay long, so we had lunch and only Bibbi, Kris, Irene Naumann and I went for a swim before hiking back up.

Another weekend, on Saturday Bibbi, Linwood, Kris and I hiked out un-chaperoned to Berijam Lake in the rain. We left the dorm at just after 5 in the morning and got to the lake at about 8:30. We ate breakfast and goofed around swimming and paddling out in an old boat that was there, but the wind was quite fierce, so we kept getting blown around. We ate our lunches at noon and headed back to school, still in the rain. The following day, Sunday, the four of us hiked out to Snake Falls for the two points that would give us ten for the weekend, since the hike to Berijam is worth only 8. With that we had each earned 40 points, with only 20 more to go to earn the pin.

We later earned points for a hike to Poombari for Christian Endeavor (CE) retreat, which was attended by most students, boys and girls, and involved an overnight stay. Linwood had the idea to make hammocks out of cut-open burlap bags and ropes. We would suspend them between two trees, with a tarp suspended on a rope above us. Bibbi claimed that he slept comfortably high and dry. My experience was different. Maybe my hammock sagged more than his did, or maybe I didn't set mine up right, but it rained hard at night, and rain dripped down along the rope under my tarp and dripped onto my stomach, soaking a part of my sleeping bag. I was also unable to straighten my back, which was sore and took some stretching to get back in shape in the morning.

Merp Week   The second week of August was designated 'Merp Week'.

"What's 'Merp' Week?" I asked Bibbi, when the announcement was made.

"'Merp' stands for Male Economic Recovery Program," said Bibbi.

"Huh? What does that mean?"

"It basically means that girls get to ask guys out and have to pay for their food and stuff," he explained. "The juniors sponsor a dance and girls are encouraged to bring a boy to the dance and pay for his food. It's basically a way for juniors to make more money since most of us guys are broke by this time in the semester. They get to have one in the second semester, too. The juniors are the class that really needs to build up their treasury, since they are saving money for their Senior Sneak and their Prom."

"Oh, I get it. It's kind of like Sadie Hawkins' Day: The girls have been saving all their money while we've been spending all of ours on them! The only problem is that I haven't really spent money on any of them, and I still manage to get broke," I said.

"Yeah, well that's the way it's supposed to work. At this time in the year there aren't so many couples as in the spring, when the seniors get their night, so by getting the girls to invite the boys they get more people and we get a free ride," he clarified.

"So, how do I get one of the girls to invite me?" I asked

"Don't worry, just about everyone gets asked. The girls don't like to leave anyone out," said Bibbi.

"That's easy for you to say," I replied. "Carolyn's probably just waiting to pounce!" I was kind of teasing him.

He grinned. "Well, you never know, do you?"

Surprisingly, the next day during first period, a new girl in our class, Lucy David, asked Bibbi to go to Junior Night with her.

Toward the middle of the week I had not been asked, and my expectations were low, but, surprisingly, one afternoon Kathy Schneck, a girl in our class from one of the off-campus compounds nervously asked me to go with her. She was a cute red-head who was very quiet in class. I was thrilled and happy to be asked.

Junior Night itself was a fun affair with a catered supper and dancing in a festively decorated gym. We all again dressed in our cleanest outfits, boys in black slacks, buttoned shirts and jackets, leather penny-loafers and white socks; girls in colorful party dresses with crinolines, heeled shoes and raw silk shawls.

I enjoyed the evening platonically, and I think that Kathy did as well. We chatted about our lives up to then and what we were doing in

India. Bibbi seemed to be engrossed in his conversation with Lucy, and I noticed that Carolyn was keeping a close eye on them from her table nearby where she was with the boy she had invited.

Grades It was approaching the end of the first quarter and grades would be coming out in mid-August when Bibbi explained the 'Free Study List' to me.

"If your grade-point average is over 3.0 and you don't have any grade below a 'B' you are exempt from Study Hall. That means that when everyone else is stuck in the Library, you can be down in the common room or in your own room and study, listen to music, chat or play ping pong as much as you want. You can be outside the library if it's a nice night and see your girlfriend if she's on the 'free-study list as well.

Bibbi seemed obsessed in making the 'free'. He was definitely one of the 'brains' in our class, more because of hard work and constant study than any obvious innate talent. His grades were always in the top range on any of our exams or assignments. Others were gifted in some subjects more than others, and there were a couple of known 'Einsteins', such as Ron Koepke, but Bibbi was solid in just about every subject. I wasn't witness to other kids study habits, but Bibbi would often stay up past lights out in the common room with special permission from Mrs. Gibbs to work on term papers and study for exams. It was a 'privilege' mostly reserved for juniors and seniors, but Bibbi somehow wheedled permission from Mrs. Gibbs to join them. The idea never really appealed to me.

The only subject that was keeping Bibbi back was typing. It is a subject that doesn't depend so much on intellect or careful study, but rather on mechanical coordination. Bibbi and his sister Mary shared a typewriter that he used to practice on whenever he could. However, as a senior, Mary was often having to type out term papers and letters to colleges, so Bibbi couldn't always get his hands on the machine.

I was not in any danger of making the 'free-study list'. I was getting a 'D' in Typing, 'D+' in Religious Education, a 'C' in Biology with limited prospects of improving my grades in the few weeks until the end of the Quarter. I was jealous of Bibbi's good grades, but unwilling to buckle down the way he did. I was also secretly hoping that he wouldn't make the 'free', since I liked having him to study with in Study Hall at night.

In the end, Bibbi got a 'C' in Typing, keeping him off the 'free' for what turned out to be one of the only times in his last three years of High School.

With about six weeks left in the semester before out winter break, dorm life marched along fairly peacefully. With Hiking Season ending, other sports and activities were picking up. Kodai School had become a competitive force in boys' basketball the previous year thanks to the presence of Hal Oliver, Bob Fletcher, David Eaton and Mike Meinzen on the school team. Now they were back for their senior year, and our prospects were good to take the State Championship this year. As sophomores we were encouraged to try out for the team, but it was understood that our roles would be secondary if we made it.

Mr. Root was in charge of the team, and began to run us in drills during P.E. to select a few of us to join the school team. Since I was fairly tall, I was selected to join in the drills, which were very rigorous. I made it through the first couple of cuts, but in the end I was dropped from consideration. Bibbi, of course, made the team along with Ron Koepke, Kris Riber and Lyn Krause.

This created quite a disruption in our dorm routines, as well as some of our classes. The team had to travel to other cities, such as Dindigul and Madurai to compete, and other schools would send teams to Kodai. Games usually started after school hours, but occasionally a game would happen early in the afternoon, and the players would be excused from class. So Bibbi, Ron, Kris and Lyn were let out early a number of times, and were out of the dorm some weekends.

When the team was scheduled to travel to Madurai for a tournament, Bibbi was desperate for some new basketball shoes. The ones he had been handed down from John were falling apart, and a pair he got from Pete Fourt, a kid from before my time, had holes in them. Finally he got 20 rupees from his parents and spent Rs. 14.25 on a new pair. With all that, he told us, he only got to play for about 5 minutes.

The team traveled to Madurai, Trichy and Dindigul, among other towns. Knowing that he would have time on these trips, Bibbi would take his books with him and spend as much time as he could, keeping up with his schoolwork. I, on the other hand, not having Bibbi to study with and whip me along, routinely fell behind when the team was on the road. In short, basketball season made more of an impact on my grades than it did on Bibbi's.

During this time, Carolyn was on the cheerleading team and attended all the home games. As such, she kept close to Bibbi and their relationship became more serious. They could be seen holding hands walking around campus and sitting on walls and chatting between classes. One evening he came back to the dorm after Study Hall and told me that he had asked her to the Fall Formal, and she said yes. He confided in me that they were going steady, which was already an open secret. She had been wearing his Tahr Pin on her blouse for a week.

I didn't have anyone I could take to the Formal, not that I wouldn't have loved to go. Johnny was taking Sue Martin (a senior!), Bibbi was taking Carolyn, and both Kris and Lyn had dates. Everyone was supposed to go, even if you went stag, which a number of us ended up doing. For the occasion we had white silk jackets tailored by Peter in the Budge and white shirts with neck ties or bow ties. It was very exciting and fun, and I wished afterward that I had had the courage to bring a date, but Linwood, Bob Rushton, Phil Turner and I sat at the same table chatting and getting up to ask a girl to dance from time to time.

When dinner was served at the formal, a number of students had been recruited to provide entertainment. There were skits and songs and music. Bibbi, Mike Aung Thwin and Hal Oliver surprised us by performing "How to Handle a Woman" from Camelot. I didn't know when they had practiced for it, but they were pretty good.

End of Term My first term at Kodai School was winding down, but the work wasn't getting any easier. In fact, a number of things had piled up, mostly due to my procrastination, and there were a number of logistical challenges for getting ready to leave campus for the break and setting up for the next semester.

While I had been doing better in Religious Ed and Typing, English and Biology were demanding a great deal of my time. We had been tasked with turning in book reports every other week, on books from a list provided by Ms. Franz. As such, we were forced to read nearly a hundred pages a day to keep up and have time to write a report. The deadline for turning in our Biology Term Paper to Mrs. Edmund was fast approaching, and we had to prepare for a final exam in her class as well.

On top of all the things we had to do, Bibbi was still traveling and playing with the basketball team since they had made it to the championship round. He was going to have to stay with the team after we had all left to finish up the season. They were going to be traveling to Coimbatore a few days after the end of the semester. As if that wasn't enough, he was also running for the office of Vice President of Senior Christian Endeavor (which was largely a ceremonial role, but which would look good on his college applications), and arranging to ship his bicycle and other personal effects back to Rajahmundry.

I realized that by the time he finished playing in the State Tournament, I would be back in Madras. He would be taking a train and coming through Madras on his way to Rajahmundry.

"Why don't you stop in Madras for a few days on your way home?" I proposed. "You could stay with me at our house and we could hang out and go to the beach."

"That would be cool!" he exclaimed. "I love the beaches around Madras, but we don't get to go there very often."

"Yeah, we have a bungalow on Elliot's Beach at Mahabalipuram. Dad was having it built when we left in May. We can also go to the gymkhana club. Plus, our cook has promised to cook all my favorite meals, so we can eat till we pop." I was encouraging him to come.

It would be a fitting end to our first term. Bibbi had been the one to make my first semester at Kodai School one of the happiest school semesters of my life. He had made the culture shock that accompanied the moves I had made all my life as gentle as any I could remember. I had five more semesters of dorm life ahead of me, but now I looked forward to them with pleasure, ready to forge ahead.

We were sitting on the wall outside Bibbi's room, flush with the prospect of a few days in Madras when Mrs. Gibbs approached us.

"Good afternoon, boys," she greeted us. "I have just received some news that may interest you. I believe I heard that Charles was interested in rooming with you, Robert, but that you and Kris Riber were planning to room together next semester, is that correct?"

"Yes, Ma'am," we both replied, simultaneously.

"Well, then," she continued, "one of the seniors who was going to room in Room 11 just informed me that he will not be returning next semester, so the other two will be taking another room together. If you would like to share Room 11, you could all room together. I only let reliable boys stay there since it's more isolated."

Bibbi and I looked at each other to gauge each other's reaction to this news. We broke into huge smiles.

"That would be cool!" Bibbi exclaimed.

"Excellent!" I added.

What a cap on my first semester at Kodai!

There were still challenges, I knew. My grades needed improvement. I wasn't as athletic as I would have liked. I was still shy around girls. But Bibbi was my friend, and now we would be rooming together. That made all the difference.

Roommate issues arose several more times during my time in Kodai. After my semester with Doug, and then my semester with Kris and Bibbi, Kris and his family went back to the States for a year of furlough. Bibbi and I wanted to keep our three-man room, so we asked Linwood if he wanted to room with us in Room 11 the following semester. Unfortunately, however, Mrs. Gibbs retired and Mr. and Mrs. Amstutz took over Wissy as dorm parents. For some reason, Mrs. Amstutz was unwilling to allow three boys in one room, so we came back from break to find that we had been preemptively reassigned. I would be rooming with Linwood in Room 15, and Bibbi would be rooming with a new kid, Kurt Johnson.

Linwood was a good roommate, very neat and organized. He studied hard and was fun to talk with about academic subjects. He was much more religious than I, and spent time studying his Bible. He liked to arise before wake-up call and exercise on the floor beside his bed, performing 50 or 100 sit-ups and pushups almost every weekday morning. Bibbi was happy with Kurt, who turned out to be his intellectual equal, if not superior.

The following semester, second semester of our junior year, Bibbi and I were reunited as roommates in Room 13. When Kris returned from furlough for our senior year, Mrs. Amstutz relented, in part due to the fact that Wissy was full, and in part due to the fact that Bibbi was one of Mr. Amstutz' favorite students, and allowed us to again room together in Room 11.

Dorm life was the heart of Boarding School life. Being a successful student started with having a happy dorm life. I was fortunate in that aspect of my time at Kodai thanks in large part to my friendship with Bibbi.

3. Boarding School Life

Schedules   Life in a boarding school is highly regimented and carefully choreographed. There were about thirty of us high school boys housed at Wissy, and another thirty or so housed in other compounds outside campus owned by various religious groups: Lutherans, Mennonites, Seventh Day Adventists, and so on. The girls on campus were housed in Kennedy, and there were others at the off-campus compounds as well, making a total of about 150 high-school students.

In addition, there were middle school and elementary dorms with about two hundred students from first through eighth grade. In all, there were about 350 students at Kodai in 1963. The whole school, all twelve grades, was smaller than the ninth-grade class at Andrew Lewis High School.

Meals, classes, assemblies, sports, social events, church gatherings, and study hall: from wake-up to lights-out, nearly every minute was programmed, with just a few slices of un-programmed time that grew more liberal as one advanced through grade levels. There were several afternoons a week that permitted discretionary activities for us as sophomores, usually in our dorms.

Much of the so-called "free time" was taken up with routine chores and tasks such as making one's bed (required) , cleaning one's space, required reading, writing letters home, sorting, re-folding and putting away laundry brought back by the dhobis and many other mundane, house-keeping tasks. As mentioned, I owned a tape recorder, and had a number of tapes with popular music of the day such as Peter, Paul and Mary; The Limelighters; Gordon Lightfoot; Bob Dylan; and The Three D's. I would often have these playing as I performed my tasks, and since I was one of very few students with music, my room was often a place where students congregated.

I was also one of several students who had a guitar. I had learned about a dozen basic chords and could accompany myself strumming out a number of songs. Bibbi was an enthusiastic singer and would join in on sessions with Peter, Paul and Mary songs, harmonizing and enjoying the music. Sam Turner and Mike Aung Thwin, who could play guitar well, much better than I could, would join us from time to time to help me figure out the right chords and pick out better harmonies. Sam's roommate, Stan Bissel, would sometimes join us with his beautiful voice. (Sam, Stan and I later formed a trio, performing songs at some events and fundraisers. We, along with a classmate, Dave Carner, performed "Four Strong Winds" at our class's Commencement Exercise.)

Academics   Of course, Kodai School's primary function was academic instruction. For six hours a day, five days a week we attended academic classes. Looking back through my report cards brings back some memories of these classes, but in general, my memories of Kodai are almost all about the other ten hours of my waking day (and some of the hours when I should have been sleeping).

Anyone looking through my report cards from those days would see a record of my academic performance and have no idea of my personal growth through these three years.

In tenth grade I took English (I got a C+), French II (A-), Plane Geometry (B-), Biology (B+), Indian Social Studies (B-), Religious Education (C), and P.E. (C). I took Chorus as an extra-curricular elective, and received a grade of Satisfactory. My tenth grade report card also disclosed that I was 70 inches tall and weighed 126 ¾ pounds.

My eleventh grade classes: English (B), Algebra II (B), Physics (B), American History (A), Typing (C+), Religious Education (C+) and P.E. (B-). I grew an inch and a quarter and gained 8 ¼ pounds.

In twelfth grade I took English (B+), Chemistry (B-), World Geography (B+), Wood Shop (B), Religious Education (A-), P.E. (B) and Chorus (S). I grew to six feet even and weighed 140 pounds.

I learned more academically during those three years than I did in the seven years of college and graduate studies that I took afterwards. Nevertheless, there are very few lessons that I could recall with any clarity. At the time we rated teachers based on whether their class was fun or boring, how 'cool' they were and how hard it was to get a good grade in their classes.

English- English class was taught by Ms. Franz. We called her 'Fuzzy' in honor of the peach fuzz on her upper lip. She wore a suit to class, with stockings and medium heels. She usually had deep circles under her eyes, probably from staying up late to grade papers. You had to work for your grade in her class and the comments she put on your essays could be very cutting. She was very professional and stern. Her classes weren't fun or boring, she wasn't 'cool', and it was hard to get an 'A' from her. My ability to write coherent sentences and the ease I had in turning in term papers in college are easily attributable to her work with me. You could not turn in crappy work to her, as she would make you redo it. 500

words meant at least 500 words and you were punished, grade-wise, if you tried to get away with less, while the reward for going over was minimal.

Foreign Language- French- Two years of a foreign language was a requirement, but because of my year in École Saint Joseph, I was placed in French II with the rest of the tenth-graders who had taken French I in ninth grade, and only had to take one year. Mr. Mapp, the French teacher, was a character, but it was easy to get an A in his class.

Green Bananas
Mr. Mapp's French class was on the second floor of the Quad, and there were only about ten or twelve of us taking the class. The room and the instruction were often disorderly. While he followed some English school lesson formula he had learned in his public school in England, carefully writing vocabulary and grammar lessons on the board, we would pass notes, fly paper airplanes, shoot peas and throw chalk at each other.

He was a short, stout, red-faced Englishman with bad teeth and a wild, balding white head. He had been serendipitously recruited to teach French when the last French teacher had come down with malaria. He had been riding his bicycle up the Ghat when he had bumped into Mr. Root at a roadside chai stand. Mr. Root was on a mission to recruit a replacement French teacher. Mr. Mapp was riding his bicycle on a tour of India.

In their conversation Mr. Root had discovered that Mapp was a retired teacher and claimed to speak decent French. His French accent wasn't as good as the French I had picked up in my fifth grade in the French nun's school, but he was able to work his way through our lessons.

Mr. Mapp was also an ex-military man who had spent time in the British Army fighting the Mau-Mau rebellion in Kenya, so he and Mr. Root hit it off as two old soldiers will. Little did Mr. Root know that Mapp loved recounting his adventures among the Mau-Mau, and could be easily distracted from teaching French by a comment or question about his experiences.

On the particular day in question, Joe Rittmann had brought a large bunch of baby green bananas to biology class which he had used, among other items, as a prop for his biology report. As we were leaving biology on our way to French class, Lyn decided that they would make great missiles. The usual supply of chalk was dwindling as the semester wound down, so the bananas would make a fine substitute.

I was, as usual, sitting in the front row, when a green banana suddenly flew past my head and struck the blackboard upon which Mr. Mapp was carefully writing a vocabulary list.

THWACK! The banana hit the board. "Who threw that?!" Mr. Mapp whipped around, his eyes darting around till they centered on me.

I donned my most innocent expression and turned to look behind me. To my dismay, somehow the bunch of bananas was now leaning against the back of my chair.

Green Bananas

"I… I swear it wasn't me." I stammered. "I don't know whose bananas those are."

"Well, you just take that bunch of bananas down to Mr. Nickel's office and explain it to him. I'm tired of your disruptions!" Mr. Nickel was the Acting Vice-Principal while Mr. Root was away.

I was resigned to being given serious detention as I picked up the bananas and stood up, my head hanging.

"He didn't do it, Mr. Mapp," Bibbi spoke up, his face red. "I'm sorry, but I did it. I didn't mean to... I was just swinging it and it slipped."

Mr. Mapp's anger cooled and his attitude changed abruptly. "Oh, Bob. I guess I'll forgive you. Thank you for coming forward. You may sit down, Charles." He pronounced 'Charles' in the French way, 'sharl'.

He went back to writing on the board, and soon green bananas were flying back and forth around the classroom. They really hurt when they struck you, but nobody made any noise other than the occasional 'thwack' of a banana hitting its target. By the end of the class, most of them had been flung out one of the open windows and were scattered on the grass below.

Science- My science classes were Biology in tenth grade, Physics in eleventh and Chemistry in twelfth. I arrived at Kodai hating Science because I had failed my science class the year before at Andrew Lewis High School in Salem. As a new kid I did not yet have the advantage of study partners and lacked a great deal of self-confidence. In addition to that, I was rooming with a ninth grader, Doug, who was taking General Science. So that first semester, I felt myself falling behind and scrambling.

~*~ Biology- Mrs. Edmund, the Biology teacher, seemed to like me, and kept giving me decent grades. Her classes were sometimes fun, and she wasn't 'cool' in any way. She was a small woman, middle-aged, and had red hair and a red face.

She was terribly disappointed when she caught me cheating on the final course exam at the end of the second semester...

Cheating in Biology Mrs. Edmund had told us that one of the questions on the final would be to diagram a leaf with all its biological parts. To prepare for the exam, I traced the leaf diagram in the book and copied the names of all the parts of the leaf onto the tracing: petiole, base, midrib, lamina, etc. I studied my drawing assiduously. I was confident. However, during the exam I was running out of time, so at the end, I just slipped my traced diagram into the exam folder, knowing it was wrong, and turned it in.

The next day I was called into Mr. Root's office. Mr. Root was behind his desk and Mrs. Edmund was in the visitor's chair. My diagram and the Biology text open to the diagram page were on his desk. My stomach sank into my shoes.

"Is this your work here, Charles?" Mr. Root asked me after giving me an intimidating stare.

"Ye.. Yes, I.. I think so," I stammered. I picked up the drawing and pretended to study it intently.

Mr. Root turned to Mrs. Edmund. "Thank you, I'll take it from here." Mrs. Edmund got up and left the room. She hadn't said a word.

"That's quite a remarkable rendition of the leaf diagram," he said. "It almost looks like you traced it."

Foolishly, I tried to bluff my way out of the situation. "Yeah, I studied it real hard because Mrs. Edmund said it would be on the test."

"Well, you should have it well in mind since the test was just yesterday. Here's a sheet of paper. Sit down and do it again and we'll count your diagram. Otherwise, you'll get a zero on it and an F on the test."

Miserably, I sat down and began to draw. It became painfully obvious within a few minutes that I couldn't come anywhere near to the tracing.

Mr. Root pinned me with his stare, and said "What do you think we should do, Charles? Cheating on a final exam is something we can expel you for."

I fought back tears, thinking about how my father would react, and how I would miss the new friends I had made over the year.

"Please don't" I begged.

"Well, Mrs. Edmund has offered to give you a different final exam. She says that she thinks you just made a mistake, and that it shouldn't end your career here. You're very lucky," he said, staring sternly. "She says she will give it to you after school this afternoon and grade it tonight. She's willing to give you a grade based on how you do. Meet her in her classroom at three-thirty.

"That's all, you may go now."

My knees nearly gave out as I stood and left the office and I leaned against the railing. I was almost physically sick, and couldn't catch my breath. It was a feeling that I never wanted to feel again. I had learned one of the most important lessons of my high-school career, and I never cheated again.

I was so embarrassed and humiliated when I went to take my test that I thought I hated Mrs. Edmund. She was there, grading the other students' exams, and unsmilingly, but gently, told me to take a seat at the back of the classroom. My face was burning, my hands were trembling, and my stomach was in knots. When I was seated in the seat she had assigned, she came over and placed an exam booklet and a sheet of questions on my desk.

"I'll pick it up in fifty-five minutes," she said, looking at her watch. The clock on the wall said three thirty-five.

I calmed myself with a couple of deep breaths and read through the questions. They were harder than the ones on the original test, but as I read, I saw that I could answer most of them comfortably.

In the end, I got an A-minus on the exam, and a B-plus overall in Biology. Looking back, I realize how big a favor Mrs. Edmund gave me.

~*~_Physics-_   Our Physics teacher was Mr. Reimer. He was "the Absent-minded professor". His classes were always surprising in ways that he didn't intend. His models of atoms would fall apart in mid-presentation; his demonstration of electricity traveling from positive to negative post sparked out; our home-made electric magnets were either too strong or too weak. Whenever one of these glitches would occur, he would begin to blink furiously, a habit which we all learned to imitate.

~*~_Chemistry-_ Mr. Neufeld, our Chemistry Teacher, was deemed "the Nutty Professor". We learned to make esters that smelled like bananas, rotten eggs, and burning hair. We learned how chemicals reacted to heat and light. The most famous event, which I got a very good look at since I sat in the front row, was how sodium interacts with plain water. The demonstration involved a large bowl of water into which Mr. Neufeld was to shave a thin flake of pure sodium off a large block. Unfortunately, the whole block slipped out of his hand and into the water. The explosion was epic, and sizzling shards of sodium flew all over the classroom. Several of us were slightly singed. Fortunately, Mr. Neufeld had been wearing his protective glasses and gloves, so he survived fairly intact.

Fly Guts   A famous bit of mischief, for which I took the blame, also occurred in Mr. Neufeld's Chemistry class. The Chemistry Lab was in the Science Block. Kodai School used septic tanks to dispose of its waste, and these tanks were located behind the Science Block. This spring, the system had backed up and overflowed, creating a stench and a perfect breeding ground for flies. We didn't know, at first, what was causing the awful smell, but it was a huge distraction from our studies.

Chemistry Lab came just before lunch, and we were in the second semester of our senior year. The weather was getting warm, and following the outbreak of the odor, there was a sudden huge increase in the number of flies. The Science Block became the epicenter of this plague, especially during the warmer part of the day. These were the days before air conditioning, so the windows were always open and the flies were free to come and go as they pleased.

Bibbi, Kris, Lyn and I sat in the four desks nearest the door (we liked to be the first ones out the door at the end of class in order to make it to lunch quickly). Our lab notebooks and texts were on the desks in front of us whenever we were not actually standing at the lab tables performing some experiment or other. The flies became quite awful pests, and we would wave our hands to shoo them away constantly, movements which caused Mr. Neufeld no end of distraction at the beginning. However, he soon got used to us flailing away and chose to ignore us.

In the warmth of midday the flies seemed to be somewhat sluggish, so that as we swiped at them, we could sometimes actually hit one or two of them as they flew away. It became our objective to swipe at them vigorously to see if we could feel their little bodies on our palms as we flailed.

I think it was Kris who began catching them in his fist.

"Watch this," he commanded in a whisper. He carefully cupped his hand behind a small group of flies that had landed on his desk and suddenly scooped, closing his fist around several of them. Then he shook his fist violently up and down and slammed the flies down on the floor. They lay there stunned, and were easily squashed underfoot. Soon we were all doing it, and competing to see who could catch the most flies in one scoop.

Bibbi soon mastered the art of it, and was able to catch a group of nine flies. Or so he claimed. "Hey guys, I swear I got at least nine that time," he hissed.

Since there were already so many squashed flies on the floor, who could tell for sure? Then Lyn came up with the idea of slamming the flies into the back page of our Lab Notebooks, where we could count them for sure. He demonstrated, scooping five or six flies off his desk, shaking his fist while opening his notebook to the last page, throwing them in and quickly closing the notebook shut on top of them.

Upon opening the book, there they were, duly squashed and fairly easy to count.

"There you are," he explained. "Six flies for sure. That makes me the champion."

Of course we all had a go, waiting patiently for enough flies to gather close enough together to make the attempt worthwhile. By the end of the period, the back pages of our Lab Notebooks were full of fly guts and crushed carcasses.

I was making one last attempt to win the contest, and scooped a good fistful of flies. Not wanting to lose any of them, I shook them vigorously and flung them into the back of my notebook.

Squished Flies

Unfortunately, in my zeal not to lose a single one, since any not sufficiently stunned would quickly fly away, I slammed my notebook closed with a resounding slap, drawing Mr. Neufeld's gaze my way.

"What is it, Charles?" he asked, seeing my guilty expression. "Did someone send you a note? Let me see."

"Uh, no sir," I said. "I just almost dropped my notebook. Sorry, sir."

"Really?" he asked, raising his eyebrows so that they arched above the rims of his glasses. "Let me see it, please." He walked over to my desk and held out his hand.

Reluctantly, I gave him my notebook, hoping he would look through the front pages and see some of my legitimate notes. The back pages were sticking together, glued by all the fly guts, so I hoped he would miss them. But, of course, he noticed that the back of the notebook had something between the pages, and soon discovered the resting place of all the flies.

Mr. Neufeld was a really cool teacher, and well-liked by most of us. When he saw what was in the last pages of my notebook, he looked disappointed.

"Really, Charles, I think you need to pay more attention in this class. It's not as if your grades are all that good. This really looks like a waste of time, both yours and mine." I was feeling awful. "Why don't you attend detention after Study Hall tonight and write me a short report about what we covered in class today? You can give it to me tomorrow."

He was giving me a demerit!

Bibbi, Kris and Lyn were suddenly all studiously busy copying notes from the blackboard into their books and thumbing through the pages in their texts, pretending they didn't know me. After standing in front of me for a few more embarrassing moments, Mr. Neufeld went back to his lecture.

"How could you let me take the rap by myself?" I hissed at them as we were leaving after class. "It wasn't even me who started it."

"What good would that have done?" asked Kris. "You should have been quieter with your book. You almost got us all in trouble. Anyway, since we never counted your last catch, I guess I'm the one who caught the most."

"Don't worry, Charlie," said Bibbi. "We'll help you write your report. I'll get Ron or Kurtis to lend me their notes and join you after Study Hall." It felt good to know that Bibbi had my back.

The sewage problem and fly plague went on for several more days, but we only caught them in other classes, which weren't quite as infested as Mr. Neufeld's class, so Kris remained the champion of the flies.

Math- I am actually quite good in Math… practical Math and Math Logic, that is. When math gets theoretical or complicated, I tend to get lost. Plane Geometry falls in the category of practical and logical, but unfortunately, I began to get out of my depth in Algebra II, so I later dropped out of Calculus and never took Trigonometry. In those days, those classes required a slide rule (we hadn't heard of electronic calculators), and I was always astounded by Bibbi's skill with one. He, Kurt Johnson and Ron Koepke would sit together with their slide rules talking about some problem or other while furiously working their slides back and forth to come up with some solution to a problem that I didn't even understand. Bibbi went on to be a surveyor; Kurt became a physicist; and Ron, a medical doctor. I stuck to basic Math.

~*~*Plane Geometry-*   Mr. Reimer, from Physics, had also been my Geometry teacher, a subject that he seemed to find boring, or at least not intellectually stimulating.   Classes seemed to consist of memorizing formulae and solving problems. We learned, but it wasn't that fun, so the learning didn't stick with me for long. It was at this point that I decided that students who weren't having fun in class weren't learning, a maxim that I tried to live by when I became a high school teacher years later.

~*~*Algebra II-*   My Algebra II class was taught by Mr. Amstutz. Mr. Amstutz was an earnest, small man, and very serious about Math in general, and quite passionate about Algebra, Trigonometry and Calculus. He wore thick, horn-rimmed glasses that made his eyes appear to bug out.   The class was scheduled for the first period after lunch, a period of the day in which our energy levels were low and concentration was difficult, so it should have been a very draggy class, but it wasn't...

Kicking the Can   Mr. Amstutz would rush into class from the teachers' dining room, usually after the bell had rung, and head straight to the board to begin writing out the day's proof. One day near the start of the semester, as he triumphantly finished this analysis of a formula, he stepped back energetically, and in so doing kicked the trash can that was on the floor behind him to one side of the blackboard. The metal can flew backwards and spewed its contents, papers and pencil shavings all over the floor. The whole class erupted.

The following day, and every day thereafter, whenever Mr. Amstutz was late, Lyn would come into class and carefully place the trash can on the same spot. And, every day, at some point in the lesson, Mr. Amstutz would step enthusiastically backwards and kick the can, to our great amusement. We tried to hide our laughter with coughs and tittering.

One interesting result of these shenanigans was that we would concentrate fully on Mr. Amstutz' delivery of the lesson.   We were anticipating the moment that he would complete his proof and triumphantly kick the can. He would look up at us periodically and see our rapt attention and launch into more detail and explanation, assuming that we were focused on the lesson. As a result, we probably learned more than we would have without the mischief, and Mr. Amstutz thought he was doing an awesome job of teaching. As far as I know, he never caught on.

Social Studies- ~*~Indian Social Studies- Our Indian Social Studies teacher, Mrs. Mitchell, was very organized and strict. I was at a disadvantage, having just recently arrived in India, while most of my classmates had lived here for years and been immersed in Indian history and culture. The text we used was also singularly opaque, having been written by an Indian Ph.D. who took pride in his erudition. I buckled down and was able to eke out a B-minus for the course, after stumbling along at a D for most of a semester.

~*~American History- Mr. Rushton was our American History teacher. He was Canadian, which should have lent the class a different perspective. Unfortunately, he was one of those teachers that seem to paint by the numbers, and we just followed the book, learning dates and names that we would have to regurgitate on an exam. He was a generous grader, and I got one of my easy A's from him. He was very lax in his class discipline, however, and we often took advantage of his class to pass notes and study for other subjects. We could get permission to go to the bathroom and leave the classroom for long periods of time, sometimes two or three of us together.

~*~Geography- Mrs. Mitchell also taught World Geography in her same strict, organized way. After going through the obligatory continental drift theory and map projections we took a deep dive into the Koeppen Climate Classification System, which I found fascinating since I had lived in four of the five main climate classifications, (all except for polar climate), as well as the sub-category of Highland Climate. My interest and participation with first-hand experiences served me well, and I got an A-minus.

~*~Religious Education- A requirement at Kodai School was taking Religious Education (R.E.) every semester as part of our academic curriculum. Although not part of the standard United States Curriculum, R.E., as we called Religious Education class, was treated as an academic course and taken very seriously by the school administration. The School pastor was usually the teacher, which, for the first two years I was there meant Mr. Reble. Mr. Reble was a gentle man with ample religious tolerance. He was not dogmatic or evangelical, and encouraged diverse opinions for discussion. I had never been in a Socratic class environment, so it took me a while to get my bearings and begin to engage with the class. That kept my grades low in the D-plus to C range until Bibbi sorted me out. Reverend Dewey took over the class for my senior year, and my grades improved, thanks more to Bibbi's tutelage than to any other reason. Reverend Dewey was, if anything, of a gentler nature than Mr. Reble.

Both men were pastors at Kodai, but for some reason "the reverend" suited Dewey better than it did Reble. A few years later, Reverend Dewey wrote a letter to my Draft Board that supported my claim to be a Conscientious Objector to the Viet Nam War when I became eligible for the draft.

Religion at Kodai   Kodai was, first and foremost, a Christian-based institution. All students were required to attend church service on Sunday mornings and Vespers on most Sunday evenings. Even Narain, who was a Hindu, (you'll meet him later), was required to attend these services. Children of diplomats and businessmen not affiliated with a church, as well as those students whose missions did not maintain separate compounds, stayed in Wissy, which was multi-denominational. The more conservative missionary groups had boarding compounds off campus where they could keep tighter control of their wards.

In those days most of the students at Kodai were the sons and daughters of Christian missionaries to India, many of whom had obtained their visas before such visas became difficult to get, and as such, had lived in India most of their lives. The writing was already on the wall that Kodai would have to broaden its student base beyond the dwindling pool of foreign Christian missionaries. Nevertheless, the School's Christian identity was well established and informed its curriculum and staffing.

My own religious background was spotty, and not deeply ingrained. Dad had been a New England Baptist and Mom was a Presbyterian. I don't recall attending church in Burma, but we were steeped in Buddhism through our many trips to the Shwedagon Pagoda, and the celebration of the religious festivals, such as the Light Festival and the Water Festival.

The first I recall joining a church was when we were in Herndon. From the age of six to about nine, I attended the local Presbyterian services and Sunday school with my mother and brothers and sister. Dad attended the Baptist church down the road for a while, but it was Southern Baptist as opposed to the New England Baptist branch he had been raised in, so eventually he joined us at the Presbyterian Church.

In Jerusalem we flitted from church to church as part of Dad's official duties. The church that I remember most there was the Anglican Church, probably because we went there twice for Sunrise Services on Easter morning. We attended the Union Church in Tegucigalpa occasionally. At some point along the way, Dad lost his zeal, and church attendance became voluntary, and therefore, rare.

I received additional religious formation while we were in Jerusalem, where I attended fifth grade at a French Catholic school run by nuns, who tried to inject religion into all our classes, and then a Quaker boarding school for sixth grade in Ramallah where I was exposed more to Islam than to Christianity. I had not developed an affinity to any specific religion, and was already fairly agnostic well before I came to Kodai.

As such, R.E. was a burden I really didn't want about a subject that I didn't find interesting. The only saving grace was that I attended it with Bibbi, Kris and Lyn, and it was a fairly un-demanding hour, compared to math, science, English and history. It wasn't an easy A by any means, and I got D+'s fairly consistently for my first year until Bibbi took me to task. Based on our discussions, I gathered that he, like me, was somewhat (though more reservedly) agnostic, or possibly pantheistic, though he wouldn't have admitted it then. He appeared to show as much affinity for Eastern philosophy as for the Lutheran teachings he had been brought up with. He kept those feelings close to his chest, only letting them surface in some of our deeper private discussions about subjects that came up in class. In spite of that, he got straight A's in R.E., and was considered to be one of the more pious students. Among the four of us, Lyn, Kris, Bibbi and me, I was considered the least religious, followed by Kris; and Lyn, a Mennonite, was considered the most pious followed by Bibbi.

After my third D+ at the end of the third grading period of my first semester at Kodai, Bibbi took me aside and explained how my grade in R.E., while not a required course in an American curriculum, would affect my GPA, which would affect my choice of colleges at graduation. He began to work with me on the reports I had to turn in and to prepare for tests. We began to engage in philosophical discussions and analyze the various sects that arose through the Reformation and whether we believed in any of their arguments.

We found in each other a great philosophical rapport, to our mutual surprise. He was more inclined to accept the basic tenets of Christianity, including virgin birth and the divinity of Christ, than I was, but he was unwilling to dismiss the divinity of Buddha. He was open to the existence of a supreme being, and committed to being a moral human being.

I began to pay more attention in R.E. so that I could mount more convincing and interesting arguments in our discussions, and found that as I concentrated more and participated more, my grades improved so that by the end of the semester I had raised my grade to a solid C.

Bibbi and I continued our ongoing discussion of religion and its place in our lives, becoming ever more in concert in our views. Bibbi was inherently more honest and conscientious than I was, but we both agreed that the most important idea we could distill from R.E. was to treat all people and religions with dignity and care, and condemn no one for their sincerely held ideas or beliefs. In our view, the greatest sin that anyone could commit was the hypocrisy of professing a set of standards and not following it. On reflection, it is a sin that I have committed often over the years.

~*~*Physical Education-* I was never a 'jock' by any stretch of imagination. I wasn't exactly the 98 pound weakling that was portrayed in the back of comic books beside a picture of Charles Atlas, but I was tall and skinny at 126-130 pounds, and I was far from being one of the athletic kids. P.E. was always a chore to me, and driving myself to become stronger and faster did not appeal. As such, I don't have many coherent memories of our P.E. classes, taught by Mr. Hall and others. I do remember being near the last to be picked when we chose up teams for scrimmages, as well as being cut from the school basketball team in spite of my nearly six-foot height. I never made it on to any of the field-day squads. I would go down to Bendy field or to the basketball courts and run around, rarely doing enough to break a sweat, but enough to garner a C or B-minus most terms.

All high school boys attended P.E. at the same time, dividing into class groups, but sharing the same teacher, so that there were some seventy or eighty of us occupying the fields of both Upper and Lower Bendy, when one of the school teams was not having separate practice. The school had a basketball team, a soccer team, a tennis team, a golf team, a volley ball team and a track team, all of which competed with other high schools locally and around India. They were coached by various teachers (Mr. Root coached basketball) during the P.E. period and before or after school, and traveled around India by bus and train. They regularly brought back championship trophies. Bibbi was on several of the teams, as were Kris and Lyn, so I was often at P.E. class without them.

Electives- ~*~*Chorus-* We were encouraged to fill out our schedules with electives and I took chorus most semesters. Our chorus directors were Mr. Hunt and Mr. DeJong. Mr. Hunt, the first semester of my sophomore year, was a typically temperamental gifted musician. I had a decent voice, but had never studied music and couldn't read notes. I was gifted, however, at learning a part quickly so that actually not being able to read the notes didn't slow me down compared to the others who could.

That didn't satisfy Mr. Hunt, who would refer to the score using terms like 'measure', 'treble', 'staccato' 'clef', 'pianissimo' as well as notes A, B, C, D, E and F, and get very frustrated with those of us who couldn't understand what he was saying. I dropped out of chorus for two semesters after that, returning in the second semester of my junior year when Mr. DeJong took over.

Mr. DeJong was much more tolerant of my ignorance, and appreciated the ease with which I could learn and memorize my parts, and the fact that I sang on key. The music he chose for us was a little less classical than what we had looked at with Mr. Hunt, and a lot more fun. I sang tenor, and got to stand next to Judy Staal, a cute senior who also sang tenor, during the spring semester of my junior year.

~*~*Typing*-   I took Typing in my junior year, as did most of my classmates, and our teacher was Lyn's mother, Mrs. Rose Krause. We used to joke that she was a true 'Kodai Rose', which was the euphemism by which we referred to cow dung patties that were encountered everywhere around Kodai, since sacred cows were allowed to roam at will.

In typing class we learned to type on mechanical typewriters, and I spent a good deal of my time unsticking the keys and changing the ribbon. If you made a mistake, you couldn't correct it without removing the page from the typewriter and erasing your error with a special eraser wheel and brush. Little by little, to my surprise and Mrs. Krause's delight, I pulled my average word-per-minute score up to 36 wpm with no mistakes, enough to warrant a solid C. Fewer than 35 wpm would have been a C-, and with 2 mistakes or more would have dropped to a D-plus. If I had made any mistakes in the time test, I would have been dropped to a C-minus. Most of the girls and some of the guys were hitting 50 or more words per minute with no mistakes by the end of the course, and Barbie Ford, whose mother was _also_ a typing teacher at Kodai, was above 60 wpm.

~*~*Wood Shop*-   With all of my required courses behind me, I took Wood Shop with Mr. Sipantzi in my senior year. He immediately identified me as quite unskilled with my hands, and kept me off the lathe and band saw, as well the other machines that could maim or kill. Sam Turner, my classmate, excelled in shop and turned out project after project: tables and chairs with beautifully turned legs and glossy, smooth surfaces. I managed to make a book stand that my mother kept proudly in her kitchen to hold her cook books.

Showers and Hygiene   Showers were an important activity during our "free time" periods, especially on Wednesday after P.E. and before Canteen. The boiler was fired up for hot water every Wednesday and Saturday for showers. Showers were available any day, but hot water was limited to Wednesday and Saturday afternoons, and cold showers were avoided as much as possible. At seven thousand feet, the night cools off quickly, and the water temperature in the pipes is in the 50's Fahrenheit.

Dorm showers were a fraught activity. On Wednesdays, upper classmen were usually released from P.E a few minutes earlier than underclassmen so that they would be first in line for the showers, which assured them hot water. As sophomores and freshmen, we would run back to the dorm after P.E. as quickly as we could to reserve a spot in line, hoping to get into a shower before the water began to cool. Since the boiler was still burning, the water wouldn't get too cold, but it became lukewarm, which wasn't as enjoyable as piping hot.

The trick was to get to your room, strip, wrap your towel around your waist, grab your soap and run to the bathroom as quickly as you could. When you got there, you would identify the boy who made it there just ahead of you and confirm that you were next after him. Then you would identify the boy who would follow you when he arrived. There was no "saving a place" for your buddies. Once you had your turn identified, you could use the facilities, brush your hair or your teeth, mill around in the warm, steamy bathroom, or go outside and sit on the wall in your towel, waiting for the bathroom to clear and keeping your eye on the boy ahead of you in line. It was understood that a senior arriving for his shower could cut into the line at any time.

It was fairly normal for us to be sitting around outside the bathroom waiting for our turn in the shower for twenty minutes or more. The seniors loved to luxuriate in the hot water, taking their time, and many of the juniors followed their example. There could be as many as fifteen or twenty boys ahead of you in line for the six shower heads. We were encouraged by Mr. Root to take no more than three minutes in the shower and to turn the water off as we lathered up, based on his experience in the navy, but a five- or six-minute-shower was more the norm, and only a few boys would turn off for lathering.

As boys will be boys, these waiting periods sometimes became raucous. One boy would whip off another boy's towel, leaving him naked, while others jeered. Objects would be tossed at the crotches of boys seated on the wall. Towels were snapped at buttocks. There was a lot of banter about the perceived masculinity of this boy or that. Mostly this horseplay was good-natured and could usually be quashed with a joke or a cutting remark, but it did make some uncomfortable, and once or twice turned to angry words. By today's standards, some of this behavior would be condemned as inappropriate or bullying, but compared to what I had experienced in Ramallah, they were pretty tame. Some boys waited in their rooms until all the jocks and upperclassmen had left the area to come out and have their showers, often getting only lukewarm water.

As teenagers, our sweat had begun to smell. Any time we exerted ourselves or became nervous we would begin to 'ripen' quickly. Since hot showers were only available on Wednesdays and Saturdays, we would often resort to cold showers or sponge baths to manage the smell. My account at Hamidia's became a godsend to me since I could acquire deodorant and cologne to mask my body odor between times. Others were not so fortunate, and would often turn to me to lend them my products.

Bibbi was quite fanatical about his cleanliness, and would frequently take freezing cold showers before breakfast. He was able to hop in, soap up and rinse off in less than a minute. There was one time when the water main to Wissy was being worked on, so there was no water at the dorm. He had played in a soccer match the evening before and felt that he needed to wash up before breakfast.

He came back to our room from the bathroom in quite a state.

"Charlie, I've got to wash up before breakfast and there's no water! Let's go down to the lake and wash up," he suggested.

"Are you crazy? The lake is freezing!" I replied

"No, really, the top layers won't be so bad. It's not like we're going to go swimming," he declared. "We just splash some water on and soap up and then splash some more to rinse off. Come on! You're a lifeguard so you're used to it."

Despite my reservations, I let him convince me and we put on our bathing suits and headed out to the lake.

At breakfast I found out why he had insisted on cleaning up when Carolyn came to sit at our table.

Liquor, Drugs and Pear Wine   Tamilnadu was a 'dry state' as Bibbi had told us on that first day. Liquor was banned for general consumption. There were no liquor stores in Kodai. We understood that adults could find an evening libation or a glass of wine or a beer with dinner at the English Club or at the Carlton Hotel. These pleasures, however, were frowned upon universally by all the conservative denominations at Kodai, and were reserved for the less observant members of the expat community. With the exception, possibly, of Mr. Mapp, almost all teachers and staff were probably teetotalers.

However, that does not mean that liquor didn't exist. The palm toddy that Bibbi had told us about was around, although I never knew anyone who had tried it.

Other drugs were also available and their use by Kodai students was severely punished if they were ever caught. Hashish could be had if one knew where to look, and I did hear of several students who partook. If being caught smoking was bad, getting caught with 'hash' was terminal. Once in a while a student would basically 'disappear' from campus, usually during class time so that no one saw them leave. Rumors would circulate, but anyone who knew for sure what had happened usually didn't want to admit it.

Our group, indeed, our whole class for the most part, was innocent of these sins. I heard in later years that one or two of my classmates had indulged in some of these illicit activities, but while I was at Kodai, I was blissfully unaware of these incidents, or even the availability of drugs, and never tempted to participate. The most daring behavior along these lines we ever tried was smoking bidis, which, while frowned upon, was overlooked by some of the more liberal staff.

There was one activity among the stories that Bibbi had heard from John that did give us ideas about things that we could get into trouble for. One of the more interesting was the tale about pear wine. During my first hiking season at Kodai any discussion of taking a day hike or bike ride to Pillar Rocks would involve some feigned wobbly walking and slurred speech that made no sense to me until Bibbi explained the inside joke.

There were a number of old pear trees in an abandoned orchard around the lake that we could take pears from. They were 'sand pears' and weren't very good to eat most of the time, being either too sour and hard or too soft and gritty. There were also some fairly decent pears on the Lutheran compound that Bibbi and I would walk over to pick and eat. Sometimes as we walked around the lake past the sand-pear trees, we would imagine the fruit into grenades that we would lob out into the lake or throw up as high as we could to watch them splat on the roadway as we made explosive noises.

Someone, though, had discovered that you could put sand pears through a strainer and get juice out of them, and that this juice turned hard after a few days in a canteen. Who this "someone" was is never revealed in the telling, but the story goes that a staff member somehow tried some of the hard pear cider and the "someone" was severely punished, maybe even expelled.

It wasn't long, however, that some students in John's class, that may or may not have included John, came up with a way to avoid staff surveillance.

Pillar Rocks

The hike out to Pillar Rocks, where we had climbed the chimney, was a fairly easy walk or bike ride. It is about seven miles with very little incline, mostly along a paved road. The rocks themselves are large granite outcroppings forming a fairly sheer cliff face. The rocks are weathered and tree-topped, and have, as recounted earlier, many shallow caves, crevices and cracks that make excellent hiding places. These cracks soon became the go-to secret repositories of so-called pear wine.

I, myself, never tried any of the pear juice, but Bibbi recounted stories John had told him about some who had. Some students claimed that they were able to "get high" on the stuff, and some tried to get girls to join them on hikes to the Rocks to take part in bacchanalian parties. Stories of these parties tended to be clearly made-up or greatly exaggerated, and Bibbi gave them no real credence. The most consistent story, however, was that the pear wine was a very good way to get diarrhea and stomach cramps so that you could get out of test days and spend a day in the "dish", the School's health office or "dispensary".

Local Staff   In addition to the kitchen and office staff, Kodai School campus grounds were maintained by a local staff of about forty men and women under the direction of Mr. Norris, father of one of the girls in our class, Sandra.

These hard-working people kept the campus swept and manicured very much behind the scenes. Our dorm rooms and bathrooms were swept and cleaned daily. Push mowers and hand clippers kept all the grass areas on campus immaculate, from the Flag Green to the lawn in front of Wissy. Firewood for the boiler was cut and split and stacked in the boiler room. The sports fields were groomed and lined. The red clay tennis courts were rolled and lined almost daily. Pot holes were filled, cracks were mended, and brickwork and stonework was repaired. Every once in a while we would see some work in progress here or there around campus, evidenced by a cordoned-off area, but in general, all this activity occurred while we were in class.

These staff members were largely unsung and unnoticed by us students. They went about their workdays quietly, and the effort of their labor was taken for granted. It was only when something went amiss and left undone that we paid attention to the work they did, such as when the septic tank behind the Science Block backed up.

They would be especially busy during the long vacation when we had left school. We would return to find fresh coats of paint and polished floors and furniture throughout the school.

For the most part, even though I would see them around from time to time, I never got to know any of them by sight, and could not have told you their name or title, or even their function. Nevertheless, their dedication and efficiency made the Kodai experience much more enjoyable.

There was also other non-staff support from services that were contracted out. On Wednesday mornings we would stuff all of our dirty clothes into our dhobi bags and cart them down to the Housemother's cottage. Our dhobi bags were picked up and taken away by local dhobis. These washerwomen would cart our bags of clothes down to Munjikal Sports fields below the Budge, where Palar Stream, which flowed out of the lake, and Bear Shola Stream merged. There our clothes were pounded clean on rocks, then spread out and sun-dried on the grass nearby. They were folded and returned the following week.

Trouble in Paradise Life at Kodai was, in many ways, idyllic. Our time was filled with activities that were mostly fun and interesting. There was little of the bullying behavior that I had experienced in other schools, partly because it was channeled into the hierarchy of class status. Upper classmen were allowed to lord it over underclassmen to a limited and controlled extent, while being encouraged by staff example to support and nurture them. For the most part, disciplinary decisions were rational and understood. We were allowed some latitude to explore our adventurous spirits, but we all understood the limits. The vices of smoking, drinking and 'loose behavior' were strictly sanctioned.

Sometime before the start of my second year at Kodai, Bibbi and I had taken to composing our letters home together during study hall. We would feed off of each other's ideas to fill out stories for our parents and make the letters interesting and informative. We had learned that in this way we could fill up the Aerogramme letter form, which always made Mrs. Gibbs happy. She would hold our sealed letters to the light to see how much we had written and look to see if our missive had spilled over on to the back flap of the Aerogramme, which could be easily seen as it was not in the sealed part of the form.

This practice made me a better letter writer. Bibbi would come up with anecdotes that didn't exactly reveal all of our activities, but gave our parents solid information about how things were going and shone the best light on some of the shenanigans we got up to. We would read each other's letters to make sure that not too much was revealed, and that we were both mostly on the same page.

Occasionally Kris would join us in letter writing and share his anecdotes with us, but he was usually busy "studying" with Maureen, and would end up dashing off a quick note to his parents just in time to meet the deadline for sending out the weekly letter home. Lyn, since he was living with his parents, found our struggles to fulfill our letter-writing chore amusing. So it was that in June of '64, at the start of our junior year, both Bibbi and I wrote home about the new students who had been assigned to Wissy. I wrote:

> *"So far, five new kids have entered Wissy and all of them are asses. One, a British kid, claims he's a Homo, but I think that that's just a bunch of bull made up to get attention; another is a religious character who always acts 'holier than thou'; another, Leslie Eidus (you know his mother in Madras) keeps lying about how cool he is when he isn't so cool after all; another is a small, quiet little boy who really isn't too bad; and the last is the worst of all. He just came today. He is a Texan and a typical one. He hates colored people, and crows about how he used to go 'ni[**]er-knocking' when he was in the States. His dad is a millionaire. He drinks, smokes and swears. I think and I hope that he'll get kicked out before he has a chance to influence anybody."*

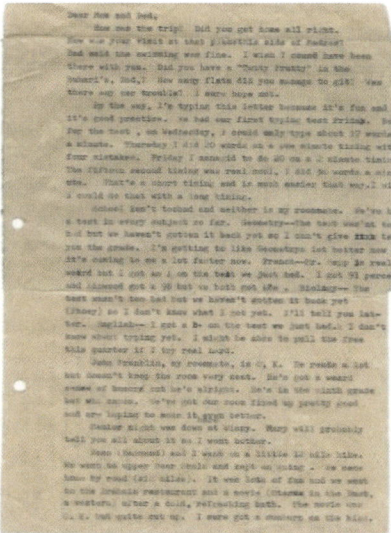

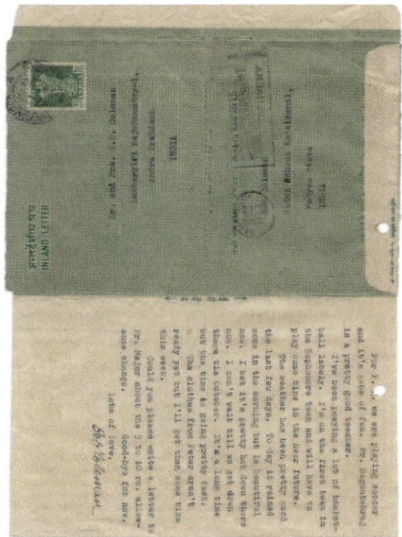

A Typical Aerogramme Form: Bibbi's Letter of June 26, 1963

Bibbi wrote a very similar narrative in his letter, although he was much more diplomatic than I was. He wrote:

"The new students here are really weird!!!! One guy is a real dope. He goes prancing around acting stupid all the time. Another guy is real quiet and seems to like to do everything by himself. Another tells everyone that he is really 'cool' in everything but he isn't quite as good as he really says he is. The last addition is the son of a millionaire from Texas. He seems to have gotten into the segregation problem in the States. He told someone that he was a 'ni[**]er hater'. That doesn't go over too well with the people around here. I don't know what will happen to his case."

The idea of a racist at Kodai was outrageous, and shocked us deeply. As multicultural kids, the concept was anathema. Even more shocking was his willingness to share this aspect about himself on his very first day at Kodai. I later heard that he had also expressed this detail with Narain, our Hindu classmate, who, being brown-skinned, took it quite personally.

In any event, Jeff, the obnoxious Texan, spent very little time at Kodai. The details of his quick departure from Kodai were cloaked in mystery, but nevertheless, he was gone within a month or so. We heard rumors that he would be continuing his education at the American School in Delhi, and we all wished him 'Good Riddance'. Not a single picture of him made it into that year's Eucy (Our school year-book, The Eucalyptus).

The other regrettable episode that came from this group of students involved 'Mr. Cool', Leslie Eidus. I guess one could argue that he brought his troubles upon himself by telling us how cool he was, but the scorn we piled on him was one of the few ugly blots on our behavior at Kodai.

It is likely that Leslie was given poor advice by his parents or someone else. His family was Hungarian and had fled their home during the Russian invasion in 1956, when Leslie was seven or eight years old. They had escaped to Canada. Leslie was quite the polyglot, fluent in Hungarian, English and French, a decent student, a decent tennis player and fairly athletic. The one thing he was *not* was 'cool'… at least, not in any way that we interpreted the concept. So, whoever told him to advertise his 'coolness' as a way to fit in to a boarding-school society, did him a disservice.

He was also unfortunate in other ways. First, of course, was his gender-bending name, Leslie. He definitely got some flak on that front.

The other was his ethnic physiognomy. He had a narrow face and a fairly prominent nose that extended straight from his forehead with little or no bridge. Based on this, Bibbi committed one of the few sins for which, in later years, he expressed deep regret. He likened Leslie to a shrew, and drew a wicked cartoon that he repeated on many notes and in the corners of his notebooks. Leslie tried to laugh it off, and even signed my yearbook with the 'nickname', but it was obvious that it seriously bothered him.

Bibbi was not a cruel person, and in fact, was one of the most tolerant and hospitable students in the school. So his treatment of Leslie was way out of character, and persisted for a long time. I would say that Kris, Lyn and I somewhat encouraged him by laughing at his comments and cartoons. As the 'class clown', I would often instigate the harassment by quietly saying "squeak, squeak" when Leslie spoke up in class.

Bibbi's Rendition of Leslie as 'The Shrew'

Leslie, admirably and with his dignity intact, stuck it out for the duration, and graduated with us the following year.

Boarding School Food   As boarding students at Kodai, we always felt half starved. Food at the cafeteria was plentiful enough, and there was enough for seconds most of the time, but of the twenty-one meals served each week (not including tea times) we found about a third of them less than appealing.

Breakfasts were usually good, and we especially liked pancakes, French toast, and scrambled eggs. Cream and syrup for our pancakes and French toast would often run out, so you had to act quickly to get your share. Their high caloric value was highly prized, besides the fact that they were delicious. Dry cereal, oatmeal, and wheateena were filling and nutritious.

Lunches were often stew or some kind of meat with rice. About twice a week we were served curry for lunch, which we all loved. There were basically two kinds of curry: wet curry and dry curry. Dry curry had a reputation of producing epic flatulence, probably because we all gorged on it whenever it was served.

Desserts were not my favorite part of the meal, except for when we got canned peaches or pears in nectar. I wasn't a fan of rice pudding or bread pudding, and couldn't stand the yellow custard we dubbed 'chinaman's snot'.

Suppers were light, and for the most part, were forgettable. We often went to bed at night wishing we had something more to eat, especially when our 'care packages' from home had run out.

And so, when we could afford it, we often headed down to the 'Budge', our slang term for the bazaar, for a good meal a couple of times a week. Sometimes we would pick something up at one of the veg (vegetarian) places, which were cheap and would serve all you could eat for the same low price, but when supper was especially bad or light, and we were really hungry and not yet broke, we headed for the Hotel State.

Hotel State   As a town in Hindu India, most eating establishments in Kodaikanal were strictly vegetarian. Most of these would provide eggs and paneer (Indian cottage cheese made from cow or buffalo milk), but of course, none would serve meat.

About three quarters of the way down 'Budge Road' was one of the few Muslim eateries in Kodai, the Hotel State. It was what is known in India as a 'meals hotel', as opposed to an inn that offers lodging. As a Muslim locale, they served meat of sorts. The chicken was very tough and stringy, and we suspected that it might be vulture meat. The beef was also tough and gamey, which we deemed to be water-buffalo meat. And, of course, at seven thousand feet up and hundreds of miles from an ocean, we didn't even consider fish as a possibility. The only consistently reasonable non-vegetarian fare was mutton, usually from goats rather than sheep.

Looking back, I realize that the Hotel State was not the most sanitary of operations and was more run-down than most of the Hindu establishments. The smells were different, as well, and one had to get used to them, which we did. Cooking aromas usually dominated, which was what drew us there. The curry smells were enhanced by meat and animal fat sizzling away. There were always more pests than in veg places, more ants, cockroaches, flies, and mice. But these were not abundant enough to turn us off, and there were fans to keep flying pests at bay while we ate.

Hotel State was a typical colonial style building that had seen better times, with high ceilings and a raised wooden floor in need of a good sweeping, made of ill-fitting planks worn bare by thousands of feet. The main area was large and often noisy, so when we went, we asked to be seated in the 'family room' which was more private, with only three or four tables. It was always a festive moment when we went, assured of delicious food and full bellies. After ordering, we would lounge back and tell jokes or gossip until the food arrived, when silence would descend. After eating, we would stay, sipping the last of our chai and planning our next visit.

Meals were served quickly on fresh banana leaves, and we ate with our fingers as there were no utensils to be had. There were a couple of kids who took to bringing their own forks stolen from the dining room, but we considered them weenies. Who didn't know how to eat with their fingers? Of course, you were criticized if you used your left hand to help push, or if the food stains crept past the second knuckle of the fingers on your right hand. Bibbi was by far the most adept of us at this skill if measured by speed, but Lyn, Kris and Linwood weren't far behind. I gamely kept at it to avoid being deemed a weenie, and soon got the hang of it, though I couldn't eat as quickly as the others, and I sometimes had to endure jibes when my hand got too messy.

The back room of the Hotel State became one of our favorite hangouts. There were places that had better chai, better rice, better raita, etc. and ones that were less expensive. But we would gravitate to the Hotel State more often than not. We would go there to celebrate or commiserate events. A high grade on a test or term paper was a great excuse. Missing supper (accidentally on purpose) due to a long hike was another one. Breaking up with a girlfriend (not me), was also a good reason. There were often other Kodai-ites there, but if we cared to, we could time it to have the place mostly to ourselves.

Our favorite fare, mutton biriyani, was expensive, costing about Rs. 2.50, (about 54 cents, US) with chai costing extra. You could get it with a hard-boiled egg on top for a few paise more. My allowance, Rs. 20 a month, would get me eight of these meals a month if I didn't spend on anything else. Bibbi only got Rs. 12 a month, which limited him even more. As a result, our outings waned towards the end of a month, and we always looked forward to the next month.

One day towards the end of a month when we were exceptionally hungry, Bibbi and I scraped together what funds we had left and found that we had about Rs. 3, enough to share a mutton biriyani meal, one for the two of us, and have it with a cup of chai. We headed down to the budge hoping that the waiter wouldn't be too stingy, and that we could get extra chutneys and mutton juice. We explained to the waiter that we only had enough for one meal, and that we would share it, and he wagged his head at us.

"Vhy doan't you ordar mutton biriyani with no mutton?" he suggested. "You have yenough money for two meals then."

Bibbi and I looked at each other and nodded. "Thank you!" Bibbi exclaimed. "We will do that. How much is 'mutton biriyani with no mutton'?"

"Just one rupee twenty-five, isn't it?" he replied.

Mutton Biriyani with No Mutton

We now had a way to stretch our meal funds, and although veg places would give us more meat-free food for our money, we felt that getting the mutton juice with the biriyani rice somehow made the meal more filling. We could also add an egg to our mutton-less biriyani if we felt like splurging.

On another occasion, when we felt we needed to fuel up for a long study session to prepare for a mid-term exam, we rushed down to the Hotel State with Kris and Lyn for our usual fare. Bibbi was nervous, as usual before a big test. He wanted to spend every possible minute cramming information into his head, and had even brought a textbook with him.

Bibbi, Lyn and Kris ate quickly, and I was trying to rush through my meal to avoid delaying them. While he waited for me to finish, Bibbi pulled out his textbook and began to skim through all the material again. Kris kept asking him irrelevant questions to throw him off his studies, and we all laughed at his frustration.

"How do you calculate the angle of the dangle?" was a typical question that Kris threw out.

Bibbi was getting flustered and began bouncing his foot nervously under the table. He tried to turn the discussion back to the subject he was studying. We all had to take the same test, so after a while, Kris relented. Bibbi went on bouncing his foot and running his finger down the pages. He was muttering to himself when we heard a shrill squeak from underneath the table. We looked under the table and saw a small brown mouse lying crushed on the floor. It had apparently run under Bibbi's bouncing foot by mistake. Bibbi felt awful about it at the time, but we all had a good laugh about it later. From then on, if we ever saw a mouse there, we would tease Bibbi that it was the wife of the mouse he had killed coming to look for her husband.

Our Impact on the Local Economy The Indian rupee was decimalized in 1957, changing its fractions from 'annas' to 'naye paise', or 'new pence', and in 1965 to simply 'paise'. However, traditions persist, and in our days, eight years after decimalization, prices were still largely quoted in annas. The traditional rupee was divided into 16 annas, which became one hundred paise. Anna coins and half-anna coins were still in circulation, valued at 6 np. and 3 np. respectively. So a half rupee could be quoted as either 8 annas or 50 paise, 4 annas could be 25 paise. It took me a while to understand prices and be able to work my way back and forth between annas and paise, but eventually it all made sense. Fortunately, there was no alternative nomenclature for rupees, so once it was explained that one rupee was 16 annas or 100 paise, I could do the math to figure out what I was spending out of my allowance of 20 rupees.

Our allowances were actually a significant part of the local economy. From 1950 to 1965, the rupee was fixed at 4.67 rupees per 1 US dollar, making my twenty-rupee monthly allowance worth a little more than 4 US dollars. With 350 students in Kodai School, our allowances added over a thousand dollars a month to the local economy. I was told at the time that the average per capita income for an Indian worker was around fifty dollars per year, which meant that we were contributing the annual income of some two hundred workers with just our allowances.

A significant portion of our allowances were spent on-campus at the various fund-raising events staged by the classes to fund things like retreats, proms, formal dances and other worthy causes. We would constantly beg our parents for extra funds for this or that purpose, and, in most cases, parents came through. But money was a constant theme in our letters home.

In addition to the Hotel State, local entrepreneurs found a number of ways to help us spend them.

Halva and Peanut Brittle- A fixture outside the front gate of the school was the Halva Man. His name was Hassan, but we called him Joker (pronounced joe-kar) for some reason that I never learned. He stood there all day, every day with his little makeshift table displaying a tray of orange halva, thick and chewy, and a tray of peanut brittle. Both of these confections were guaranteed to loosen one's fillings, and many of us spent time at the dentist's office during our long winter breaks having the damage repaired. The halva was cut into fairly uniform squares which he would sell for 2 annas or 12 paise (p) in modern currency.

If you went with several people, you could sometimes get five squares for 8 annas. The peanut brittle was broken into random sized pieces and you could choose a size to fit your budget, or he would put 2 annas worth into a cone made from discarded newsprint. The actual amount seemed to vary based on his mood, or how quickly his product was selling that day. Almost every time we came back from a hike or a meal in the Budge we would stop by and buy a piece of halva or peanut brittle.

Joseph's Confections- (on campus below the Science Block) Joseph somehow talked his way into a shack on campus with a small kitchen in which he cooked up all manner of candies, mostly chocolates, which he sold for 1 anna or 6 np. apiece. He wasn't there during my first year at Kodai but showed up during my junior year. I was soon a regular customer, and became completely addicted to his sweets, especially the marzipan center dark chocolates.

I didn't connect the consumption of his products with my acne problem, though I should have. My pimples got larger and breakouts more frequent after he set up shop. I assumed that this was just part of my teenage curse. This was before the days of Oxi-10. Bibbi seemed immune to acne, though that was possibly due to the fact that he rarely bought chocolates because he needed to conserve his money for real food.

Hamidia's Sundries Store- Hamidia's Sundries was a crowded space with all manner of processed dry goods and canned goods on shelves. Most products were of Indian manufacture, but there were also some more exotic items such as canned sardines, smoked mussels, and Italian pastas. Since I had an account there, I could usually avoid spending my allowance there, but occasionally would have to dig into my pocket when the monthly amount he had agreed to with my dad was exhausted. Other kids would go there to buy soap, toothpaste and other essentials. Once in a while, after the owner got to know me better, he would let me exceed the limit one month and recover the amount out of the next month's quota.

Spencer's- Another store that we frequented was Spencer's. It carried many of the same things as Hamidia's, plus a few more exotic items such as English orange marmalade, pickles and Spam. Hamidia's was cheaper for the shared goods, such as soap and toothpaste, but didn't carry items that appealed mainly to western palates. Spencer's was managed by Mr. Henderson, our cafeteria manger's husband. As with Hamidia's, some kids had small charge allowances at Spencer's.

Vegetarian Restaurants- There were a number of vegetarian (veg, pronounced 'vedge') restaurants. They were mostly small, and specialized in dishes preferred by their owners, but all made some variation of chutneys, sambar, a lentil-based vegetable stew in tamarind-flavored gravy, and rasam, sambar's soupier cousin, served with rice. Potato masala dosai was one our favorite veg meals. Okra (bhindi) masala and eggplant (brinjal) masala were also great meals, served with rice and chapattis. Idli, patties made from rice and lentil flour and steamed, were also on our list, with sambar and coconut chutney. Although idli is commonly considered a breakfast dish, we would eat them any time, as they were one of the cheapest meals. One of the eateries offered thali meals, which featured a variety of these vegetarian concoctions served on one plate with rice and chapattis.

All of these meals were very spicy and filling, although they digested quickly, leaving one hungry for more. The primary advantage of veg restaurants was price and quantity. For 1 rupee 50 paisa or even less at some places, one could eat one's fill.

Peanut and I J vendors- At any gathering of people off campus, and in certain parks and public spaces, vendors would walk around with boxes harnessed to their chests with peanuts and fried chick-pea and lentil flour pieces we called "Indian Junk" or simply "I J". For as little as 1 anna (about 6 np.) one could get a scoop in a paper cone made of old magazine or newspaper. These were salty and crunchy. These vendors also sold bidis, homemade Indian cigarettes, which some boys liked to take on hikes to smoke when staff wasn't looking.

Kodai Talkies- There was a theater, of sorts, near the Munjikal Sports field, below the Budge. It was a large, enclosed barn-like structure, with cloth walls that could be raised or lowered, depending on the occasion, where movies were shown on the weekends. For the most part, the movies shown were Tamil melodramas filmed in Ganesh Studios in Madras or one of the millions of Hindi productions filmed in Bombay or New Delhi, and didn't attract us much. Every once in a while, however, a Hollywood production would make its way to the theater, and we would head down to sit on the wooden benches (no chairs) and enjoy the show with some I. J. The price of entry was about one rupee.

The only movie I recall seeing there was "The Roman Spring of Mrs. Stone" with Vivien Leigh and Warren Beatty. The subject matter, sex and murder, made it fascinatingly inappropriate for Kodai kids, and much more interesting than the films that were periodically screened in the gym at School. Sam, Phil and I snuck off one Saturday afternoon to watch it. Bibbi decided not to come with us because he had to study for some test or other. I'm sure I did too, but I wasn't as conscientious as he.

Bike Rentals- Those of us who didn't own our own bike often rented bikes to go off on jaunts around Kodai. Rides around the lake were pretty easy, and rides out to Pillar Rocks or up to Bear Shola were easy and fun. We could also ride out to the golf course to play nine holes, saving the time it would take to walk out there. The bikes were rented from Shadrach, who had a shop near the intersection of Seven Roads. He had about a dozen bikes that were in various stages of disrepair, but he kept them all running well enough for easy rides. He could often be seen riding one bike and steering two more with one hand as he ferried them from his dwelling to his shop in the morning or back to his shack in the evening. These were the bikes that needed extra attention to make them passably road-worthy. If you were going to head down the Ghat, you needed to let him know so that he could make sure that the brakes were in good shape, the tread on the tires was sufficient and the handlebars and steering were tight.

Rentals ran anywhere from 8 annas to 1 rupee for a morning or afternoon up to 5 rupees for a long weekend. You could also rent by the half hour if you just wanted to accompany someone special around the lake.

Tea Stalls- Tea stalls served hot, sweet, spiced tea with milk, or chai, and hot coffee with milk and sugar. There seemed to be no such thing a black tea or black coffee, nor iced tea or coffee. The mixtures were kept over a low flame and stirred before each order was served.

Chai Wallah at Work: The Three-Foot Pour

An adept chai-wallah would scoop out a ladle of tea and pour it into a cup held at arm's length, making a stream of liquid up to three feet long that landed precisely in the cup with almost no splash or spillage. This pour served two purposes: it re-oxidized the tea, and cooled it to a (barely) drinkable temperature. A cup could be had for about 4 annas (25 np.).

Punt Rentals- During the spring semester, the weather was often gentle and fine and the Lake inviting. After church on a Sunday, many couples would take advantage of the weather and head out for some private conversation. Mr. Root had binoculars, and kept an eye on a good portion of the Lake, and would often have couples into his office for a quiet, uncomfortable chat if they seemed to be taking too many liberties. Those of us who didn't have girlfriends would sometimes rent punts to go out and harass these fortunate couples, just to make sure they weren't having too much fun.

Occasionally, during May break, we would get together with a couple of friends and take a punt out to the middle of the Lake and dive in. During May break at the end of our junior year Bibbi and I got Lucy David and Rani Vandeberg to join us for one such outing. My parents were out on a punt of their own, so we had to behave ourselves.

Kodaikanal Golf Club- About two-and-a-half miles from the school, the Kodaikanal Golf Club offered a fun way to spend one rupee and a Saturday morning or Sunday afternoon pursuing a pimpled white ball around a beautiful hilly expanse. Lyn's dad was on the board of the golf club, so Lyn got to play for free, while Kodai students got a special rate of 1 rupee per round. For most of us, these charges did not come out of our primary allowances, however. Parents could sign their students up and green fees would be sent to the school to be billed directly to the parents account.

I don't recall exactly how many holes the course had, not eighteen anyway, but you could replay some holes to complete a classic 18-hole round. Bibbi was an avid player and would often charge out to the course for a quick round. He had a caddy that would carry his clubs for tips and give him inside information on improving his scores. I didn't go often after learning the basics from Lyn, but occasionally we would get some girls who wanted to go, and we would accompany them gladly. I played with a putter and two irons that Lyn lent me so I wouldn't have to rent clubs for an additional fee.

Postage- We were required to write a letter to our parents every week, and we could purchase Aerogrammes for 10 np. each from our

House Parent. The preferred practice was to purchase ten for one rupee, but that meant tying up money that could be used for other things, and there was the danger that they could be "borrowed" by other students or soiled before being used.

Haircuts- Every month or so, we would decide that we needed to get our hair cut. This realization would usually occur when there was going to be some event that involved mixing with the girls, such as a prom or class trip. We would head down to the budge to visit Muthu, the barber. He would basically just trim us up with his scissors and thinning shears, and clean around our ears and neck with his straight razor. Bibbi and I would usually go together and thumb through old Tamil language magazines with pictures of current movie stars while he worked on the other. To get a haircut, you had only to sign Muthu's register which he then sent to the school, which billed your parents. If you wanted any hair products, such as Brylcreem or a comb or brush, you had to pay for them.

During our senior year, Bibbi took on the task of being the editor of the school's yearbook, the Eucalyptus, or "Eucy" as it is fondly referred to. This was in addition to his other extracurricular activities, Student Council President, and first string basketball and soccer teams. Each year the editor of the Eucy, along with the rest of the Eucy staff and its staff sponsor, would select a staff member to be honored on the 'Gratias Agimus' page to be singled out for special thanks. The person selected was often an influential teacher or pastor, or one of the helpful staff members.

Under Bibbi's leadership, however, the Eucy staff chose to honor local entrepreneurs and merchants who meant so much to us. The Gratias Agimus page in the Eucy of our senior year included six honorees: The Halva man (no name given) who stood outside the school's front gate at Seven Roads; Hamidia's store; Muthu, the barber; Peter, the tailor; the Hotel State; and the K.M.U, or Kodai Motor Union (not the Kodai Missionary Union, also known by this acronym), which provided transportation for field trips and excursion. Such a Gratias page had rarely been seen, and spoke volumes about how important these businesses were to our class as a whole, and to Bibbi personally.

4. A Couple of Capers

Orchids from Shembug   Another John-inspired adventure also involved sneaking out of Wissy at night and riding rented bicycles down the Ghat to Shembaganur, the Jesuit compound. I later discovered that this was a fairly common enterprise in early morning missions, but less so during nighttime raids. Our mission was to steal orchids for the corsages for our Prom dates.

Bibbi was an experienced cyclist, and had ridden bicycles for many years in India, both on the plains and in the mountains around Kodai. My own riding experiences were mostly limited to horseback riding, and I had only ridden a bike regularly for the three years we had lived near Washington, D.C. when I was eight and nine years old. During winter break, Bibbi got around Rajahmundry, where his family lived, on a bike all the time, and had taken long, intercity bike rides, so the idea of riding the few miles down the Ghat to Shembaganur (Shembug) didn't strike him as a big deal.

Linwood, my 11th-grade first-semester roommate, tells a typical and interesting story of one of Bibbi's many biking adventures during the off season:

Bibbi's parents and mine (Linwood relates) *lived only a few hours by train from each other, mine in Ellamanchili and Bibbi's in in Rajahmundry, in the state of Andhra Pradesh. It wasn't so difficult to arrange a bike trip that would start at my parents' house and end up at his. Missionary friends of Bibbi's, located approximately half way between our two towns, offered an easy overnight for this two-day, 143 kilometer, bike trip. We did a brief test run to missionary friends of mine, to make sure that we were prepared for most eventualities.*

When the big day came, we equipped ourselves with lots of water and some snacks, and set out.

Bibbi was so much fun to cycle with. He would chat up the owners of the local tea stalls when we stopped for a break, and he was easy to chat with while we were cycling. He was a stronger cycler than I was, so even though I had a 3-speed and he only had an India one-speed, I found I had to work a bit to keep up with him.

The first day, when it was time for lunch, we stopped at a small local restaurant and asked the staff if the water was boiled. Of course they said "yes". We looked at each other and decided to go for it. Bibbi was always up for an adventure. (Happily there were no long-term consequences of drinking whatever it was that they served us.)

We had no maps of the area, and when we asked people how far it was to the next town, we were always told that it wasn't very far.

In spite of our fine lunch, we were famished at the end of the first day. And although the supper we had with Bibbi's missionary friends was very nice, we had expended a lot of energy on the ride and the next morning we still felt hungry. I think that each of us ate 6 eggs for breakfast.

On the second day, as one might expect, my bike came down with a flat tire, and my repair kit was clearly not up to the challenge. Bibbi, ever resourceful, managed to flag down a truck and I was able to put my bike in the truck and arrange to meet Bob at the edge of town. (For some reason, the truck wouldn't take both of us and our bikes.)

We limped along back to his parents' place, walking our bikes, where we spent a few enjoyable days, before I took the train back to my parents' house.

According to Bibbi, then, a midnight jaunt down to Shembug would be a piece of cake and a fun lark.

With Bibbi's encouragement and constant nagging, I had finally screwed up my courage to ask Nita, a classmate, to the junior prom. As I have said, I was terribly shy around girls, especially about expressing any interest in them. My shyness stemmed from the fact that I always built up unattainable fantasies about girls I felt attracted to, and was never willing to risk having the fantasies shattered. Also, I suffered from fairly severe adolescent acne, and was often impaired by red spots or worse on my nose, forehead and chin. At one point I heard that a girl I was quite partial to had described me as "Tall, dark and pock-marked". That one cut to the quick, and I didn't get over it for some time.

Nita was a very cute blond girl, and she was very popular with guys, especially the twelfth graders. Her family was living in Madras, and during the winter break, our families had enjoyed several outings to Elliot's Beach at Mahabalipuram, near Madras, together. At one point on a ride home, our bare knees had actually touched for a few moments. (What a thrill!) We had enjoyed each other's company, or at least I had, and so I thought I might have a chance with her.

I finally got a moment alone in a covered walkway between classes with Nita and stumbled my way awkwardly through my invitation.

"Um, hi, Nita. How are you?" I started.

She smiled a bit nervously, and answered "Fine." Nita had a way of smiling with her mouth and eyes while frowning with her face.

"Um, well, if…, I mean, would you come with me to the Prom?" I lowered my voice so as not to be overheard, and looked down at my shoes while I spoke.

When I raised my eyes, Nita's smile had faded and she had an exasperated look on her face… not a good sign. She tried to let me down easily, I think, but she turned me down.

"Oh, Charlie, I'm so sorry. I was expecting someone else to ask me. Someone I am really hoping to go to the Prom with. One of the girls told me she thought he was planning to," She explained. "I hope you're okay if I go with him instead."

What could I say? Totally humiliated, of course, I said, "Sure!! I'll go to plan B."

When I told Bibbi what had happened, he seemed genuinely upset. He knew how hard it had been for me to build myself up to ask Nita out. In fact, he had been the one who had encouraged me.

"I guess I'll just skip the Prom." I said.

"No way!" he exclaimed. "That would make you look like a loser. You know that all the girls will know that Nita turned you down by this afternoon. You gotta take someone else and have a good time!"

"I don't know," I said. "Most of the girls that can go have already been asked, I think, or they're in couples."

"I don't think so. What about Radha, or Lucy, or Irene, or Barbie?" he suggested. "They're cute and fun, and I don't think they've been asked yet." Bibbi was going steady with Carolyn, so his prom date was set.

It was not only the girls who knew about my humiliation at Nita's hands. After lunch break a number of guys had let me know that they were aware of the situation.

Friends were sympathetic. "Don't worry, Charlie. She's the loser, not you," was a typical refrain.

Others were not so kind. "What were you thinking? She's way too hot for you." I wasn't about to let those guys have their laugh at my expense.

So, after reloading my courage, I had asked Irene Naumann, one of the smartest and sweetest girls in our class, who (surprise!) accepted my invitation. When the prom came around, she was a delightful, if platonic, companion. We had a wonderful time. Her hand trembled in mine every time we stood up to dance. She was shy and gracious and laughed at my jokes. It was a wonderful evening.

***

With my prom date secured, Bibbi reminded me of John's adventure of securing orchids for his prom dates. Orchids are fairly common around Kodai, and there are a number of sholas that give them a natural habitat. But the ones that grow naturally are fairly plain, with greens, browns and yellows being the dominant colors. At the Jesuit compound in Shembaganur, however, the monks or priests cultivated more exotic species with gold, white, purple, blue, pink and yellow tones. These exotic beauties would show our esteem and express our love for our prom dates. We would be able to present them with corsages that would be the envy of all the other girls. We had to do it!

The pre-dawn raids of prior times had been detected by the priests, and they had arranged to be alerted by the school when there was to be a formal event so that they could intercept the raiders, a number of whom had been caught and received punishment. As such, a midnight raid was our only option.

The ride down to Shembug was harrowing, at least for me. We snuck out of the dorm an hour after lights out, wearing our sneakers and dark outfits. I wheeled my rickety rental bike as quietly as I could to the compound wall with Bibbi and Mike Aung Thwin pushing their own ones silently along. Then Mike and I passed them over one by one to Bibbi, who had jumped over to receive them.

We had the light of a gibbous moon to guide us, but the Ghat is a treacherous, twisting, steep road, and my biking skills were not the best. Bibbi and Mike were both skilled cyclists. And, having attended Kodai for many years, they were very familiar with the Ghat's twists and turns. They soon left me behind. Every once in a while, they would pull up and wait for me to catch up, and then throw themselves back down the road, leaving me behind again. Bibbi kept reminding me that we had to get down quickly so that we could make it back to the dorm before anyone missed us and so that we could get a good night's sleep before 6 a.m. wake-up.

"Come on, Charlie!" he would exhort me every time I caught up with them. "Just let the bike go." or "You're wearing out the brakes!" or "We haven't got all night." and "We'll lose the moonlight!"

The trip down only took us about twenty-five minutes to cover the three miles or so, but that was twice as long as Bibbi had calculated.

The Jesuit compound was surrounded by an eight-foot wall. By standing on one's bicycle seat as it leaned against the wall, one could reach the top of the wall to pull oneself up. There was a friendly tree just inside the wall at the point we chose that gave us a way down into the compound, and then a way back out. Bibbi and Mike went over while I held their bikes steady. With no one to steady the bike for me, I found that I couldn't balance myself on the bike while reaching up for the top of the wall.

"Guys!" I called softly. "The bike is too wobbly. I can't get on top of it."

There was a whispered conference on the other side of the wall. "That's okay," came the reply. "We'll get one for you, too. See you in a few minutes."

So, I was left outside as lookout, and to guard the bikes, even though there was absolutely no one astir.

It must have been less than half an hour, but waiting outside the wall standing in moonlight, it seemed to take forever. Finally, I noticed the tree above the wall beginning to shake, and seconds later saw the top of Bibbi's head peek out. Bibbi came over first, and I guided his foot down onto the bicycle seat. Once there, he carefully handed me down the orchids before climbing off the bike. Then he held the bike for Mike. Within minutes, both boys were standing beside me admiring their prizes.

Bibbi's bike had a basket on the front in which he had brought a soft sweater and some tissue. We carefully wrapped our orchids in the tissue and nested them in the sweater, placing twigs to keep the folds of the sweater from falling in on them.

Both Bibbi and Mike had steady girlfriends, and therefore wanted first choice on any orchids. That was why they had wanted to be the ones to go in first. Since I was taking Irene, not my steady girlfriend, and my second choice, they figured that whatever I got would be good enough. So I got the smallest orchid of the three. But as it turned out, it happened to be the most colorful and exotic when we got them back into the light. Irene seemed well pleased when I presented her with it.

The return up the Ghat was a slog. The average grade of the Ghat is between 4% and 6%, and although we flew down, relatively speaking, our return averaged barely over walking pace. Indeed, as our bikes had only one gear, we were forced to walk them at some points, and then strain to get them going again in less steep areas. Bibbi, the most experienced cyclist among us, would probably have powered himself through the steep parts, but luckily for me, Mike was happy to walk whenever I found that I had to get off.

The moon deserted us about a mile before we reached the lake, which meant that it was close to one in the morning. Getting the bikes back over the compound wall was a real strain, especially since we needed to do it as silently as possible. Mike, arguably the strongest one of us, went over first, standing on his bicycle seat much as he had done at Shembug. Then I went over after passing the orchids carefully up to Mike, and Bibbi began to hand the bikes up to us. They kept scraping against the wall, and we were sure that someone would hear, but finally all three bikes were up. We got Bibbi up with a towel rope, and we left the bikes chained together just inside the compound wall below the dormitory and made it to bed at around two.

The Slog up the Ghat

As news of our exploit spread through the School, I was approached by some of the same students who had been critical of me asking Nita to the prom who now thought that maybe I should be taking someone hotter than Irene. Looking back, I'm sure I had a much better time with Irene than I ever would have with Nita, if only because I would have been so terribly nervous. At the time, though, I was happy to accept their admiration.

Capture the Flag   Not all of the adventures I had involved Bibbi or repeated adventures that his brother John had told him about, though most of the worthwhile ones did.

There were times when Bibbi, like Kris and Lyn, was also involved with girlfriends, or spending time practicing for or participating in various sports tournaments, that left me without my usual companions. These interludes drove home to me the lesser status that I held in the group, unable to equal my friends in either of these arenas so important to kids our age. During these times when I felt left behind, I found ways to venture out with other classmates.

One such adventure occurred during the first semester of our senior year. Narain Mahtani had joined our class during our junior year. He was a handsome boy from a wealthy Hindu family living in Kandy, Ceylon (Sri Lanka, today). He had the gift of gab and a great sense of humor. He was also one of my fellow lifeguards.

Narain's roommate was Phil Turner, brother of my classmate, Sam. Phil was a year behind us. Phil and Narain made an incongruous pair. Phil was tall and freckled with long limbs, a square jaw, and straight brown hair. Narain was fairly short, brown-skinned, with an oval face under jet-black hair. He wore thick glasses and a puzzled expression on his face most of the time.

Narain and Phil became good friends, and when I was not otherwise busy with my buddies, Bibbi, Kris and Lyn, I would often hang out with them.

Narain was particularly disgusted with most of the school's menu, so he and Phil would often head down to the Budge (the Bazaar) for meals or snacks. If I was around, they would happily let me join them.

Narain always seemed to have plenty of money, no matter what day of the week or time of the month, and Phil was usually broke. My allowance was adequate, although sometimes Narain would lend me a couple of rupees if I had run low. These loans I would often pay back by tapping my account at Hamidia's Sundries to buy some food and cooking up a meal on Narain's hot plate in the dorm, usually spaghetti with tomato sauce.

The Budge was about a fifteen-minute walk from the dorm, and during the week we could usually find an hour at around five in the afternoon a couple of times a week to head down for a bite to eat.

In a small green expanse of land at the start of the Budge, several active local chapters of India's many political parties had planted their flag poles to display their colors to their constituents. Both Phil and I were agnostic as far as Indian politics was considered, but Narain, a Hindu whose family had been displaced from the Sindh region of Pakistan during Partition, had strong opinions on the subject, and could identify a number of the flags that flew there. We could all identify the Communist Party flag, the hated hammer and sickle, which Narain especially abhorred.

One afternoon, towards the end of a month, both Phil and I were tapped out, and my account at Hamidia's Sundries was empty as well. This fact became apparent as we were walking down to the Budge and Narain asked us where we wanted to go to get something. Both Phil and I said we weren't really hungry, which was, of course, a lie. Boarding school boys are always hungry.

"Don't worry, guys," said Narain. "I'll spot you. You can pay me back later."

"I already owe you nine rupees!" Phil griped. "That's my whole allowance for next month already gone. I'll have to starve all next month as it is just to pay you back."

I didn't owe Narain anything at the time, but I didn't want to start out a new month in the hole, so I said "Let's just walk down and get some pakoras for a rupee or so."

The Budge

We were just passing the flag poles. Narain looked up and scowled. "I'll tell you what, guys. I'll pay for our meals and you won't owe me anything if you take down that... that bloody communist flag for me."

"What?" exclaimed Phil, "How do you expect us to get it? If we tried to pull it down, we'd probably get arrested."

Narain laughed. "Ha, ha! I don't care how you get it. Bribe someone or whatever. But if you get that bloody flag for me, you won't owe me for any meals for the rest of the semester! Those bastards were the ones who were so rude to my family, jealous of our wealth and success, so we had to leave Sindh."

Phil and I looked at each other. I could see his mind already thinking about how he could get his hands on that flag. We nodded at each other, and he said "Okay, but you have to give us a couple of weeks to figure out how to do it, right, Charlie?"

Having been down the Ghat to Shembug and skinny dipping in the lake, a nighttime foray seemed a plausible way to proceed, so I said "Right. We'll get it for you. Let's go eat."

Narain immediately began asking how we were going to do it, but I shook my head at him.

"Uh-uh. Leave it to us. We'll come up with a plan, don't worry." I said.

Phil said "Yeah, the fewer people who know about it ahead of time, the better."

We arrived at the Hotel State and were shown to a table. I ordered an extravagant meal of mutton biryani *with* mutton *and* egg, and chai. Phil did the same. We ate heartily and took our time.

Mutton Biriyani with All the Fixings

By the time we were done, it was almost time for supper at the School. We skipped the School's supper, and laughed happily when the other guys came back down to the dorm to get ready for Study Hall, complaining about it.

"How did you guys have money to go to the Budge?" Bibbi asked me. "I thought you said you were broke. It's the end of the month and we won't get our allowances for two more days."

"We made a deal with Narain," I answered. I told him quietly about our commission to swipe the communist flag from the Budge.

"I don't know, Charlie," he said. "That could get you into real trouble if you're caught. The commies in this town are pretty powerful people."

"Yeah, well, I guess we better not get caught, so don't tell anybody." I said. "The fewer people who know about it the better. We'll just have to be extra careful."

Phil and I began making plans the next day.

Phil had lived in Madras State with his family for many years and spoke quite a bit of Tamil. Also, he had been in Kodai since grade school, and so knew many of the vendors and workers in town personally. His first idea was to try to get one of them to swipe the flag for us one night.

"I like that idea, but how are we going to get someone to do that? We can't pay them," I said.

"No, but I could give them an old pair of jeans or a pair of shoes," he said.

I laughed. "Do you know anybody your size? Or mine? And besides, once you begin to ask people, everyone will know it was you who got someone to steal the flag. That word will probably get back to Mr. Root through one of the local school staff. I think we would be more likely to get caught that way than if we do it ourselves."

"Well, what's your idea, then?" he asked.

"Well, there's no moon these nights for the next four or five days, so we should sneak out after lights out, the later the better, and get it ourselves. We just wait till all the shopkeepers have gone to bed and pull it down. The season cottages are all empty right now. It shouldn't be too hard." I said

"What if we're caught?" he asked. "I've already gotten six demerits this month. Any more and I'll get Saturday detention and they'll write to my folks."

"Why would we get caught? Guys sneak off campus almost every night, certainly every weekend." I wasn't going to tell him about my own exploits, but he already knew.

"Yeah, you guys always seem to get away with it. I get caught every time I step out of line. It's just my luck that Mr. Root will be riding by on his motorbike when we're crossing the road." He had a point. Phil did get his full share of demerits.

"Well, first thing is, we can't tell anybody about this. Bibbi said that swiping the flag is gonna raise a stink with the commies. Nobody can know it was us, not even Sam," I warned.

"It sounds like you already told Bibbi," he pointed out. "And of course Narain will know it was us because we have to give him the flag. And Tim was asking me why I wasn't at supper, so I told him that Narain treated us to supper, and that we had a deal with him."

"No way!" I exclaimed. "Tim doesn't know how to keep secrets."

"Yeah, well, I didn't tell him what we were going to do."

"I'll swear Bibbi to silence, and we can both work on Narain," I said. "He won't be able to show off the flag, and he has to understand that up front. Otherwise, we won't do it, and we'll have to pay him back for yesterday's feast."

"Don't worry about Narain," said Phil. "I've got some things on him that he won't want me to talk about, so I'm sure I can get him to keep mum."

"Like what?" I asked.

"I promised not to mention to anyone. Anyway, it's just embarrassing stuff... stupid stuff. It's about a girl that he likes, but he's sensitive about it, so he won't want it to get out. Besides, he'll know that if we get caught, he'll get in trouble too," he replied.

"So, anyway, I think we should do it ourselves," I insisted. "Let's plan for Tuesday night. If we leave campus at midnight, the whole town should be asleep, and we shouldn't take more than about half an hour, start to finish. Tuesdays are kind of dead, anyway."

We agreed on Tuesday, and went into the details of the operation. Phil would set his alarm and come by to wake me up, since we would have gone to bed at ten o'clock. I would wear my jeans to bed and have my black windbreaker by the door with my sneakers. With luck, Bibbi and Kris wouldn't wake up. Narain would probably be aware, but that wouldn't be a problem.

At the appointed hour, I was shaken awake by Phil's hand on my shoulder. I was in the single bed, with Kris and Bibbi in the bunk beds of room 11. We didn't speak. I grabbed my sneakers and windbreaker and we headed to the bathroom to finish dressing. The dorm was as silent as the proverbial tomb, and the night was dark and moonless. We slipped down to the gate below Phelps dorm and prepared to climb over. A noise froze us in the deeper shadows against the wall. The noise became a soft crunch of boots on gravel. We heard the gate rattle and then a clicking sound. The soft crunching resumed and went on by outside the wall, heading off toward the Boat House.

"The Gurkha!" whispered Phil.

"Whew!" I breathed.

In all my nighttime escapades from the School over the three years I was there that was the only time I ever ran into the School's night watchman. I had never even been aware of the Gurkha guard patrolling at night. He was always in his little kiosk by the main gate, and we always had to avoid exposing ourselves to his field of view as we went about our risky business, but I hadn't even known that he patrolled the School and checked the gates.

"Yeah," said Phil, when I mentioned this. "He goes on patrol around the outside of the School three times each night, usually at around midnight, then at two and at four. He has a clock that he has to punch with a key at each gate. That was the clicking sound you heard."

We waited for a good while in the shadows after the footsteps faded and until our hearts settled back to their normal rhythms before climbing over the gate. We headed the opposite way that the Gurkha had gone, hurrying toward Laws Ghat Road, hoping that we would get past the Main Gate before he made it around the back of the campus. It wouldn't do to run into him.

There was no one around. We moved like shadows, only our breathing making any sound. The night was still. We made it past the Main Gate without seeing anyone, and headed off to the Budge road, past the empty cottages that families rented during the May season. We stopped in the shadow of some trees and surveyed the flagpoles. There were a good number of them, long bamboo poles planted in the ground. The poles were about six inches thick at the base, and tapered to about two inches some twenty-five feet up. The flags were all hanging limp against their poles. It was so dark that we couldn't tell which one held the communist flag!

"Now what?" I asked. "We can't pull them all down to see which one we take."

"I'm trying to remember…" whispered Phil. "I think it was on the pole farthest away from the road. Remember when Narain looked up? When I looked up, it was behind the DMK flag."

"I don't know what the heck you're talking about, but if you think you know which one it is, let's get started." I moved to the pole he had indicated and looked up to see where the line that held the flag was tied. To my dismay, it was well above my reach! As a security measure against miscreants from another political party, the flags were secured by lines tied to a cleat about ten feet off the ground.

"We're gonna have to climb up on something to reach the rope," I said.

"No, here, just give me a boost," said Phil

I made a stirrup of my hands, and he stepped into it. I straightened up. He was just able to reach the hook where the line was tied, and began to work it with his fingers. I was leaning my back on the pole, which was rather bendy and wiggled as Phil worked at the knot.

Phil was not a light guy, and after about five minutes, my shoulders and arms began to get tired, and my fingers, laced under his foot, began to burn. I was also having to work to balance Phil as the pole swayed.

"How's it coming?" I whispered.

"I can't get this damned knot!" came the reply. "Did you happen to bring your pocket knife?"

"No. Dammit! I left it in my other pants. How much longer? I'm beginning to get tired down here," I said.

"I can't get it," he said. "We'll have to come back with a knife."

"No way!" I hissed. "Let's switch and let me try."

Having spent my last long break learning to sail in King George Harbor in Madras, I had gained a bit of experience with ropes and knots, especially wet ones, and hoped that I would be able to succeed where Phil could not.

Phil climbed down and we switched positions. I reached up and felt the knot. With the knot still so high over my head, I couldn't get a good feel of it.

"I've gotta get higher!" I stated.

"Maybe you can stand on my shoulders," said Phil. "Come back down."

I stepped out of his cupped hands. He squatted with his back to the pole. I stepped onto his knee and lifted my other foot to his shoulder. I brought my other foot up onto his other shoulder and began to pull myself up the pole as Phil rose to a standing position underneath me, sliding his back up the pole for balance. It really felt precarious, and the swaying of the pole didn't help. But now the knot was well within my reach and I could work it.

Little by little I could feel the strands slipping. Back and forth I moved it until I identified which strand was slipping. In two more minutes I felt it begin to give, and a moment later the two ends came apart. I pulled the flag down, hoping that it was the right one. I couldn't see us having to repeat the operation on another pole.

The flag reached my hand, and I told Phil to lower me back down. He slid his back down the pole to a squat, and I stepped off. We studied the piece of cloth in my hand to see what we had managed to retrieve, but it was too dark to really tell. There was a lone street light a few shops into the Budge, so we made our way to it.

"Hallelujah!" said Phil. We had captured the right one.

Mission Accomplished: The Actual Flag

The next day we took the flag to Narain.

The walk back to campus was uneventful. We kept to the shadows passing the Main Gate and went back down the Laws Ghat Road. We toyed with the idea of climbing over the Dish Gate, but there were staff quarters near them, and we would have to approach Wissy from the Houseparent side. We decided to go back to the gate on Lake Road, even though it would take us an extra few minutes. Our mission had taken nearly an hour.

"Awesome, Guys!" he exulted. "You actually did it! Now what are you going to do with it?"

"What? No… here. You take it. It's yours. You told us to get it for you, and we did. And don't forget your part of the bargain. I'm feeling hungry already." I pushed the flag at him.

"I don't want that dirty rag, fellows," he said. "I just can't stand to see it flying up there over the Budge. Don't worry. You've earned your meals."

"You can take it back to Ceylon with you as a souvenir," I said.

"No way! I wouldn't dare try to take that thing through customs. Communists are not well regarded there, and my family wouldn't understand why I even had it. If I told my mother that I had stolen it, or had it stolen, she would punish me. Just throw it away. Or maybe we should burn it. It's just a rag, anyway."

"We can't burn it or throw it away after all that work," Phil declared. "We'll keep it."

For a few days, no one seemed to notice that the communist flag was no longer flying over the Budge. We kept our exploit secret, per Bibbi's advice, although I did show him the flag at one point. He was duly impressed, but counseled continued caution. In the end, we were fortunate that we heeded his advice.

The Monday following our excursion, unbeknownst to me, a delegation from the town council came to the Principal's office to complain that someone had stolen one of the party flags from the Budge. They wanted to know if anyone on campus had any idea of who it might have been. If we had spread word of our misdeed at all, it would surely have reached an official ear somehow. But as only four of us knew about it, and no one asked us, the missing flag was deemed a mystery.

Lyn heard about the complaint from his dad and mentioned it during a break between classes. Bibbi and I looked at each other, and he rolled his eyes at me. I gestured wiping sweat off my brow, but neither of us said anything. In the end, the flag stayed hidden in my tape recorder case, and made it back to the States with me.

5. Laying Plans for Manjampatti

Hiking Season   John Coleman had always been an avid hiker and recounted many of his adventures at family mealtimes during long vacation on the plains, and told Bibbi separately about many of the pranks and mischief he had been involved in with his classmates.

A couple of these stories centered on hiking at night. Under certain conditions, students were allowed to set out at dusk or after dark to one of the known nearby rest houses that were strategically located along the roads providing shelter for hikers where they could rest, prepare a meal or spend the night. Bibbi had heard tales from John, and was always intrigued with the idea of night hiking. During hiking season, the skies above Kodai often clear up after a monsoonal afternoon thundershower, and at seven thousand feet altitude with no light pollution, the stars and planets sparkle brilliantly. Night hiking was definitely on our agenda of things to do when we became upper classmen.

Ten weekends in the first semester of the School year (June through October) are designated for earning the coveted Tahr Pin award. These weekends are during the start of the monsoon, the wettest months of the year, when it can rain as much as twelve inches a month in the Palani Hills. This is one of the conditions that make earning a Tahr pin quite a feat. If you're lucky, you will enjoy good weather in the mornings, with thunderstorms holding off until mid to late afternoon, and you can get most of your hiking in before it starts to rain. Many of the longer hikes that entail an overnight stay have destinations that include some sort of shelter such as a rest bungalow or a cave, to keep dry in. Night time temperatures in the heights can drop into the upper forties. Rain gear, sleeping bag and dry socks are required equipment. This is 'Hiking Season'.

During hiking season some on-campus some weekend activities are curtailed. Kids not involved in hiking can often find themselves on an empty campus, bored with nothing much to do. Most of the staff members are also involved in hiking, so all students are encouraged to take part in at least some of the hikes.

(January, February and March are the driest months in Kodai, with only about five or six rainy days each, and would be much better for hiking. Temperatures are still chilly at night, dipping into the fifties, but the days are pleasant and usually bright. However, these drier months are all about team sports such as soccer and basketball, and getting ready for Field Day, so most students are practicing and conditioning for their individual events. These are also the months when the Proms are scheduled and classes take their field trips. By March, daytime temperatures can climb into the low eighties.)

There are many delightful day hikes in the area that can be accomplished in a few hours with a packed lunch. Pillar Rocks (seven miles, fairly level), Devil's Kitchen (four miles, fairly level), Silver Cascade (about two-and-a-half miles, mostly level), Dolphin's Nose (three miles, 1500 feet down and back), and Gundar Falls (nine miles, fairly level) to name a few. These hikes were the most popular, especially among couples, for obvious reasons, as well as for boys who weren't that into hiking, and girls who weren't that enthusiastic about spending nights out of their relatively comfortable beds, or sharing meals and campfires with horny adolescent boys. It was also true that none of us looked, or smelled, our best after a night of sleeping on the ground in our clothes and skipping showers. Overnight hikes were, therefore, usually segregated and chaperoned. Nevertheless, hiking season was always looked forward to with great enthusiasm because it gave us the excuse to get off campus, even if only for a few hours. Every hike is rated and earns points towards an award to be handed out at the end of the season. Two main factors are considered in the point awards. The first factor is distance... the longer the hike, the more points. The second factor is elevation changes over the length of the hike, with more extra points for uphill portions of the treks than for the downhill ones. Other more subjective factors were also considered, as I found out later on.

The roads in Kodai had all been clearly marked with both milestones and kilometer markers. Milestones were large stone blocks painted white with the mileage painted in black numerals, and kilometers were large stone blocks painted yellow with the kilometer number in large black numerals. Between these markers, every furlong was marked with a smaller white block numbered one through eight unless it coincided with a kilometer marker. In this way, we could measure most of our hikes very accurately.

A furlong is one eighth of a mile (220 yards) and one fifth of a kilometer (200 meters), so that every five miles, or eight kilometers, the larger marker was half white and half yellow, each half with its corresponding number.

Once off the marked roads, distances became more subjective, and we learned to take ingenious shortcuts, some of which shortened the actual hike's distance, but may have extended the duration, especially if one got lost or had to retrace one's steps.

Five Mile/Eight Kilometer Marker

There were avid hikers among the staff, including Mr. Root, the Vice Principal, Mr. Shaw, Mr. Neufeld, Mr. Hunt and Mr. Rushton, to mention some of the male staff hikers. Mr. Root had a set of Topographical Geological Survey maps that were used to calculate the distances and elevation changes of sanctioned hikes from which points were assigned. Staff and student members of the Hiking Committee would get together to evaluate each new hike and decide how many points it was worth, and sometimes to reevaluate point awards for hikes that may have been incorrectly graded.

Tahr Pins and Bragging Rights   The coveted award given to each student who managed to exceed the point threshold of 60 points set by the staff at the outset of each season was a silver Tahr pin.

The Nilgiri Tahr is an elusive wild goat (once misidentified as an Ibex) that is an endangered species in the Western Ghats and is a phenomenal mountain climber.

Accordingly, it was almost impossible to achieve the point total needed to earn a pin by sticking to hikes with little elevation change, or to the shorter day hikes. Ambitious hikes were usually two or three day affairs with challenging drops and climbs, and were rewarded with high points and bragging rights.

In addition to the individual awards, there was also an informal competition among grades, with the individual scores for each member were added together to see which grade won the bragging rights for the season. That award often went to the sophomores or juniors, since seniors were often distracted by other concerns, such as improving their GPA's or getting in every possible minute in with their girlfriends before the end of their Kodai career. Occasionally, an ambitious freshman class would attempt to take the Class Honors.

The most coveted individual coup, however, was to get the most points of any students from any grade. This was not an officially recognized feat, but all serious hikers would try to earn it. Bibbi was a serious hiker.

Most of the hikes are well-known and mapped. Some of the more exotic hikes are less well-known, but there was usually an experienced hiker familiar with the trail to lead the way. In those days, these leaders were usually upper classmen or staff members who had been at Kodai for years. Having arrived at Kodai at the start of my sophomore year, I was not familiar with any of the trails that first year.

Hiking 101 Staff members would announce an organized hike and invite students to sign up. Short hikes were open to just about anyone who signed up with few limits. Large groups were divided into subgroups of eight or so with a leader assigned to each subgroup. These hikes were quite often coed, and would leave soon after breakfast with a packed lunch and return by tea time. Longer overnight hikes would have a limited number of spaces, usually a maximum of eight to twelve depending on the staff leader, and were almost always limited to just one sex. Female staff led girls' hikes and male staff led boys' hikes. Popular leaders would get more students trying to sign up, while some staff had to recruit students to meet the minimum. No hikes were allowed to start with fewer than four people.

Before setting out, hike leaders would review the route on a topographical map. These maps were very detailed prepared by the Geological Survey Service of the Indian Government. Landmarks and trail forks would be carefully studied and discussed with all hikers. Gear was checked to make sure that essential items were packed. Each hiker was assigned to a small group that would keep together, and each small group had a leader. That was the way it was supposed to work, and for the most part, it did. Sometimes a group would rush ahead while another would fall way behind, but for the three years I was at Kodai we never lost anyone.

Most of the longer hikes, after leaving town, led through sholas (forests), across streams and brooks, along ridges and into valleys, taking us up and down mountain trails, many of which would open up to spectacular vistas of the dusty plains thousands of feet below, or to views of distant peaks. These were the hikes that attracted us. For the romantics among us, these were glimpses of unconquered territory that cried out to be explored. In our day, most of the information available about hikes was anecdotal, handed down over the years.

The hikes had names, and trails and destinations were mapped out on the Geo maps, but the rules we followed were mostly intuitive and enforced by the Hiking Committee. "Jump-off" points were identified through landmarks and kilometer markers. There were no helpful road signs.

In modern times, there is a whole detailed Hiking Guide that is published, with detailed information of rules, equipment, and rewards that we never got to enjoy. I have heard that there is a "Gold Pin Award" and an "Outstanding Hiker Plaque" for hikers who earn a Tahr Pin every year through their Middle School and High School years. Some hikes today even have posted signs to keep hikers on the right track.

Planning Begins   I had developed a love-hate relationship to hiking in my sophomore year. The views were spectacular around almost every twist in the trail. There were soaring granite outcrops, distant peaks, waterfalls, valleys, and glimpses of the plains. Brocken spectres, ghostly apparitions that appear when your shadow projects onto a cloud below you as you stand at the edge of a precipice, were a phenomenon that mesmerized me. Vegetation was lush and fragrant. Fellow hikers were good company. Fellowship around the campfire included singing and storytelling. It was also a welcome break from the boarding school regimen. Even today, these pleasures would call me back out onto the trail.

Hikers on a trail

On the other hand, I was often wet and cold. My feet blistered, my knees scraped. Pack straps dug into my shoulders. I often had to hustle, gasping for breath more than I wanted to keep up with the group and reach our destination by the appointed time. My muscles took their time in adjusting to the demands, and I would ache for a day or two after every hike. I got shin splints and twisted my ankles a number of times. Sleeping on the ground was painful. Camp food could be delicious, but was often awful and had to be eaten in difficult conditions.

But the mind works in mysterious ways, and teenage bodies heal quickly. When the aches wore off, my blisters popped, my knees scabbed over and my swollen ankles subsided, I would begin to look forward to the next trek convinced that I was now in better shape and that the weather would be friendlier. Occasionally it worked out that way.

After hiking season of our junior year, Bibbi began enthusiastically planning for our senior hikes. As upper classmen, we were permitted to organize our own hikes without having to rely on chaperones. As juniors we had gotten permission from our parents and Mr. Root to go on several unchaperoned hikes, including a couple of overnight hikes, so the groundwork was laid. Bibbi had used his status as a student hike leader to get extensive time studying the topographical maps that Mr. Root kept in his office. He also tapped into Mr. Root's extensive knowledge of the area.

Bibbi told Mr. Root about his brother John's idea of a combined hike to Manjampatti and Kookal, but found Mr. Root to be dismissive of the idea: It would take too long; there were no trails to follow; the trek would be too steep; It would be impossible to find a staff chaperone willing to go; and so on. Not wanting to be argumentative, Bibbi kept his thoughts to himself.

Bibbi was an excellent map reader, and soon identified a track on the topo map between Manjampatti and Kookal that appeared to avoid most of the steepest parts. As we were roommates, he shared his ideas and excitement about the prospect with me, and he began to assume that I would be included in the adventure. The problems would come from things that were not shown on a topographical map, such as vegetation, rock slides, and other changes caused by monsoon rains such as gullies or mud flows. Not much thought was given to these, though, since we had encountered all of them on regular hikes in the area and judged that we could deal with them.

The unknown, unconquered territory was right in the middle between the two known destinations, Manjampatti and Kookal, so if we encountered an impassible obstruction, we would have to retrace whichever route we had taken in to get back home. Bibbi and I discussed which way around to plan the hike: from Kookal down to Manjampatti or from Manjampatti up to Kookal.

Great White Hunter Mr. Root, vice-principal, ex-navy, was known to many of us as "the Great White Hunter". He was a compact, fit man with a military crewcut and bearing, and piercing blue eyes. During the winter break, when students had left campus, he would break out his hunting rifle and head out to the back country to hunt game, mostly deer or wild boar.

Great White Hunter

We heard about these expeditions from our classmate, Lyn, whose father was the principal of the School, and who stayed in Kodai through the break.

In the off-season, when we boarders had gone back to our families to spend the holidays on the plains, Lyn and Mr. Krause, his dad the principal, would spend most of their time at the Kodaikanal Golf Club, sharpening their skills and playing in tournaments. Indeed, the plaques and cups kept in the cases of the trophy room at the Club are covered with their names. In the evenings they would get together with other staff, and Mr. Root would tell them about his latest exploits. Lyn actually accompanied Mr. Root on one or two of his hunts at nearby Vembadi Shola, and witnessed the bagging of a large boar, of which they all partook after it had been cleaned and cooked by school staff.

Mr. Root showed Bibbi where some of his hunts had taken him on the topo maps, including the area around Kookal and the non-preserve areas of Manjampatti Valley. When Bibbi pointed out how near those places were to each other on the maps, Mr. Root told Bibbi about a time that he had reached a part of the Kookal ridge that actually looked down into Manjampatti, but that it had looked too steep to traverse. And anyway, he said, he was tracking a small herd of deer that had gone into a nearby shola.

"I think we should start from Kookal." I opined. "Kookal is a little bit nearer than Manjampatti it looks like on the map, and we get there without too much change in elevation."

"What difference does that make?" asked Bibbi. "Either way will be the same overall, and if we do Kookal first, we'll leave the hard part all to the end, when we're worn out."

"Yeah," I said, "but if we have to turn back for some reason, like if we can't find a path, wouldn't it be better to do that from Kookal than from Manjampatti? If we have to turn back from Manjampatti, we'll have done all of the hard parts with none of the rewards. The way back to civilization will be a long one."

"You're right about that," said Bibbi. "But I don't think we'll have to turn back. Look here at the map. The way out of Manjampatti to Kookal is no steeper than the way in. If we compare the topo lines going in from Mannavanur, they're the same as these going up to Kookal from Manjampatti. We can even choose a gentler climb out, like through here, if we have the time." He ran his finger along the map as he explained. I understood that lines closer together meant steeper terrain, but the differences he was showing me seemed minimal.

"The other thing is that going down is more dangerous than going up if you don't know the path. If you slip or fall on the way down, you can get really hurt, but if you slip on the way up, at least your momentum will be going against gravity. You're leaning forward, so you might bang your knee or scrape your hand, but at least you'll probably fall forward into the hill."

As the relative newbie to hiking, I saw the logic and I had to give in. So, it was decided that our route would take us first to Manjampatti, and then, hopefully, up to Kookal.

One evening Bibbi brought the topo maps he had borrowed from Mr. Root into evening study hall, which was held in the library. Regular study hall was from seven to nine in the evening, and all students in boarding were required to attend. From nine to ten was detention for students serving demerits (one demerit equals a half hour of detention), and available to students who needed to catch up on assignments. The staff member supervising study hall that night was Mr. Rushton, who was one of the more lenient professors. He allowed me and Bibbi to sit at a table in the stacks and go over the maps as long as we whispered quietly. Bibbi showed me where the hike would take us, and we began to plan out the stages, trying to identify where we would be able to spend nights and what we would have to carry with us.

"So, here's our route," said Bibbi.

The route took us about half way around the Forty Mile round, a road that followed the ridge line at about a 6,800 foot altitude.

"We follow the road to Mannavanur, and from there we find the trail that takes us down. The question is whether we should catch a ride out to Mannavanur or hike. If we go on a regular weekend, that would give us a day to hike down to Manjampatti and back up to Kookal, which would be a full day, and we would only get to spend about an hour by the stream. If we go on a long weekend, we can spend the night down in Manjampatti."

Mannavanur is a tiny village that sits directly above the southern end of Manjampatti Valley. From there, we would hike down a steep path that descended about 3,000 feet to the mountain stream that flows into Manjampatti. We would follow the river downstream, dropping another thousand feet or so over the next few miles, looking for a good site to camp for the night.

"I think we should catch a ride," I opined. "That way we save all our energy for the hard parts of the hike."

"Yeah, that's right, but on the other hand, hiking to Mannavanur would give us an extra seven points," Bibbi explained.

Bibbi traced the route out with a ruler, and it looked like the Kodai to Manjampatti leg would be about twenty-five miles or so, maybe more, and would drop us about 4,500 feet once we left the road. That seemed to me to be very ambitious.

Bibbi assured me, "Don't worry. Others have done it and have come back up by bus the next day."

By "others" I understood that his brother John had claimed to have accomplished this, and that he was not about to shrink from it.

One of my first hikes in my sophomore year had been down the Coolie Ghat to Tope via Vellagavi, which I had undertaken with wide-eyed assurance that I could accomplish anything I put my mind to. It had taken a good part of the day to get down to the river and find the camp site even though we had taken most of the short cuts down the Ghat trail. Returning the following day up the twisting Coolie Ghat after a morning swim, had been more than I could take, so Bibbi and Kris had given me money to catch a bus while they climbed back up the Coolie Ghat. Comparing distances on the topo maps, it looked like we would have to go about three times as far to reach Manjampatti. Needless to say, I was skeptical.

Indeed, when Bibbi talked with Mr. Root about the trek to Manjampatti, Mr. Root informed him that hiking down and back from Manjampatti was recommended as a three-day hike, and suggested that if we wanted to hike down to the valley and up to Kookal in two days, we should consider taking a bus or lorry to Mannavanur and set out from there. That didn't sit at all well with Bibbi, who was bent on competing for the high point total.

Girlfriends… and Other Stumbling Blocks   Our planning hit stumbling blocks early in the first semester of our senior year. Our two best friends, Lyn and Kris were the companions we had expected to accompany us on the hike. In order to go on an unchaperoned hike as upper classmen, the School required that at least 4 experienced hikers be included. When we had started talking about the journey, both of them had been enthusiastic at the idea. But as hiking season got underway and we were planning our conditioning hikes as required by the School, they kept finding excuses not to sign up. For one thing, Lyn had been elected Class President, and Kris was Class Vice-president. Those duties kept them busy on many weekends. Bibbi reminded them that he was Student

Council President with extra duties, and they could be worked around and delegated.

A more difficult problem was that both Kris and Lyn had acquired girlfriends and weren't that interested in spending their weekends on grueling non-coed hikes. Kris was dating Maureen Aung Thwin, a most exotic beauty in our class, and was spending every possible moment with her that he could. He was our Class Vice-President, and she was Class Secretary, so they had many opportunities to be together. Lyn was dating Rona Nordeen, a cute eleventh grader with long blond hair and a cute, crooked smile, and while possibly not as serious about it as Kris was, wanted to spend time with her while he could. Since Carolyn had returned to the States at the end of our junior year, Bibbi was currently unattached.

Another problem we ran into was my grades. Bibbi, Lyn and Kris were all A and B students. My grades were hovering just above a D at C-minus. As such, I was in danger of being required to attend Saturday Study Hall until they hit a solid C or better.

There wasn't much we could do about the girlfriend problem, other than try to break them up somehow. As to my grades, though, once again, Bibbi took me under his wing and worked with me on completing assignments and preparing for tests. By mid-term I was getting a solid B in Math and Physics, and an A in English. I was still at a C in Shop, Typing and History, but my average was now an acceptable C-plus or B-minus.

I had always been a decent student, though given to making smart comments in class that were disruptive. I sat in the front row of class whenever I could so that I could not be ignored. Teachers were often frustrated by the interruptions and sometimes bumped off from their teaching track. I won't say that they took it out on me in terms of my grades, but possibly they scrutinized my work a little more than most in order to find ways to take me down a peg. From my vantage, I always felt that I was pigeon-holed in a low "C" bracket, no matter how hard I tried. But in hindsight, maybe I was to blame for a lot of my less than stellar academic performance.

In any event, I was, in the early days of my career at Kodai, designated the Class Clown of the Class of '66, and kept the reputation throughout my tenure at Kodai, even when I was not the one who initiated the ruckus. I suspect that it was my way of standing out from the crowd, since I didn't excel in any sport or other School activity.

Grade Recovery   Bibbi was a genius at making schoolwork fun. He made up funny and fun mnemonic rhymes and sequences of letters to fix things in the memory that could then be easily recalled on quizzes and tests. From him I learned 'Please Excuse My Dear Aunt Sally' as a way to memorize the Order of Operations to solve Algebra problems. For years I thought that he was the one who had invented this mnemonic. Additionally, he introduced me to Roget's Thesaurus and showed me how to expand my vocabulary and avoid repetitious use of adjectives. He used a stop watch to set limits to activities so that I found myself actually racing to complete an assignment that would have bogged down without the deadline. In short, he made learning fun for me and gave me skills that have served me well many times over the course of my life.

Bibbi himself was a serious scholar, and enjoyed studying and acquiring knowledge. He could often be seen in spare moments sitting on a wall with his history or science book and soaking up every drop of information he could. During our senior year, a freshman who had been assigned to monitor the piano block and make sure that all students were indeed practicing, tells a tale that illustrates how seriously Bibbi took his studies.

Midterm exams were approaching, and Bibbi was spending every chance he could to lock in his facts and dates. As a piano student, he was assigned to a practice room for one of his periods. Here is how Bob Edwards, the piano practice monitor tells the tale:

"I was a 'piano checker,' at Kodai. It was my responsibility to make sure all scheduled pianos in the back of the gym were being filled with the assigned piano students, and that they were actually practicing, and not skipping out (or entertaining unscheduled guests). I must have been in 9th grade. Bibbi was one of my 'victims.' The 'job' called for opening the practice room door, and making sure the assigned person was there, as well as making sure he or she wasn't just playing 'chop sticks.'

"One day, when I checked on Bibbi, he was indeed playing chords, but he was playing random chords with one hand, and had a book buried in his lap. He was studying, and just playing a few chords with his right hand. I guess he was hoping I would assume piano practice was going on, and hoping I would not open the practice room door. I suppose I could have given him a demerit, but we both had a good laugh, and I told him to keep on studying. No need to disturb the study with random chords. He was most grateful, as I recall. "

Bob closed the door and went on to check the other rooms.

Still Two Members Short   Without Kris and Lyn, we were still two members short of the minimum of four we needed.   At first we tried to humiliate Kris and Lyn, teasing them about being henpecked, but we soon gave it up as a lost cause.   They took our teasing good-naturedly, putting us down for not being able to have steady girlfriends, even though Bibbi did, off and on, though he was currently between girlfriends.

"Chuck you, Farley!" said Kris, employing one of his favorite spoonerisms one evening when I was trying to shame him into joining the hike. "Just because you've never had a steady girlfriend, or any girlfriend at all, for that matter, doesn't mean you can put me down for having one. You should try it sometime."

"I wish I could!" I replied.   Realizing how pathetic that made me sound, I added, "but even if I did, I wouldn't let her keep me from hiking with my friends."

"Hah! That's what you think," he said.   I suspected he was right.

I never had a girlfriend, although I longed to, and often found myself day-dreaming about one or another of the eligible girls at school. My fantasies floated from Nita to Emmy, to Karen, to Bonnie, to Cathy, to Chellie, round and round.   I never worked up the courage to actually approach any of them in any serious way, but behaved more awkwardly when I was in the throes of infatuation.   The blurb by my picture in my senior Yearbook includes the sentence: "[..] and he is always pulling practical jokes or teasing the girls."   I had never progressed past the Middle School behavior level concerning girls.

Lyn and Kris knew that we were planning to make the hike over a long weekend when there was traditionally a dance that they wanted to attend with their girls, so the idea of them leaving school for three days was out of the question.

"It's our senior year!" said Kris.   "What do you think?   After next semester we'll probably never get to see them again."

So, we were stuck with the problem of finding suitable substitutes. We were somewhat limited as to who we could get to go on the hike with us, since most underclassmen couldn't go without a chaperone, and each member had to be able to count on getting their parents' permission, and have decent enough grades.   Our classmates Sam and Phil didn't qualify grade-wise.   Narain, Kurt, Leslie, Stan and Robert did, but weren't hikers. The Loch End boys, Joe, Ron and Tim, were rarely allowed to skip Sunday services.   We could have tried to recruit a couple of juniors, but would only consider it as a last resort.   The only guys left in our class were

Linwood and Dave. If we couldn't get them both to join us, we would have to recruit a staff member, or even worse, one of the juniors.

We approached Linwood first, since he had been my roommate for a semester, and his family lived near Bibbi's on the plains. Linwood was a slender, wiry, athletic boy, of about five-foot-seven, with a flat-top haircut, who excelled in sprints and longer races on Field Day. Every morning, before the wake-up monitor rang the bell, he would hop out of his bed and do fifty or a hundred pushups and a like number of sit-ups. If anyone would be in shape for our planned hike, it would be him.

Linwood was very intense and passionate about his studies and spoke in short, excited bursts when discussing any of his pet ideas. He, unlike me or Bibbi, was very devout and could often be seen studying his Bible, so we weren't sure he would be willing to give up a Sunday church service to go on our hike. He was, though, an avid hiker, and had been on several hikes with us before.

I joined Linwood at his table one afternoon at tea-time, and explained what we were planning, and that we needed to get at least two more people in order to get permission from the school.

"Hey, Linwood," I began. "Bibbi and I are planning a big hike for the three-day weekend. We were planning to go as a group of four, with Kris and Lyn, but they're finking out. They don't want to leave their girls for the whole weekend. We were wondering if you wanted to come."

"Where are you guys thinking of going?" he asked.

"Bibbi wants to try to see if we can hike down to Manjampatti and then find a route up the other side to Kookal. It's bound to be a strain, but Bibbi thinks you can make it if I can," I said.

"Oh, wow!" exclaimed Linwood. "That's the hike that his brother John wanted to do a couple of years ago. No one's ever done it. But, are you sure you got it right? John was thinking of going to Manjampatti from Kookal because you can see the way from up there."

"Yeah," I agreed. "When we staged it out on the topo map, it worked better starting with Manjampatti. Plus Bibbi says it's more dangerous breaking a new trail going downhill than going up. Do you think you want to come with us?"

"Definitely!" he said. "Count me in, as long as I can get permission."

Bibbi's parents had always given permission for John to go on unchaperoned hikes, and so Bibbi would probably have no problem. My parents wouldn't have any problem with me going either.

Now all we had to do was to get Dave to come along. Dave was a mission kid. His parents and grandparents had been in India for decades, but had their roots in the U.S., somewhere in the South. Dave spoke with a distinct drawl that set him apart from the usual washed-out accents of the rest of us. Dave was a quiet person, laconic, but with a great sense of humor. He was easy to be around. It was up to Bibbi to recruit Dave. As long term Kodai kids, they had known each other for many years, and Dave's older siblings had known Bibbi's older brother, John, and sister, Mary.

Dave lived off-campus at the Lutheran Compound, so Bibbi spoke to him during morning break one day. Off-campus students generally left back to their home campus after the end of the school day, and before any after-school extra-curricular activities. Those involved with sports teams, such as soccer, baseball and basketball stayed on for practice, but afternoon tea and Wednesday night Canteen were not part of their schedule.

Dave told Bibbi that he wasn't sure he could join us. His excuses sounded lame, but Bibbi was cajoling and convincing, and soon got Dave to give the idea serious consideration.

Over the next week or so, Bibbi kept up his campaign to convince Dave, showing him the maps and the route we were planning, highlighting the possibility of seeing elephants, bison, tahrs, and even possibly tigers. He told him about the hikes he and John had been on, and highlighted the benefits of getting away from the school for a long weekend. In the end, Dave gave in, and agreed to ask his parents for permission, possibly secretly holding on the hope that they might deny it.

With Dave tentatively signed on, we moved forward with our plans. The first step was to get letters from our parents that showed that they understood our intentions, and that they gave us permission to go on the hike. Blanket permissions were not accepted for so ambitious an undertaking, and Mr. Root wanted letters that confirmed that they understood where we were planning to go and what possible perils we might encounter. The words "tiger country" should crop up in the letter. So we wrote what we needed in our weekly letters home, making sure that we downplayed the dangers while getting the required language into their permission letters. We emphasized that there had been no tiger attacks in Manjampatti for several years, and that we would make enough noise and sleep with a campfire burning to scare off any curious beasts that might happen to be around. Somehow, Bibbi got Dave to show him his letter home to make sure that there were no coded messages trying to get his parents to deny him permission.

A week or so later, Mr. Root informed us that all of our parents had written to him giving us permission to go, and that he had responded assuring them that he would make sure that we were well-prepared with all necessary equipment and information. He told them that he would go over the rules of safe hiking with us and what to do if we confronted any difficulties along the way.

"You boys will be hiking over Sunday, so I expect you to set aside some time for devotion on Sunday morning," he directed. "Who will lead it?"

Both Linwood and Dave offered.

"I was already planning to take my Bible along," said Linwood.

"That's fine, then," said Mr. Root. "You can handle it together."

As you can tell by now, hiking is taken seriously at Kodai, and serious hikes are taken very seriously. The route we were proposing to take combined two serious hikes with the added element of forging a route through virgin territory. Off-trail hiking is generally discouraged, since it is easy to get disoriented and lost. Most hikes had well-marked trails and there were familiar landmarks that helped hikers know where they were. So Mr. Root's concession that we would be allowed to proceed with our plan was a testament to his trust in Bibbi.

6. Getting Into Shape

Conditioning Hikes   All students were encouraged to hike, but in order to take on any of the longer, more arduous hikes, they were required to complete two or three of the easier hikes first. Hikes are categorized as A) easy, B) intermediate, C) hard, and D) challenging. To go on a 'C' hike, students had to have completed a 'B' hike. To earn a Tahr Pin, High School students had to complete 3 'C' hikes and 3 'D' hikes in addition to their conditioning hikes, all within the 10-week hiking season. It was possible to complete two 'C' or even a 'C' hike and a 'B' hike in one weekend, and, in pursuit of our goals, we often did.

I don't really recall what our first conditioning hikes were that season, but I'm sure we hiked the Upper Lake circuit one Saturday morning before breakfast. We started out before dawn and hustled around the west end of the lake and up the hill to the north of the lake, along Observatory Road out to Lake View, and then back along Upper Shola Road and Upper Lake Road. We were back in time to wash up and get to breakfast.

We also walked out to the golf course with Lyn at least once and played 18 holes with him. Like the Upper-Lake circuit, you could hike it without a back-pack, although you had to carry your clubs (rented or borrowed in my case) around the eighteen holes. Lyn had great fun showing me how to address the ball and hit it, something which I was hard pressed to accomplish. I got a little better at putting on the "browns" (greens made of hard-packed sand), and managed to get my club head to hit the ball on most swings, but I didn't keep my score. Bibbi, Dave and Linwood were regular players and did quite well. Lyn, of course, beat us all handily.

The hike to the Golf Club is exactly 20 furlongs from the front gate of the school, two and a half miles. We took it at a leisurely pace, and made it in about forty minutes. We carried a packed school lunch, and since Lyn had his clubs at the clubhouse, we didn't have to carry anything else. We would be given water to drink at the clubhouse. At the time there were fewer than the standard eighteen holes, fourteen or fifteen, I recall, and holes six and seven shared the same fairway, so that you had to give way to groups playing in the opposite direction.

In order to complete a standard eighteen-hole round we had to repeat a couple of the holes. In addition, on this particular day, one of the more spectacular holes had been rented by a film company for a bucolic scene in one of their epic Bollywood productions. We paused to watch a beautiful actress dance her way barefoot down a slope with her sari flowing out behind her.

The occupation of this fairway by the film crew meant that we had to play an alternate hole a third time. This was fine with me, because I got to practice a known hole over and over again, and figured out how to avoid losing my ball and how to land in favorable spots on the fairway.

We finished our round by about noon, and walked over to the film production's hole to watch the action. The beautiful actress in a spectacular sari was still going through the scene that had her running barefoot down a hill towards the camera. Now there were young girls skipping along with her throwing rose petals at her feet. A wind machine was making her hair and sari flow out behind her. There was a camouflaged carpet laid down for her to run on. Loud Carnatic music played, to which she danced along. She wore a delighted, excited smile and her eyes sparkled as she ran. We watched her do this three more times while we ate our sandwiches. Each time she was asked to go back up the hill to do it over, she scowled and yelled at the director and the cameraman. An attendant came to wipe her brow and touch up her makeup. The smile was back when she got ready to repeat.

We walked back to school, arriving at mid-afternoon. We turned in our hike chit in the office to get credit for the "A" hike, and went down to the dorm to wait for tea time. We were now ready to take on more strenuous longer 'C' and 'D' category hikes.

Mount Perumal   For some reason, the hike from school to the top of Mount Perumal was granted 'D' hike status. The hike does involve quite a bit of elevation change, though not as much as most 'D' hikes. Also, none of the way is very steep, and the trail is pretty smooth with much of it along the graded road. The peak is about 15 miles from Kodai, and can be reached in about 4 to 5 hours at a reasonable pace. The route drops a little over 2000 feet down the Ghat to the start of the ascent, which takes you back up the back of a long, gently rising ridge about 1000 feet. If you take the cutoffs down the Ghat, which we always did during daylight, you can shave a couple of miles off the way down.

During my junior year, I had discovered that you could leave the school on a Friday after supper and hike down to Rest-a-Bit bungalow near Perumal Malai before full dark. There, you could spend the night in relative comfort very near the start of the ascent. The following morning, at first light without anything but your canteen to weigh you down, the three-mile walk up the ridge was a fairly easy stroll. You could then return to Rest-a-Bit for a camp breakfast before heading back up the Ghat to school in time for lunch. In that way, you didn't miss any of the Saturday night activities. And you got credit for a 'D' hike.

So, as part of our conditioning hikes, we decided to go back to Perumal. Bibbi, as he usually did, was into keeping track of the night sky, and got us scheduled for the hike to Perumal on what he hoped would be a clear, moonlit night (if it didn't rain). We would hike down to Rest-a-Bit bungalow as usual on Friday night. Then, if the night was clear and dry, we would leave our packs at the bungalow and walk up the mountain before going to bed.

Mt. Perumal in the Moonlight

And so we did. This was one of the most magical hikes I have been on. The night was clear and dry, with only a slight chill that was easily kept at bay by our vigorous walking and our windbreakers. The trail up the hill is mostly out in the open, with no sholas or clefts to deal with, and the night sky was blazing above us. The moon threw our shadows leaping across rocks beside us. The night was quiet and still, with only the sounds of our breathing and footfalls to be heard. Occasionally we would stop, and all sound would cease. Looking back, we could see the lights of Kodai and a couple of the surrounding villages. In accordance with the hike requirements, we got to the top of the mountain, and continued until the trail began to descend on the other side, proving that we had indeed made it to the top. There, we stopped and took in the 360 degree view and soaked in the joy of being alone, in the silence, on top of the world.

Before starting back down we each picked a spot to take a leak, leaving our marks on Perumal.

On the way back down, Bibbi pointed out constellations to us. The Southern Cross, which had been behind us on the way up, shone in front of us on the way back down. We were back at the bungalow by lights out (ten o'clock), tired and ready to sleep. The next morning we arose at first light and made it back to school in time for Saturday breakfast. Pancakes, if I remember correctly.

Tope Another conditioning hike that we often took was down the old Coolie Ghat to Tope. This popular hike, which had been one of the first I went on, leads to a rocky stream with many rock pools and tumbling waterfalls. Although the distance down to Tope from the Kodai School gate at Seven Corners is only about 9 miles, the way back is quite a bit longer unless one has the stamina to use the cutoffs on the way back. The trail drops more than 5,500 feet. The old Coolie Ghat snakes back and forth following a more manageable incline, and was originally used by coolies and donkeys to ferry Westerners and their possessions up to the hill station to escape the hot season on the plains. Ladies would be transported in palanquins borne by two coolies. Like modern-day athletes, coolies' active lives were usually over by their thirty-fifth birthday.

The cutoffs of the Coolie Ghat basically bisect the twists, going straight up (or down) the mountain. Cutoffs are usually a 30-degree or more of slope, which is barely manageable on the way down, and almost impossible on the way up. Taking the cutoffs down as much as possible is what makes Tope a 9 mile hike. On the way up, the distance is closer to 15 miles following the old Coolie Ghat.

We set out in the chilly morning with back packs containing light sleeping bags, two packed lunches and fruit. I had some extra Cadbury chocolate bars from Hamidia's in mine, and we had some oatmeal to cook up for breakfast. It was to be an overnight trek, and we hoped to be back at school for lunch the next day.

For this hike we had a staff leader, and there were about 12 of us. Bibbi was asked to take the lead, since he knew the way, and Mr. Shaw, the staff leader would bring up the rear to make sure that there were no stragglers. I set off determined to keep pace with Bibbi, which was easy enough until we reached Vellagavi, where the Coolie Ghat road drops over the edge of the mountain. Bibbi began to go straight down every cutoff we came to. On a steep descent over rough ground, one has to take careful, mincing steps, shifting back and forth to take advantage of secure footing. You can't take your eyes off the trail in front of you for fear of stepping into a patch of loose rock or gravel and sliding down onto your butt. Bibbi seemed to dance down the trails with a syncopated gait, and soon left me behind. Every once in a while he would wait for me, Linwood and Dave, who were trying to keep up with him, to be sure that we could find the next cutoff. Then he would continue to dance down the hill.

"How are you doing that?" I shouted. "You look like you're skipping on a hop-scotch grid."

He just laughed and dove down the next cutoff, his hair flopping up and down with each jump.

As we went on, I got better at imitating Bibbi's gait and timing. I managed to keep closer to him and at least come out of one cutoff before he disappeared down the next. The trick seemed to be to focus all one's attention on the trail ahead and where to place each step without regard to the length of each stride. But by the time we made it to the bottom of the Ghat, where the trail leveled off a little, my thighs, shins and calves were screaming with pain.

Bibbi called a short halt to wait for some of the others to catch up when we reached the side of Levinge Stream, which we would follow down to the place where we would set up our camp. It felt good to take off our hiking boots and sweaty socks and plunge our blistered feet into the cool water. Soon, though, after only about fifteen minutes, about half the group had caught up with us, and Bibbi decided that it was time to push on so that we could gather firewood for the camp fire and set up as much as possible before the others came. Then we would eat one of our packed lunches, and spend the afternoon swimming in one of the pools nearby.

The path beside the stream led through boulders which had washed down the mountain in flood seasons over the years. In some parts it was necessary to climb over the rocks using both hands and feet. At one point my foot slipped into a crevice and my boot got stuck. I had to take my foot out of the boot in order to wiggle it free. There was more than one skinned knee in the group by the time we got to the camp site beside one of the larger pools. The afternoon had turned hot, so in spite of our resolve to ready the camp before the staff leader brought up the slow group, we decided that we deserved a swim before starting the work. There were only boys on the hike, so we just stripped down and went into the nearby pool, sitting under the waterfall at the top of it.

The slow group arrived while we were in the water, so, of course, when we heard them and got out of the water to greet them, our clothes had disappeared.

"Hey, guys. It's not funny! We can get sunburnt or cut our feet on the rocks," I whined.

Our pain delighted them, and they stood back watching us try to discover where they had hidden our things. Once we left the banks of the stream, the ground became rough and painful on our tender feet. We took awkward steps grunting with pain. The late morning sun beat mercilessly down on us.

Bibbi, applying reverse psychology, climbed back into the pool and settled into the cool water. "That's okay, guys. You can set up camp and gather wood. We'll come up in a little while."

They kept us begging for our clothes for a few more minutes anyway, before giving in and showing us the tree they had hung them in. Bibbi managed to climb the tree and retrieve them… quite a feat when one is naked. Thankfully for him, at least it was a fairly smooth-barked tree.

After we ate the contents of our packed lunch, Mr. Shaw, our staff leader, surprised us by taking a pot out of his backpack, which he filled with water from the stream and boiled to make chai. He had some powdered milk and spices and sugar to boil up with the tea leaves. After the pot had boiled for ten or fifteen minutes, he declared the water purified and the tea ready to drink… but nobody had cups! Well, almost nobody. Bibbi had a tin cup in his pack, and my canteen was equipped with a cap that doubled as a three-ounce mug. The other boys had to take turns sharing Mr. Shaw's cup.

We spent the afternoon gathering firewood and kindling, exploring the area around our camp, choosing spots to bed down in, gathering leaves and grass to soften the ground under our sleeping bags, and jumping into the stream whenever we felt hot. There were several natural water slides that we could shoot down, but it had to be done with a pad of some sort to avoid 'butt-burn'. We used folded T-shirts or towels.

After a while, I felt my nose beginning to burn, so I spent as much time as I could among the trees that grew along the stream, in the shade. An under-classman, my ex-roommate, Doug, was not so prudent, and was turning red.

We had a nice fire going as the sun set and we pulled out our second packed meal which turned out to be a curry flavored sandwich with an apple. We always enjoyed anything with curry in it, so we thought the meal was excellent. We were all pretty tired from our exertions of the day, so after a few stories and songs, we straggled off to our sleeping bags, and were drifting off before nine. There was a soft moan coming from Doug's sack as he tried to find a comfortable position that didn't aggravate his sunburn. Mr. Shaw had some sort of balm that he administered, and Doug finally quieted down.

At about 1200 feet of altitude, the air was much thicker and warmer than Kodai, but there was still a cool feel to the dawn. By 6 or so, we were almost all awake and Bibbi was stoking the fire that had burned down to embers during the night. Dawn mosquitoes were out, so the smoke was a welcome companion to the warmth of the fire. Mr. Shaw sent me to fill the pot with water from the stream, reminding me to go upstream from our latrine and campsite, while Bibbi organized a team to find some suitable leaves to use for plates. Mr. Shaw had brought some oats down the hill along with the tea, powdered milk, sugar and spices. We boiled up the oats to make oatmeal which we ate with our fingers off the banana leaves that Bibbi's team had found nearby. Unfortunately, there weren't any bananas growing at the time.

I washed out the pot and brought more water for chai, which we drank as before, sharing cups. After a quick dip in the stream to wash up and cool down, we hurriedly cleaned up the camp and doused and buried the fire. We were packed and ready to head back up the hill before 8 o'clock, giving us about four hours to make it back up the hill for lunch. Unfortunately, when Mr. Shaw counted heads we discovered that Doug was missing.

Mr. Shaw called out Doug's name, and we joined in creating quite a chorus. We walked up and down the stream and out to the sides, a hundred yards or more in each direction. There was no reply. We were all getting worried. Mr. Shaw asked us to think about the last time we had seen him, and one of the boys said that he had been with him in the stream when we were washing up.

Frantically, Mr. Shaw ran back down to the water where we had been washing up and walked down the stream calling Doug's name. We followed along, beginning to feel really scared.

Bibbi ran ahead jumping agilely from boulder to boulder, and spotted a towel on a rock by one of the deeper pools. "I think I see his towel!" he shouted, and soon we all ran up to the pool.

Late Start   At first we didn't see him, but then there was a splash, and he emerged from under the waterfall at the head of the pool. He was surprised to see us all standing around staring at him. He had come to soak his sunburn in the pool, and had found a little cavity behind the waterfall, where he could soak peacefully in the backwash. Due to the sound of the water all around him, he hadn't been able to hear us calling. Mr. Shaw was both relieved and angry at the same time.

Where's Doug?

As a result of Doug's adventure, we didn't hit the trail until almost 9 o'clock, which meant that we would probably not be able to make it back to campus in time for lunch, which had been the plan. A couple of us still had an apple or an orange in our backpacks, and I had a very soft Cadbury's bar in mine, but we had eaten all the food we brought with us, and tea time was a long way off. This predicament did not sit well with any of us, but especially with Bibbi, whose growth-spurt metabolism demanded lots of food. We all let Doug know how displeased we were with his delay.

So Bibbi asked Mr. Shaw if he could take a couple of the stronger hikers and ascend the Ghat via the cutoffs, rather than follow the switchbacks with the rest of the group. In this way he hoped to make the trek in a bit over 3 hours, rather than the normal four-and-a-half that it usually took. If we made it up to campus by half past twelve or so, we should be able to get to the cafeteria in time to get something before the kitchen closed down. The staff there, especially Cruz and Jackie, would have pity on us and give us something to eat. Mr. Shaw agreed to letting some of us forge ahead, but limited the breakaway group to the four of us who were seniors: Bibbi, Linwood, Dave and me. Doug was a tenth grader, so thankfully, couldn't join us. Phil, my flag caper companion, was an eleventh grader, and begged to be included, arguing that he was an upper-classman, and should be allowed to join our group.

I somehow let Bibbi convince me that I was capable of powering up the hill with him, and he sweetened the deal by telling me that he thought that today's lunch was "dry curry", one of our favorite meals. So, five of us set off up the trail heading for the first cutoff, leaving the others to follow along at a more leisurely pace using the switchbacks to take the climb more gently.

We followed the stream up for a few furlongs, clambering over boulders and wading through shallows wearing sneakers, until we arrived at the path that led to the Ghat road. There we changed into our hiking boots, and emerged shortly onto the shoulder of the old coolie Ghat.

The first cutoff was just a few yards up the road, and we charged up to it determined to make the climb in record time. Up to that point, we had been chatting away, talking about the trail, Doug's misadventure, food and girls; happily offering profanity-laced opinions on all of them. Once we started up the cutoff, the talking died down very quickly, as breath was needed for another purpose. From then on, talk was limited to sharp warnings or exclamations: "Watch that branch!"; "Slippery patch!"; "Ouch! S--T!"; and so on.

At the end of the fourth or fifth cutoff we paused to look back and admire how far we had come. We were already well above the stream, and could see the others just turning the first switchback. Then we looked up, and saw how far we still had to go. We couldn't see up the actual slope very far, but there were telephone poles set along the cutoffs that marched up the slope. We figured that we had only come about one eighth of the way, if that.

Not every switchback had a cutoff. Some switchbacks were stacked so tightly that there was an almost vertical wall between them with no path.

Up the Coolie Ghat

On these, we had to follow the road, which could have given us a chance to catch our breath a little, but Bibbi was so intent on making it back to school in time for lunch that he would increase the pace on these stretches, almost totally negating any respite we might have gained. After going along like this- cutoff, cutoff, switchback, cutoff, cutoff- I, for one, was almost totally drained. I gathered what breath I could and asked for a short halt.

My other companions looked grateful, but Bibbi seemed annoyed. I suggested that we should take a five minute break after every fifth cutoff, but Bibbi thought that would add about 30 minutes to the climb and mean that we wouldn't make it to school until almost one o'clock, and most of the lunch would be gone. We settled on a three minute break after every 6 cutoffs, which Bibbi calculated would get us to the entrance of the school shortly after noon if we hurried once we got to Vellagavi.

It was now around 9:45, and we had been climbing for about half an hour, and still had more than an hour and a half of straight uphill ahead before arriving at Vellagavi. The sun was beginning to bear down on us, and we were still low enough on the climb to feel the heat from the plains, making us sweat, especially under our backpacks. We had filled our canteens from the stream and dissolved some halazone tablets in them to purify the water, so at every break we drank a few swallows. The water didn't taste very good, which kept us from drinking too fast or too much, probably a good thing, since it made it last longer. Nevertheless, by the time we got to Vellagavi, some of us had finished our supply.

From Vellagavi the climb would be gentler, but we would still be rising about 800 feet over the 3-and-a-half mile leg into Kodai. On a typical day, the walk from Vellagavi to Kodai would take about an hour, but that was after a leisurely walk out and a break for lunch before starting back. Who knew how long it would take after an arduous climb made at top speed. I did not express my doubts aloud.

Wild Blueberries We resumed our climb, stopping for 3 minutes after every sixth cutoff, which sometimes meant every ten or fifteen minutes, and sometimes after twenty minutes or so, depending on how many switchbacks we had to take between cutoffs.

Along one stretch of the road on one of the switchbacks, I noticed bushes around us with little blue fruit hanging from the branches. Linwood said he thought they were wild blueberries, so I tried one of them. They were, indeed, sweet, ripe, wild blueberries. I called out to the others, and we agreed to take our 3 minute break early so that we could gather and eat some of the berries. Bibbi wasn't wild about the idea, but checked his watch and agreed to go along with it. I filled my hat with them as quickly as I could, knowing that Bibbi would get us moving after 3 minutes flat. I gathered a few dozen between mouthfuls so that for about a mile I was happily gorging on fruit.

We got to Vellagavi just before 11:30 in the morning, having completed the difficult part of the climb in just under 2-and-a-half hours. We found some shade to rest in for a few minutes, enjoying the cool mountain breeze that hadn't been evident until we crested the last steep rise. Bibbi found a small stick and began to scratch some numbers in a patch of dirt on the ground. My stomach was beginning to react to the unaccustomed bounty of fruit with ominous gurgling. Linwood, Dave and Phil sat down with their backs to a eucy tree and took off their boots while I looked around hopefully for a place to relieve myself. There was nowhere for me to go, but the feeling eased up a bit after I passed some gas.

In what seemed like a few seconds, but was probably a few minutes, Bibbi announced that, according to his calculations, if we kept up a pace of 3.2 miles per hour, we could make it to campus by twelve-thirty. Anything under about 3.5 miles per hour was a leisurely pace by Bibbi's standards, so he felt that he was giving us great news. But it was still up hill much of the way, although after the steepness of our previous climb, it would seem almost level, so we agreed that we might be able to keep the pace up.

As we set off from Vellagavi, my gut was beginning to gurgle more ominously as the blueberries worked their way into my system. Knowing that I would need a bathroom sooner rather than later, I set off briskly, to Bibbi's great delight, since I was usually the slowest member of our group.

"Wow, look at Charlie go!" he commented to the others.

I replied, "Yeah, well, I'm gonna need to go to the 'B' pretty soon, and I'd rather do it at school."

They all thought it was quite a joke and laughed. I didn't think it was funny at all.

After a few furlong markers had slipped by, he reckoned that we were doing better than 3.5 miles per hour, which would get us to the campus gate about 10 minutes before lunch. However, by the time we reached Bryant's Park which gave us a downhill track to the gate, I was in such a hurry that I was almost running. We burst onto campus at 12:27, having made it back from Tope in less than 3-and-a-half hours: possibly a school record. If so, it was a record that I celebrated in the bathroom in the quad.

Lunch was, indeed, dry curry, but by the time I got out of the quad bathroom, there was only a small plate that Bibbi had asked Cruz to save for me. It was okay, though, since I didn't feel like eating very much.

Final Plans Tope was our final conditioning hike for our trek to Manjampatti. We were now technically fit and could apply for the permission from Mr. Root. The three-day weekend was coming up, and we anticipated needing every minute of it to accomplish our goal. There would be a lot of thought and preparation to put in over the next few days to make sure that we had everything we needed.

We started by making a list of the meals we would be taking with us: breakfast, lunch and supper on Saturday (we would eat supper before departure on Friday); breakfast, lunch and supper on Sunday; and breakfast and lunch on Monday. The school would reimburse us one rupee for every meal we would miss, so we would each get eight rupees towards the cost of our supplies.

Lunches would all be on the go, so we opted for sandwiches, bologna and cheese (a lunch pack from the school kitchen) on Saturday while we were still in the cool heights, and peanut butter and jam for Sunday and Monday, since bologna and cheese would probably spoil after a day in a backpack. For breakfasts we would take some hard-boiled eggs for Saturday morning, and oatmeal to be cooked for Sunday and Monday. Saturday and Sunday suppers would be chapattis and rice, with lentils and sambar. We would take tea, spices, sugar and powdered milk for chai. We would take six apples and three oranges each. We would need pots and plates and utensils. We would need cups. We needed to remember flashlights, matches and a first aid kit.

The list kept getting longer and longer even before we sorted out what clothes and personal gear we would need to bring. I was planning to take an air mattress as well as a sleeping bag that I would need to borrow. As the list grew longer, I realized that the glorified book-bag that I had been planning to use as a backpack, and had used for my previous hikes, would not be big enough to accommodate my share of the load. I would need to find a better one somewhere. I didn't want to borrow one from the school's store of extra backpacks, though. Many of them were damaged and fraying, most of them smelled of old socks and mildew, and none of them had been good enough for their owner to donate or give away.

Saturday:
  Breakfast: hard-boiled eggs & bananas with bread and jam & peanut butter
  Lunch: School sandwiches and fruit
  Supper: curried lentils & rice, chapattis, sambar, chai

Sunday:
  Breakfast: oatmeal & oranges & chai
  Lunch: Peanut butter & jelly and fruit
  Supper: curried lentils & rice, chapattis, sambar & chai

Monday:
  Breakfast: oatmeal & oranges & chai
  Lunch: Peanut butter & jelly and fruit

Food
  2 lbs rice, 2 lbs lentils, curry powder mix, sambar powder mix,
  3 dozen chapattis, 1 lb. oatmeal, 1 box tea leaves, 1 box powdr milk,
  1 lb. sugar, 1 jar peanut butter, 1 jar jam or jelly, 1 doz. apples
  1 doz. oranges, 2 loaves of bread, 1 box cookies,

Meal prep
  1 pot, 1 frying pan, 1 box matches

A Very Hopeful List

At the end of every school year, seniors who were heading off to college would donate all of their decent cast-offs to the annual White Elephant sale that was held in the school gym. This generally included a lot of their camping gear; canteens, backpacks, sleeping bags, and the like. I knew that Doug (he of the Tope hike delay) had acquired a sturdy backpack of decent size, and asked him if I could borrow it for the Manjampatti hike. He was planning a short hike for that weekend, but I reminded him of his misadventure in Tope, and that he was an underclassman, and could be subjected to certain tribulations. So he reluctantly agreed to trade backpacks with me for the weekend. His biggest objection seemed to stem from the fact that his backpack had padded straps, and mine didn't. I explained that I usually stuffed a sock under the straps if the pack was heavy. Doug also agreed to let me take his sleeping bag, which was a little too large for easy carry, but would keep me warm in the two nights we would spend in the highlands.

Bibbi and I walked down to the budge after our showers the Wednesday before our departure to purchase the bulk of the supplies. Since I had an account at Hamidia's Sundries Store in the budge, I volunteered to bring matches, soap, crackers, powdered milk, sugar, tea leaves, peanut butter, jam, and Cadbury's chocolates. I also purchased a two of tins of sardines and some canned peas and carrots there to enhance a couple of our meals. The store clerk agreed to let me draw upon my next month's allowance of twenty rupees in order to pay for it all. From there we went to a couple of the stalls to where we bought two loaves of bread, sambar powder, chapattis, a pound of rice, and a pound of dahl, with the money the school had given us. We hoped to get the packed lunches, apples, oranges and hard boiled eggs from the school kitchen at tea time on Friday.

That evening after supper, Linwood, Bibbi and I met up in our dorm room and spread the purchases out on the beds. To these we added a frying pan, a pot and three Sterno cans that we had scrounged from somewhere. We divided the items into four roughly equal piles, one for each of us. We eyed the resulting piles with trepidation. The pile with the pot in it was going to be hard to fit inside a backpack that was already stuffed with extra clothes, shoes, plates and utensils. The backpack I had borrowed from Doug happened to be lying at the foot of my bed, and Linwood picked it up. We then compared it to Bibbi's backpack, which he pulled out from under his bed. Neither one of them looked like it would accommodate the four-quart pot inside it along with all of the other stuff. Linwood's backpack was in his room, so he ran to get it.

The circumference of Linwood's backpack was slightly larger than mine or Bibbi's, so the pot was able to nest in the bottom where it could be stuffed with all the rest of Linwood's supplies and gear. It wasn't that heavy a pot, so Linwood was okay with it, but it did make a hard bulge right where the pack rested on his lumbar region. Thinking about the descent to Tope with a much lighter backpack, I was glad that it hadn't fit into mine.

We each chose one of the piles of supplies, leaving the fourth one to give to Dave the next day. Bibbi reminded us to leave room for the lunch packs and other things we would be getting from the kitchen on the day of our departure. I began to stuff the softer items I would carry into the bottom of my pack, and lined the side next to my back with my folded towel. By the time I had packed my share of the supplies and my clothes into the backpack, I realized that my air mattress and sleeping bag were not going to fit. They would have to be tied to the top of the pack once it was filled. Oh, well.

It was Wednesday night, and we were late for Canteen. Linwood wasn't going to go, but Bibbi and I wanted to get in a couple of dances, so we ran up the stairs and joined the party already underway. Canteen, our weekly opportunity to be near and actually touch girls, was an activity we always looked forward to.

Canteen Interlude For us, boarding school denizens, Canteen on Wednesday nights was one of our primary social pleasures, especially for those of us who didn't have steady girlfriends we could spend time with. Lights were dimmed and music played. There was always a staff chaperone to make sure that dancers kept at least four inches away from their partners, and that girls' skirts and dresses touched the floor when they knelt. I was very self-conscious, and would have been mortified if I had ever been singled out for dancing too close. I was also very shy about asking girls to dance with me, and would wait till there was a fast dance to ask, and hope that my chosen partner would agree to keep dancing with me when a slow dance came up. I wasn't a bad dancer, but always got tongue-tied and had a hard time making small talk, so it wasn't too often that girls would stick with me through more than one or two dances during a set.

Bibbi had no such limitations, though, and danced almost every dance. Even when he was between girlfriends, he could dance as much as he wanted because so many of the girls were interested in gaining his attention. Besides that, he was a wonderful conversationalist, so he always danced and chatted away with all the choice girls at Canteen. By the end of the evening, details of our upcoming hike had spread to all the girls and many of the boys. It helped me get some extra dances in, too, when girls began to ask me about it, giving me a handy subject to talk about and keep their attention. I happily basked in the reflected glory of being Bibbi's friend.

Canteen was about as close as I ever came to having any real encounters with the opposite sex, though not for want of wishing.

Let me digress for a moment since we are on the subject:

Sex at Kodai Kodai was an inherently heterosexual place. Its Christian missionary base lent a biblical interpretation to its overall nature. By today's standards it would probably be deemed homophobic. We made jokes about boys we perceived to be a little swishy. Thursdays somehow became identified as "fairy days" and should not have any social activities scheduled. We were aware of several teachers who seemed to like members of their own sex and watched carefully to see who frequented their company. It would be naïve to believe that nothing ever happened, but the conservative nature of the denominations dominating School management kept such proclivities under very tight rein, and there were no scandals while I was there that I heard of.

Boy-girl relationships were tolerated, if not encouraged, and strictly monitored. Only High School students were allowed to date, and couples blossomed and bloomed, especially in the spring semester, and especially among upper classmen. Bibbi, Kris, Lyn, Ron and Stan were the on-campus studs in our class, and each one had at least one girlfriend during high school, if not two, or even three, though only one at a time. Others of my classmates had steady dates from time to time, but these flings were not as carefully watched. I always aspired to be in their club, but never managed to get up the courage to let a girl know I was interested.

That said, as in any pubescent community, hormones raged. The School Administration made elaborate provisions to let off some of the steam and reduce tensions. Sports and other physical activities were a big part of the plan. Most of the real jocks, including Bibbi and Kris, were on sports teams with grueling practice schedules. Teams often traveled to other schools, usually on overnight trips, bringing home trophies and championships. Hiking, swimming, biking and other strenuous activities helped as well.

Staff members would show up randomly in the nooks and corners where couples could disappear. These hidden spots were especially popular when one or two of the more tolerant staff were on duty. We were certain that Mrs. Henderson, the cafeteria manager, added saltpeter to our food, which, at the time, was believed to lower libidos.

Elective classes and extracurricular activities, such as band, chorus, class plays and the like gave boys and girls controlled spaces in which to interact. Several couples grew out of choir practice or acting together in a school play. Couples who were in two different grades would join the same elective program to be able to hang out with each other during the class.

On top of that, there were the sanctioned boy-girl activities. On Wednesday nights we got an hour and a half of Canteen, a regular dance event for high school students. There were refreshments and low lights and music with a dance floor. These chaperoned dances were one of my weekly highlights. The girls from Kennedy would dress nicely and we boys would don our cleanest clothes after our showers.

Girls who weren't in a steady relationship would all sit on one side of the room, and hopeful boys would walk around near the refreshment table plucking up their courage to ask one of them to dance. It usually took several tunes before things got moving and the ice was broken, during which time the established couples would have the floor to themselves. I heard from Bibbi that they preferred it when the rest of us got out on the floor, because the chaperones would catch them if they danced close when they were the only ones out there.

I could usually get in several dances in an evening, carefully avoiding the girl I really wanted to dance with for a while so that she wouldn't guess that I was interested. Then I would swoop in when a slow dance started. I thought I was being clever, and hiding my feelings, but I found out years later that my method had been detected and identified. To my chagrin, one or two of my targets found it flattering, and would possibly have welcomed further advances from me. If only I hadn't been so shy!

Wednesday nights after lights out became known as 'squeak nights'. The stimulation of close proximity to the opposite sex created tensions that were released in private under the covers, and the creaky bed frames told their tales. Many accusatory jokes were made the following morning, and many denials as well. Not willing to believe that girls were not afflicted with the same tensions and desires, Kennedy dorm was dubbed 'The House of a Thousand Candles', which set our fantasies flying.

There were those rare occasions when rumors flew about this couple or that couple "doing it", and in one infamous case that arose in my first year, seemed credible. But for the most part, relationships didn't pass the surreptitious 'making out' stage.

The credible rumor that circulated involved one of my classmates, who shall remain nameless, with a girl from a higher grade. They were observed on several occasions, or not observed, better said, taking a punt out into the middle of the lake and then disappearing from view into the bottom of the boat. The boat drifted here and there, at some points venturing close enough to shore to offer a glimpse of their supine forms to prying eyes.   What was actually going on was the subject of speculation.   Once the rumors began to fly, and they were subjected to a conference in Mr. Root's office, their travels on the lake ceased.   There was never any confirmation of hanky-panky that I heard of.   The relationship was probably more than a serious fling, though, for years later, I heard, they married and had two children together.

Bear Shola was another hot zone for couples. Just over a mile from the School, it offered a secluded place for couples to walk and sit on rocks and listen to the waterfall.   The lush vegetation screened couples from prying eyes, and emerging couples were seen exiting as they straightened their clothing.   On the whole, though, supervision and Christian principles kept our most basic instincts under control.   Needless to say, as much as I would have liked to be involved in these activities, I never was.

Erotica was essentially unavailable at Kodai.   There were a few books in the library that depicted male and female anatomy, and there was even a very basic sex-ed primer.   Certain issues of National Geographic were also popular reading in the library. My own go-to girlie pics were basically the women's underwear and swimsuit sections of the Sears catalog, but that was only available to me when I was on vacation.   So it was quite an exciting shock to the system when Jerry Haley arrived during our junior year.   He was a class year behind us, but a little 'wiser' and more worldly than most of us, having spent several years in the States.   He had a tape recorder with a lot of newer music, including the Beatles, who were all the rage.   He also had two issues of Playboy secreted in his footlocker. He was instantly popular with all the upper classmen, and the Beatles and Playboy became the new pinnacle of dorm culture.

The Girls at Kodai   As a teenager, and even before, I was always obsessed with girls.   I had my first (and only) declared girlfriend when I was five or six years old, in Rangoon, Burma.   Prinnie Anderson lived in the house across the road from us, and was about my same age. She liked to come out when I was riding my tricycle so that I would let her ride it with me standing on the back axle holding on to her shoulders.

We took to meeting each other almost daily after school and visiting each other's homes for after-school snacks.   I think our parents thought the relationship was cute, so we agreed to be boyfriend and girlfriend.

In Honduras I had a short exclusive friendship with my next-door neighbor, Desiree Osborne, but it mainly involved sitting in the branches of a mango tree by the fence between our houses and holding sticky hands as we talked and ate the mangoes we plucked from the branches.

I was also interested in Linda Matamoros for a long time, but she was more interested in my best friend, Glenn Tilton, so, although I often rode my horse up to her house in Las Lomas to watch TV sitting with her and her mother on their couch, my interest, although probably noted, was largely rebuffed. We did correspond with each other for several months after I left Honduras.

In Kodai, my lack of success with girls was even more pronounced, mainly because of a sudden shyness that afflicted me as my hormones increased and my fantasies about girls became more vivid. Additionally, I was susceptible to unsightly breakouts of adolescent acne, which made me very self-conscious. My brother Johnny, however, while just as acne-prone as I was, had no such shyness, and within weeks of arriving at Kodai was already going steady with Sue Martin, a senior, while he was just a freshman. He had several steady girlfriends after that.

There were several long term dating relationships at Kodai, none of which, unfortunately, involved me. These often coincided with the spring semester, when the weather in Kodai cleared and warmed. Bibbi was active in this scene, as were Kris and Lyn. Bibbi's romance with Carolyn Morgan during our junior year was possibly his most serious fling. Carolyn was a sweet, gentle girl, a brain, and an amazing athlete. She shone on Field day in several events. She was one of two Black girls in our class, with Terri Oliver, and Bibbi fell head-over-heels in love with her. Unfortunately for the romance, she left Kodai on furlough early in our senior year.

Although I never had a steady girlfriend, I fell in love with many, many girls during my three years at Kodai, sometimes more than one at a time; however, I never managed to forge any kind of a serious relationship with any of them. There aren't many who escaped my daydreams, but a number of them stand out as real heart-throbs. I would satisfy my yearnings by asking them to dance with me in canteen, or teasing them awkwardly, just to be able to talk to them and get them to notice me.

One of the first girls to catch my eye was Judy Staal. She was a year ahead of me, but I got to sit and stand next to her in chorus since we were both singing tenor. She was cute, vivacious and funny. She would laugh at my whispered comments and cause Mr. Hunt, the director, some exasperation at times. Judy had a pixie haircut and clear, regular features with a ready, slightly mischievous, smile. Standing next to her and occasionally brushing shoulders with her was enough to capture my attention.

Every boy in my class and in other classes as well, was in love with Maureen Aung Thwin. However, she was usually spoken for and going steady, most notably, with Kris during our senior year. She was smart and sassy, with shiny black hair, almond-shaped eyes and golden skin; an exotic beauty that caught the eye and the imagination.

Maureen's close friend, Cathy Scott, was another beauty in our class. Cathy's older sister, Cyril, and her older brother, Foster, were very socially active, but I don't recall that Cathy was much of a dater.

That said, she was very attractive and was often the target of my teasing and my fantasies. Notably, I tried to get her attention at our Senior Sneak class getaway by squirting her with sea cucumbers, which are slightly disgusting, squishy tubular animals which eject a surprising stream of water when squeezed. Needless to say that while my actions attracted attention, they did not endear me to Cathy.

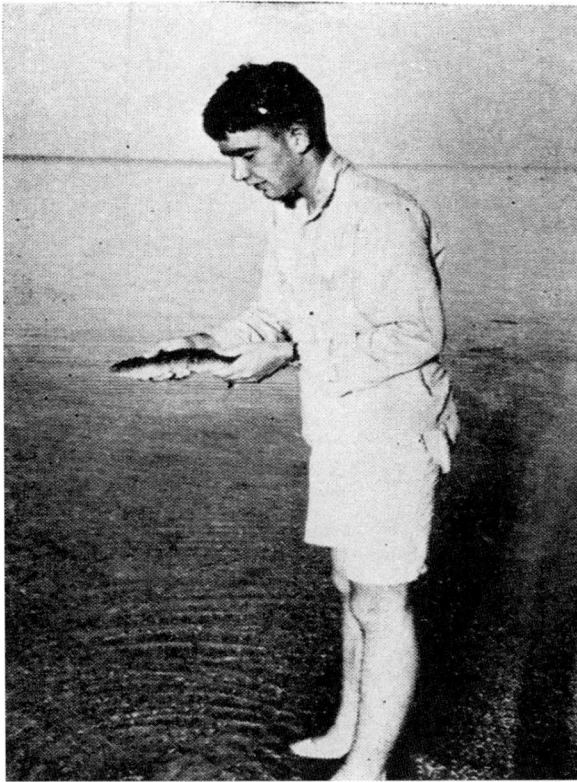

I Show How to Squirt a Sea Cucumber

Chellie Eaton was another of the girls I fell in love with several times. Our senior yearbook describes her well: "Chellie is known for her blonde hair, cute smile (usually accompanied with a blush), and her knack for attracting admirers of the opposite sex." Chellie was Canadian, but had been born in India and was equally at home in western clothing or Indian saris. I was entranced with her either way.

Bonnie Norton joined our class during the middle of our junior year, and quickly became one of my favorite fantasies. Also a Canadian, Bonnie was cute and pert with soft eyes and smooth skin. I got to go swimming with her in the lake a couple of times, and was totally smitten with her.

Nita Firmage, who turned down my invitation to the Prom, Irene Naumann and Barbie Ford, who went with me to the junior and senior proms, also from our class, were other girls I admired and who were mentioned in the story of my escapade to Shembug earlier in this narrative. Nita was the one I fantasized over, but Barbie and Irene were actual dates, so my memories of them are genuine and warm.

I also fell in love with many girls from other classes. Among the class behind ours, there was Hope Dexter, Margie Graham, Carol Gibson, Rona Nordeen (who later dated Lyn), and Laura Servid. Only three come to mind from the year before that, Jennifer Henchcliff, Karen Burall, and, of course, Emmy Riber, who plays a part later in the story.

My fantasies about all these girls almost always involved them making the first move, as whenever I contemplated making a move for real, my palms would sweat and my tongue would grow two sizes in my mouth. In my heated brain, Chellie would put her head on my shoulder during a slow dance in canteen... Cathy would play footsies with me... Bonnie would get scared of something while we were swimming in the lake and grab me around the neck... Laura would ask me to the Sadie Hawkins day dance... Margie would get hurt on a hike, and I would have to carry her... Emmy would allow me to drive her around the 40-mile Round (...oh, wait, that really happened) and we would stop and kiss at beautiful scenic points (that didn't). The situation would always progress from there in my adolescent imagination and lead to more and more intimate encounters.

None of these girls, other than perhaps Emmy, and maybe Nita, were ever aware of my feelings toward them or my thoughts of them, as far as I know. Several mentioned how I flirted with them in their notes in my senior Eucy, but didn't seem to attach any significance to it.

***

When we got back to the dorm from canteen, Linwood came over to our room shaking his head. "Guys, we've forgotten one of the most important supplies."

"What!" we asked him. What could we have left off of our exhaustive list?

"There's no TP on the list", he told us.

We had all suffered through hikes without toilet paper, and knew that things could get very uncomfortable without it.

"Depending on how much we eat, we'll probably need almost a half roll per day for the three of us, that is, if nobody gets diarrhea," said Bibbi. "To be on the safe side, we should take two full rolls with us. Glad you thought of it, Linwood."

"Well, I've only got a tiny bit left, and maybe not even enough to last till we get our next roll next week," I said.

"Yeah, me too," said Linwood. "That's why I thought of it when I went to the bathroom a little while ago."

"Let's pool what we have and see where we are," said Bibbi.

Pooling our supply came up with the equivalent of about half a roll, and would undoubtedly be less by the time we left on Friday.

A Tale of TP Toilet paper was one of those things that the school rationed out carefully. There had been a time in days long gone by when, according to legend, it had been plentiful. However, some dastardly students had snuck out one dark night and wrapped Mr. Root's motor cycle with multiple rolls of it, which had then stuck to the chassis with the morning dew, making a royal mess. It was a hilarious stunt, but from then on, each boarder was allowed only two rolls per month, one every other week, which we guarded jealously, locking it away when we were out of our rooms.

Every once in a while, someone would forget his roll of TP in the bathroom and have to rely on the generosity of others to make it through the month. We suspected one student in particular of going into the bathroom every time he heard someone leave and harvesting any TP that had been inadvertently left behind. His room was next door to the bathroom, and we often saw him ducking in and out of it after someone had left. In fact, once when Narain suddenly remembered that he had forgotten his roll, he returned immediately and witnessed our suspect leaving the bathroom with a roll of TP about the same size as the one Narain had forgotten.

"Hey, is that my roll of TP I left there a few minutes gone?" asked Narain.

"Uh, no," said the suspect, "I, uh, brought it with me just now."

Either he was a brazen liar, or he had really brought it to the bathroom himself. Narain's roll had disappeared, and while he couldn't prove that the roll being carried away was his, he let several of us know what he suspected.

At some point, Bibbi and I (my idea, as Bibbi was much too gentle a soul to conceive of such an underhanded plot) decided to set a trap for the TP purloiner. Bibbi had a small remnant of a roll that he felt he could afford to lose to the cause. We got a red chili from the kitchen which we scored with a pocket knife. Then, unrolling a few squares, we dragged the scored surface of the chili along the next dozen or so squares and carefully re-rolled it to make it look untouched. This Bibbi left in the bathroom one afternoon after making enough noise to assure that our target would hear that he had come and gone.

I have to hand it to him. Although we tried to pay attention to see who followed Bibbi in, we never saw him. Yet the toilet paper was gone when we went to check about 15 or 20 minutes later. Had it not been for the trap we set, we would never have been able to say for sure who it was. In fact, for a while we thought that our plot had failed because several days went by with no visible results. We began to think we had done something to tip our hand. Maybe he had discovered the tampering. Maybe he was impervious to chilies. Maybe he had suffered in silence. We had almost given up on catching our prey.

However, a few days later it became obvious that we had scored a home run when our victim ran screaming from the toilet stall and, kicking off his pants, jumped into the shower, shirt and all. I wasn't there at the time to witness the ruckus, but Bibbi was close enough to hear the wails, and others actually saw what happened. From then on, for at least the rest of that semester, no more rolls of TP disappeared.

Final Details Bibbi spoke to Dave the next day at morning break to give him his share of the supplies and to ask him if he could bring two rolls of toilet paper from his compound. They didn't have the strict rationing over there that we did, and so he allowed that he could easily get two rolls, but wasn't sure that they would fit into his backpack with all the supplies we were giving him. Bibbi explained how we had divided up the loads, and that Linwood was stuck with the pot. Dave, laid back as always, said that he would figure out how to fit it all in. This turned out to be a very lucky arrangement for us in light of subsequent events.

So, by Thursday afternoon, we were all ready and only had to get through Friday to embark on our high adventure. As it was the Friday before a long weekend, several of our teachers had scheduled quizzes or assignments that had to be turned in, but thanks to my new-found study and work skills, I was able to turn in at lights out without any qualms and got a good night's sleep.

Friday's quizzes and assignments passed unremarkably. Our pending departure after supper was on our minds, and we spent our breaks gathering up the last-minute items that needed to be in our packs. Mr. Root called Bibbi into his office to remind him of the essential items that we had to have with us: extra socks; first aid kit, flashlights, matches wrapped in plastic, and more. He also wanted to make sure that Bibbi had a good compass and a copy of the topo maps of the area. Bibbi went over our planned route with him, which Mr. Root wanted to know, he said, half laughingly, in case he had to send out a search party for us.

At around two in the afternoon, the almost daily monsoon thunderstorm let loose with a vengeance, thundering rain down on the roofs of the walkways and soaking the campus. We kept our fingers crossed that it would clear up in time for us to leave after supper as planned. It was because of the consistency of these monsoonal downpours that we had decided not to leave right after school. There was nothing more miserable than starting out on a three-day hike with a soggy pack and wearing wet shoes and clothes.

At teatime, Bibbi, Linwood and I went back into the kitchen to ask Mrs. Henderson, the school's head cook, for our lunch packs and apples and oranges for the hike. Mrs. Henderson was Scottish, and true to the stereotype, tended to be stingy. She was reluctant to give us the quantity of oranges and apples that we had planned to take, even though we reminded her that we wouldn't be on campus for any meals on Saturday or Sunday, or most of Monday. And she laughed when we asked for hard-boiled eggs. So, she went into the storeroom and brought us three apples and three oranges each, just half the quantity we had been hoping to take, reminding us that the school had reimbursed us one rupee for each of the meals we would miss. We hoped that Dave would have more luck at the Lutheran compound.

The rain was tapering off when we took the lunch packs and fruit down to the dorm and added them to our backpacks, which were already bulging. Bibbi went over Mr. Root's list of essential items with us, and I added an extra pair of socks and a flashlight to my pack as well. I was going to have to tie Doug's sleeping bag to the outside of the backpack as there was no way that it would fit inside. Linwood said that he was glad to have the pot in the bottom of his pack, since it gave him a solid base into which he stuffed all of the soft items he was taking: socks, t-shirts, a towel, his bible and squashed down remnants of rolls of toilet paper. Bibbi put the topo maps and compass into a plastic bag, and stowed them in an outer pocket on his pack.

Treasure from Jackie and Cruz

Last minute preparations done, we sat on our bunks and waited for the supper, willing the rain to stop, and psyching ourselves up for the coming adventure. Bibbi again went on about how we were going to be pioneers and trailblazers. He pulled out the topo map and showed us how he was going to identify the point at which we should begin our ascent out of Manjampatti based on a bend in the river and the shape of the hill that would take us to the ridge that led out to Kookal. It didn't look far on the map compared to the distance we would already have covered. Nevertheless, we were allowing for a full day to cover the twelve miles or so that it looked like we would have to travel to reach the caves.

Soon enough it was supper time and we went up to the cafeteria to eat our last school-cooked meal for the next three days.

***

The kitchen staff numbered around fifteen who labored under the stern gaze of Mrs. Henderson, a ruddy-cheeked, blue-eyed Scottish matron who kept her dark hair tied in a severe bun. To our dismay she held very conservative ideas about how food should be prepared, usually thoroughly boiled and tasteless. It was only when she turned the staff loose to cook up Indian fare that we got savory, well-seasoned food. On special occasions, such as the Field Day feast on Bendy Field, the whole crew would turn out with great pots and pans of biriyani, and ladle out generous portions onto our banana-leaf plates as we sat cross-legged on the ground to eat with our fingers.

In the cafeteria, though, only three or four of the kitchen crew interacted regularly with us. Bibbi made sure to ingratiate himself to these staff members in the hopes of getting favors, such as larger portions, second helpings and extra service. Bibbi assured me that our very survival depended on keeping these guys on our side. Having been at Kodai School since first grade, Bibbi knew the ropes.

Of the staff members we had most contact with, Cruz was the youngest. He cut a dashing figure with a thick head of oiled black hair brushed straight back under his starched white garrison cap, and a chevron mustache accenting his ready smile and straight white teeth. He was gregarious and enjoyed engaging us with stories and kitchen gossip. He would let us know what menus were being prepared for the week so that we could plan our runs to the Budge.

During one particular period of tension at the border between India and Pakistan Cruz confided in us, with a grim expression, that he was going to volunteer to join the army and go fight the Pakistanis. I'm sure he would have made a fine soldier, but the dust-up at the border died down before he could register.

Cruz took a liking to me and made a point of greeting me cheerfully whenever I entered to cafeteria. He would quietly bring extra bread or fruit to the table I was sitting at, which made me a popular tablemate, especially with Bibbi. I gave Cruz some clothes and shoes that I had outgrown at the end of my first semester, which earned me his undying loyalty.

Jackie was older than and not as engaging as Cruz with a craggy face under bushy eyebrows. He was more taciturn and smiled less than Cruz, but seemed to be especially solicitous of our group in his gruff way. He would stop by to chat and bestow extra goodies at our table. Sometimes he would walk briskly past our table, and in his wake, an extra portion of rice or curry would magically appear near an elbow.

Velu stayed behind the serving line and wielded the ladle, so we made a point of greeting and complimenting him to ensure that the ladle was dipped to the bottom of the stew or curry to bring up the heavier, more filling morsels, and that it was full when it reached our tray.

Thanks to these three individuals, we ate well when the meals we liked came along, and knew when one of our less favorite meals was coming so that we could make other plans. All of this favoritism was performed surreptitiously, and with sleight of hand to avoid the watchful eye of Mrs. Henderson, who would frown furiously if she caught sight of it.

The rain had stopped, and the skies were clearing quickly. We were already dressed for hiking, and all of our classmates stopped by our table to wish us luck in their own special ways. A couple of them talked about how to set a signal fire if we got lost, one of them asked if we knew how to make a stretcher to drag a wounded companion out of the bush, another offered the advice that we should pee liberally around our campsite to ward off tigers, and so on. We took it all in stride, knowing that they were mostly just jealous. Girls who stopped by our table were more encouraging, especially, it seemed to me, when it came to wishing Bibbi luck.

Bibbi, as usual, went back through the chow line for seconds and thirds, and then ate my dessert, rice pudding, which I didn't like. He always had a prodigious appetite that went along with his seemingly boundless energy, and he was storing up for the less bounteous days to come. Linwood and I went back for some more rice and mystery stew, which was good enough to be one of the more popular meals when compared to some of the other fare we were given. Our favorite meals were always the curries seasoned by the local cooks using spices that Mrs. Henderson, with her Scottish upbringing, just couldn't understand.

While we waited for Bibbi to finish eating, Cruz and Jackie came over to say goodbye as well. Cruz leaned close to me and shyly, in his clipped accent, told me to come to the back door of the kitchen when we were leaving. Intrigued, I took Bibbi and Linwood with me to see what they wanted. The back door of the kitchen opened before we could knock, and Jackie quickly handed us a burlap rice sack and closed the door with a quiet wave. We understood that the contents of the bag were to be kept secret, so we quickly walked it down to the dorm, where we spread the contents out on my bunk.

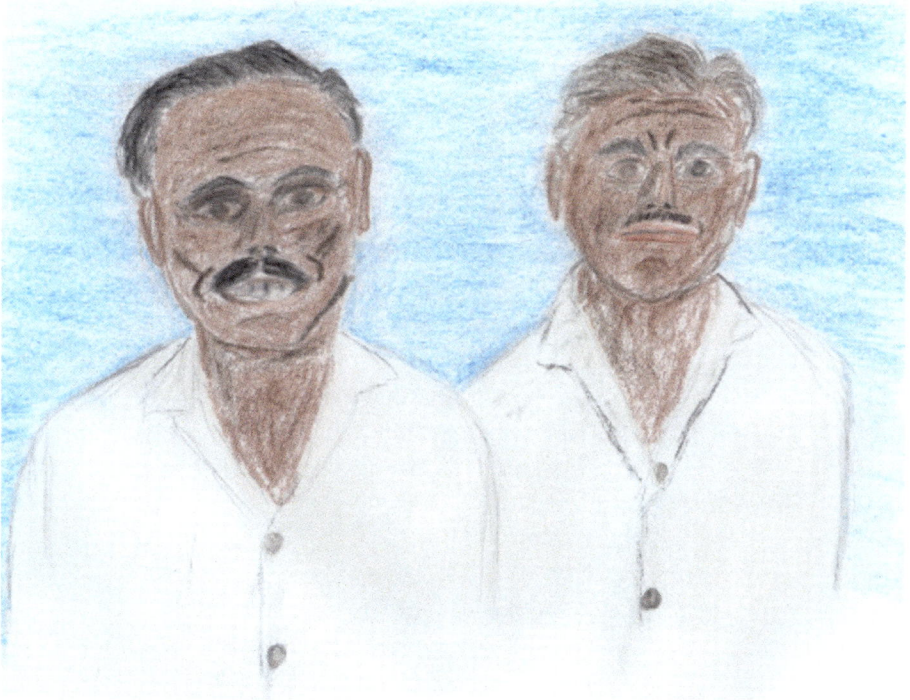

Cruz and Jackie

Jackie and Cruz had given us treasure. Lying on my bed were three oranges, three apples, six tangerines and six hard-boiled eggs. The eggs were still warm. We gathered around the side of the bed and stared at the bounty. Linwood, in full Panglossian mode, said that he hoped Cruz and Jackie hadn't stolen them. He said that he wouldn't feel right taking them if they were stolen, and thought that maybe we should return the items to Mrs. Henderson.

Bibbi gently assured him that while Mrs. Henderson might not be aware of the transfer of the items to us, we deserved to have them because we would be missing at least eight meals and two tea-times, which, since we definitely ate more than one rupee worth, would more than pay for their cost. Linwood was not fully won over by the argument, but allowed himself to be convinced enough to agree that we should keep them. We divvied them up, wrapped them in clean underwear, and put them into our bulging backpacks, making sure that they were in places that would not get squished.

A Stop at the Dish   We had arranged to meet Dave at the Dish at 6:30, and we were already late, so we donned our backpacks by setting them on the bunk and sitting in front of them to thread our arms through the straps before standing up. It took me two tries to get to my feet, as the weight of the pack pulled me over backwards on the first try. Once up, I had to lean well forward to center the weight over my feet. We laughed nervously about how heavy our packs were, and headed out to the Dish.

Dave was waiting for us at the Dish with a similarly bulging backpack. He had walked over from the Lutheran compound after their supper there. He said he was hoping to get some help from us with the weight of his pack, because even the short walk over from his compound had been a struggle. We let him heft our packs and see how stuffed they were to disabuse him of the idea. There was a scale in the Dish, so we decided to weigh our packs to see if we needed to distribute the loads any more evenly. Bibbi went first, and his pack weighed just over 45 pounds. Linwood's pack weighed 42 pounds. Mine weighed just shy of 39 pounds, and Dave's pack weighed in at 43. They all looked at me, obviously thinking about shifting some of their extra pounds over to me. Bibbi, however, ever the human calculator, quickly realized that the most they could do would be for each of them to give me one pound, which would make hardly any difference. So we settled that I would carry the first-aid kit and halazone tablets that we were there to pick up.

Annie Putz, the school nurse, was a small, prune-faced German lady with a thick accent and a crusty bedside manner. Her job was to make sure that all students were up to date on the impressive number of vaccinations and boosters that the World Health Organization required of foreigners in India, and to attend to the scrapes and bruises that were part of daily life at a boarding school. She had been in India since before the end of the Second World War, and would sometimes tell tales about the British and living through Partition, when India and Pakistan were separated. Her Kodai position was actually her retirement life, after a long, active nursing career with several missionary clinics. Her job with us was to sign off on our fitness for heading out, and to make sure that we had the first-aid essentials and water purification tablets that we would need on our hike. The first aid supplies consisted of Band-Aids of various sizes, disinfectants, gauze tape, adhesive tape, halazone tablets, ace bandages and other essentials. She took our temperatures and listened to our hearts and lungs, and finally, satisfied that none of us was about to expire, she signed our permission slips which she would then send up to Mr. Root.

I added the first aid kit to my backpack as we had agreed, and went back to the scale to weigh it. It now weighed 39.5 pounds, which I rounded up to 40 when I reported it out to my companions.

7. The Hike - Part I: Into the Valley

Bibbi Sets the Pace By then it was after seven, and dusk was deepening. We were eager to get underway so that we could arrive at Poombari guest bungalow, where we would bed down for the night in time to get a good night's sleep and be up by six the next morning. Poombari was about 11 miles from the school, and Bibbi, as usual, was hoping to make it in record time. By taking the Observatory Road out of town, the hike to Poombari normally took about four hours. Bibbi calculated that if we kept up a pace of four miles per hour, we could get there by 10:30 and get about seven hours of sleep.

We shouldered our packs and set out from the Dish at a little before seven thirty. Stars were already visible as the sky was darkening to a deep indigo. As an experienced hike leader, Bibbi knew that it was essential to set the pace right from the start. The first quarter of a mile or so was downhill towards the lake, and Bibbi took advantage of the slope to set a blistering pace with long strides and swinging arms. We all fell in with him and walked single file along the shoulder of the road. We passed the north arm of the lake onto Observatory Road, which soon started to climb up to Upper Lake Road. There, the pace and the 40 pound packs began to take their toll.

Bibbi kept his stride as we started up the hill, and Dave and Linwood seemed to follow easily enough along with him. I was already feeling the strain, but managed to keep on their heels. Bibbi periodically checked his watch every few minutes as we marched along, at one point telling us that we were going too slowly and needed to pick up the pace even more. Somehow, we did, and the next time he checked his watch he smiled and told us we were perfect.

"What do you mean: 'Perfect'?" I asked him, panting a bit.

He pointed to his watch and said, "One minute and fifty-two point five seconds," as if that answered my question.

"What does 'one minute and fifty-two point five seconds mean?" I panted.

"Well," he explained, "one minute and fifty-two point five seconds per furlong means that we complete one mile in fifteen minutes. That's four miles per hour!"

"How do you figure?" I asked.

"There are eight furlongs per mile. One minute and fifty two point five seconds is one hundred twelve point five seconds. Eight times one hundred twelve point five is nine hundred seconds, which, divided by sixty seconds per minute is fifteen, fifteen minutes. One mile per fifteen minutes equals four miles per hour"

"When did you figure all that out?" I wondered.

"It's one of those calculations that my brother John and I figured out on one of our hikes," he replied.

"Oh." That explained it. We were once again following John Coleman's footsteps.

If you have ever tried to walk at four miles per hour over any distance, you will quickly learn that it is an exceptionally fast pace. Race walkers average between 7.5 and 8 miles per hour, and power walkers average 4.5 miles per hour, with no added weight. We were carrying forty-pound packs.

Upper Lake Road leveled out after a half mile or so, and we seemed to settle into our pace a little better. I was still bringing up the rear, but the cool evening air was invigorating, and I seemed to be hanging in there. We hiked along without much talk until we reached the Solar Observatory, where Bibbi told us that we had covered about two and a half miles, so we only had about eight and a half to go. If we kept up the pace we were on, he calculated that we could indeed make it to the Rest Bungalow by ten thirty. I wasn't at all sure that I would be able to stand another two hours and twenty minutes, but I kept that thought to myself.

In fact, it soon became obvious to me that I was not going to be able to keep up the forced-march pace that Bibbi was setting. I knew that day trips to Poombari Rest Bungalow and camping ground allowed four hours for the hike each way. And that was carrying only a day pack, maybe ten pounds or so. Bibbi had us trying to make it in a little over three hours. I felt I had to invent ways to slow us down a bit, or I would soon become that much-maligned member of the group, the slowpoke. First I asked to stop for a moment claiming that I had a stone in my shoe, which gave me a moment's breather while I removed my boot and shook it out. After another while, my shoe came untied somehow. At another point, Linwood asked for a hand readjusting his straps and the padding he had stuffed between the pot and the small of his back.

At each of these stops, Bibbi would look up at the night sky and study the brilliant stars overhead. At seven thousand feet up, the equatorial sky is filled with stars, with the Milky Way slashing splendidly across the whole sky. He pointed out the planets that were visible, Venus, Mars and Jupiter, and began to enumerate the various constellations that he knew: the Pleiades, the Southern Cross, Cepheus, and several more. Recalling our night hike up Mount Perumal, I began to ask him questions about stars that caught my eye, realizing that as he looked up to where I pointed and responded to my questions, the pace became more endurable. From then on, I was able to keep up, and we all settled into a comfortable, swinging rhythm that permitted conversation and good-natured banter.

First Night on the Trail   In the end, it took us nearly three and a half hours to reach Poombari, arriving there at around eleven p. m. The night was lit only by starlight, with the moon not expected to rise until early morning, and it would be only a sliver of a crescent. The campsite was very dark, and the bungalow was locked. A notice on the door told us that the staff would return at around eight in the morning, and that there were to be no fires allowed without staff supervision. So we unrolled our sleeping bags on the front porch, where we would be somewhat sheltered from the dew and any rain that might fall. Our flashlights gave us some assurance that the floor was fairly clean. I was the only one who had brought an air mattress, so I spent a few minutes blowing it partially up, just enough to give me a little padding.

It didn't take us long to fall asleep after the vigorous walk. We bedded down in our clothes, without washing up or brushing our teeth. I was happy to have Doug's well-insulated sleeping bag, as the night temperature had quickly dropped to around 50 degrees. Sometime during the night a stray rain shower went by, causing the eaves of the porch to drip, but fortunately there was little wind, so we didn't get soaked.

First light awakened us just after 5 in the morning. There was a fairly thick mist around us, but it was close to the ground, which allowed the sun's approach to light up the forest around us. It was the promise of a bright and glorious morning. As usual, Bibbi spoke first, reminding us that we would be hiking about 19 miles before we could rest, and that he hoped we could reach a decent spot to camp by three or four in the afternoon.

We rose quickly and spread our sleeping bags out on the porch wall to air out while we took care of morning rituals. Dave had brought a small folding camp shovel, which we used to bury our poop, since the camp outhouse was also locked, and would have been very smelly had we been able to access it anyway. Then we sat at a camp table and ate our hard-boiled eggs and an orange. With no fire, we only had water from our canteens to wash down the eggs, which we did sparingly, since we didn't know when we would be able to fill them again.

Bibbi went over our route for the day. We would continue to follow the 40-Mile Round for about 10 miles to Mannavanur. There we would need to find the head of the trail that dropped down into Manjampatti, which he had been on a couple of times before, but which was hard to find. He was sure that someone in the village would be able to show us where it was. From Mannavanur the first five miles or so of the trail dropped steeply down around four thousand feet to where we met the river, which we would then follow for another five miles or so, dropping another eight hundred feet, until we could find a familiar area that he had camped at on one of his previous trips.

Setting Off at Sunrise   At around six o'clock we were ready to start out. The sun was chasing the mist away as it came up over the hills to the east. We set our packs on the porch wall, which was about three feet tall, and squatted down to slip our arms through the straps. With grunts and groans we stood up, shouldering the weight. My collar bones shrieked at the abuse as the straps dug in, and I could see by their expressions that both Dave and Linwood were also feeling the pain. Bibbi just looked happy to be getting on. We hooked our thumbs under the straps to relieve some of the pressure, and started off towards the road. Our legs were stiff from the morning chill and the strain of the previous evening.

As we came out of the trees surrounding the rest bungalow and hit the road, the sun chose the moment to peak through a gap in the hills and light up the paddy terraces stretching down the side of the hill below the road. The rice plants were emerald green with the sun glinting off the water in the paddies around them.

As we walked along, one terrace after another caught the rising sun's rays, setting each alight in its turn. There were very few people about in the village below the paddies, though several of the houses had smoke rising from their chimneys. I've seen many photographs and paintings attempting to capture the scene we were seeing, but this is one that had to be experienced.

The first mile or so of our hike that morning was fairly gently downhill, so Bibbi took advantage to set a good pace, not quite as grueling as the one he had tried to set the night before, but still faster than a normal walking pace. The tightness in our legs soon eased, and walking became easier. We had about ten miles to go to Mannavanur, and he wanted to get there by about nine thirty in the morning.

After that first mile, however, the road began to climb, though not steeply, and the pace again became an issue for me.

Terraced Rice Paddies

I took a page from Bibbi's book, and began to time our furlong markers. I found that working back and forth between minutes and seconds really complicated my mental calculations. I found that we were passing a marker every 2-and-a-quarter minutes, which I finally calculated to be a little less than 3-and-a-third miles per hour. With ten miles to go, we would cover the distance in 2 hours and 50 minutes. We could slow to about one furlong every two minutes and thirty seconds (3.0 mph) and make Mannavanur in 3 hours and 33 minutes, which would get us there at right around 9:30.

"Hey, Bibbi!" I hailed him when I was sure of my mental calculations. "We're going too fast!"

He gave me a puzzled look. "What do you mean?"

"Well, you want us to get to the Mannavanur cutoff at 9:30, right? And it's about ten miles, right?"

I explained my reasoning to Bibbi, and he went silent while he followed my mental calculations. After a couple of minutes he gave out with one of his signature belly laughs and slapped me on the back.

"Wow, Charlie!" He grinned. "You've passed your final exam in Algebra!"

We slowed the pace a bit, laughing. Bibbi explained the joke to Dave and Linwood, and they joined in the laughter. We all became much more talkative as we pressed on with a little more breath to spare.

The road continued to rise for about 4 more miles, rising about 900 feet from Poombari. We were traveling through Palani Hills Forest Conservation Area, with very sparse population. We passed only one small group of people walking toward Poombari who smiled broadly and wished us a good day. We must have been an interesting picture to them with our backpacks and hiking gear. The men were walking mostly unencumbered and barefoot, with their dhotis tucked up between their legs. A lady in a silk sari carrying a basket gracefully on her head followed along behind them.

A View to Mannavanur   The sun was well up when we reached the edge of the forest and the top of a rise. We had covered more than half the distance to Mannavanur, and it was nearly eight o'clock. Bibbi thought that we had earned a breather, so we dropped our packs and went to sit on the wall at the side of the road. We were overlooking a wide valley surrounded by forested hills. We could see a small lake to the south, that Bibbi reckoned was Mannavanur Lake, and a little to the east of the lake we could make out a tiny village surrounded by rice paddies, which we figured was Mannavanur itself. My heart lifted at the sight of our next destination, and by the fact that our road ahead appeared to be mostly downhill.

Hiking is always easier when one's destination is visible, and even though I knew that Mannavanur was only about half of the day's objective, I felt renewed as we started off again. I had taken a pair of thick socks out of my backpack, and stuffed one under each of the straps across my collar bones to add to the padding that came with the straps. It gave me some relief. I was gratified to see that Dave had watched what I was doing and followed my example. I knew that I wasn't the only one feeling the strain.

We set off again down the road at a good pace. We were getting used to the weight of our packs, and I was getting better at keeping the weight centered over my feet, which eased the strain on my back. The sun was behind us, and there were clouds making their way across the sky so that we moved in and out of bright sunlight. Furlong markers passed steadily by, and more people were coming out along the road. There were no vehicles traveling in either direction at that hour, except for a lone bullock cart that seemed to be carting a load of rice. We saw women heading out into the paddies when Bibbi figured that we were about a mile from the village.

Finding the Way Down   We turned right off the main road onto a service road that took us down to the village of Mannavanur. Most of the villagers had headed off to their day's labor, or were in their houses attending to chores. Very few were out and about. We flagged down an old man who greeted us with a gap-tooth grin. Bibbi asked him if he could please tell us where the trail down to Manjampatti Valley started. The old man gave us another toothless grin and replied with an unintelligible stream of sound, all the while shaking his head from side to side in the Indian affirmative. I thought I heard the word "Manjampatti", but it was garbled. He pointed us down the road, so we salaamed and thanked him and went on.

We met another man with a pole over his shoulder about a hundred yards further on, and Bibbi again greeted him, and asked him if he could tell us where the foot trail down the Manjampatti Valley began. This man replied, "No Yengleesh", so Bibbi repeated "Manjampatti", and pantomimed walking with two fingers across his palm. Then Dave spoke up, addressing the man in fluent Hindi! I was amazed, and from the looks of them, so were Bibbi and Linwood. (Although Tamil is the local language of the area, most people study some Hindi in school. At that time, the government was pushing to make Hindi the official language of India along with English.) Dave's Hindi was actually better than the man's, but soon he understood what we were asking and pointed out the way and gave us directions we should follow.

We thanked the man and headed off down the way he had indicated. Around a bend we saw an old woman in a ragged sari squatting demurely under her sari beside the road ahead of us. We seemed to be passing an area that was used as the village toilet by those without running water. The woman stood up and walked away without acknowledging us before we got near, and left behind coal black turds steaming in the morning light. Dave, whose parents were doctors, commented that the old woman was bleeding internally, probably from a stomach ulcer, and was probably quite ill.

As we proceeded down the road, Bibbi began to recognize landmarks from his earlier trips with his brother John, Tim Lomperis and his dad, and we became surer that we were on the right track. We had to follow the service road out the back of the village until we came to a shola beyond some paddy fields on our left. There were people already out in the fields tending to the rice plants in the paddies. They eyed us curiously, but returned our waves and salaams when we passed near them. As we passed more paddy fields, we hugged the left-hand side of the road, keeping our eyes peeled for the start of the trail down the mountain. The shola began a few feet below the road, and if we hadn't been looking for it, we never would have found the trail. Linwood spotted a break in the trees and called Bibbi's attention to it. The trail dove down into the shola, taking us between the paddy terraces.

We Start our Descent   Bibbi looked around for the landmarks that would confirm that we had indeed found the right spot, and satisfied, led us over the side of the road into the shola. There in the shade we stopped for a few minutes to eat some apples and secure our packs and tie our boots in preparation for the descent. We had been on the road for nearly four hours, and still had at least four more hours of hard going ahead of us. The first three miles or so would be steep descent of nearly 2000 feet. Bibbi would take the lead, and I would bring up the rear. We reminded each other to leave some space between us and to be aware of what was happening in front of us to avoid bumping into the person ahead. I asked Bibbi to take it a little slower than his usual pace so that we could keep up, especially since none of us was familiar with the trail. He gave me a sheepish grin and a chuckle that told me what his plans had been, and agreed to hold to a reasonable pace.

We shouldered our packs and set off Indian file, with Bibbi at the front and me at the back. Dave followed Bibbi, and Linwood was in front of me. It became apparent very quickly that my request to Bibbi to ease up on the pace had been unnecessary. The trail was so narrow, slippery and steep that only a tahr could have sped down it. The ground under the trees remained damp, and required careful placement of feet to avoid a fall. All of us, Bibbi included, spent time on our bottoms. We grabbed onto saplings and branches near the trail to steady ourselves, and had to be careful not to allow them to snap back and hit the man behind. As the last man, I didn't have to worry about the man behind me, but I kept letting Linwood know when he wasn't doing a good job of it.

In most areas, we were descending one foot for every three to five feet of trail. There were rocks and roots that gave our boots purchase, but they meant that we had to keep our eyes glued to the ground with every step. We didn't have much time to gaze around us and take in the beauty of the shola. Birds would fly up at our approach, but I couldn't tell what kind they were since I couldn't spare a glance. Cautionary warnings would float back from Bibbi when there was an obstacle to be negotiated, but other than that, we all just concentrated on the next step.

About an hour on we broke out of the trees onto grassy slopes. We could see down the valley to the north with occasional glimpses of the lowlands beyond. The ground was just as steep, but now there were no branches to steady ourselves with. The sun was warming quickly, and we were soon sweating. Bibbi calculated that we still had another mile of descent until we reached the stream that we would follow down to our camp spot.

We stood gazing out over the valley ahead of us. The stream's flow was hidden in thick foliage, but we could follow its course leading off to the left. We saw birds flying in and out of the trees and heard their calls. Bibbi pointed out a Malabar squirrel high up in a tree a short way off. It had a tan face and belly, a black back with a bright red saddle across its shoulders. Its tale was long and fluffy, tipped with tan.

After a sip of water and a short breather, we headed on. The trail was more defined here, and the footing wasn't as slippery. Bibbi picked up the pace somewhat, but he was still going cautiously, and we weren't having trouble keeping up with him, so I didn't bring it up. My knees and shins were complaining from the strain, and my shoulders and collar bones felt raw. I was determined not to be the one to slow us down. About twenty minutes later, Bibbi held his hand to his ear and said he heard running water.

Lunch by the Stream   We reached the stream at around noon, and soon found a flat-topped boulder in shady spot to stop for lunch. We dropped our packs and took off our boots to immerse our feet in the water. My feet had held up pretty well, but both Dave and Linwood were tending to blisters. I had a spot on the back of my left heel that felt sore and chafed, so after soaking my feet in the stream for a few minutes, I put a bandage on it. We took out the peanut butter and jam to make sandwiches. The bread was somewhat squashed, but we managed to make something edible with it. Sandwiches were followed by an orange for dessert.

We had each used up about half a canteen of water, so Bibbi suggested that we pour the good water into two canteens and fill the other two with water from the stream into which we would put halazone tablets.

That way, by the time we finished the good water, the stream water would have been purified.

We had hiked about twelve miles so far that day, (and ten the evening before) of which the last three had been in steep descent. As usual, Bibbi was calculating every detail of our march forward. According to him, we had about four more miles as the crow flies to the camping spot we were aiming for, but as we would be following the stream, the actual distance would be closer to seven or eight miles on the ground. We still had some 2,500 feet to descend, but the drop would be much gentler going forward. As it was now just past noon, if we went about two miles per hour, we would arrive at our destination by about 4 in the afternoon.

So, all too soon, we pulled on our boots, gathered our gear and prepared to forge ahead. I hefted my pack up on to a convenient boulder and squatted down with my back to it to thread my arms through the straps. My legs turned to jelly as I tried to stand up, refusing to straighten up under the weight of the pack. I tried again to no avail. Meanwhile, Bibbi had his backpack on and was waiting impatiently for the rest of us to join him. I saw Linwood force himself to his feet with a grimace, but Dave was still struggling with his pack. I laughed nervously and asked Bibbi to give me a hand getting up. I hoped that once I stood up I could stay on my feet.

For the next mile or so there was a well-defined path that followed the stream. The problem was that it followed the waterway closely, twisting and turning, so that we made less forward progress than Bibbi liked. At one point we actually seemed to be traveling away from our destination according to Bibbi's compass. It was a blessing that the stream was not descending very quickly, so that over that mile, we probably only dropped three hundred feet or so. Bibbi looked for a way to cut off some of the twists of the stream, but any cut-offs would have meant climbing up fairly steep terrain from the stream bed.

After a while, the stream made up its mind and headed us in the right direction for a while, aiming for a fairly narrow gorge between two hills. We entered the gorge at around two in the afternoon. Based on his topo map, Bibbi estimated that we were at about 4,000 feet altitude, only slightly lower than when we had reached the stream, and that we would be descending more than 1500 feet in the gorge, which was about a mile long. The path we had been following seemed to peter out at the head of the gorge. The stream made its way through a jumble of rocks and boulders. We stuck to the right bank of the stream, which wasn't quite as steep as the left bank, and made our way carefully over the boulders.

Several times the bank forced us quite close to the water, which was flowing very fast, and the footing became perilous with spray and moss. The stream wasn't wide: I could throw a stone to the other side easily; but it was unruly, skipping around and over boulders and splashing wildly down its bed. It made quite a racket.

We exited the gorge and the stream calmed down to a pleasant burble. Bibbi called for a short rest and a bit of planning.

"This is about where we saw the elephant the last time I came here," he stated calmly. "We need to be on the lookout from here on."

"Which elephant was that?" I wanted to know.

"The one I told you about when I told you how John and Tim wanted to hike from Kookal down to Manjampatti," he replied.

"The one that charged at you?" I asked.

"Yeah, that one, but he never charged."

Linwood had heard the tale, but Dave had not, so Bibbi gave him a short version. Here is the full account:

Manjampatti Prelude   The idea for the hike we were on today was born on a hike Bibbi had gone on with his brother John, their friend Tim Lomperis, and Tim's dad. This had also been on a hike down to Manjampatti Valley, which was a game preserve and one of the more exotic hikes the School sanctioned. As avid, experienced hikers, John and Tim were very familiar with the geography of the area, and were always on the outlook for alternative hiking opportunities.

There was a dramatic incident during the hike that made it quite memorable. After descending into the valley, Bibbi, as he often did, was leading the group along the stream, followed by Tim's dad, then Tim and finally John. The stream bed and banks are strewn with huge rocks and boulders that have washed down from the heights over the years, and runs through bedrock outcroppings. In all, it is a very rocky passage.

They had taken their time during the day, hiking all the way out from Kodai, and were arriving at the point we had just reached fairly late in the day. Daylight along the stream bed was fading.

The group was approaching what appeared to be one fairly large boulder beside the water, when the boulder suddenly shifted and began to move. It quickly resolved itself into a large elephant, which turned and faced them aggressively. John and Tim ducked quickly off the trail and behind a tree. Tim's dad moved more slowly to join them, but Bibbi froze, since he was the closest to the beast. The elephant shook its head and scuffed its feet. Then it trumpeted and waved its ears, all signs that it was getting ready to attack.

Bibbi Alone with the Elephant

"Bob!" hissed Mr. Lomperis from his safe position behind the tree. "Back away! Slowly!" Mr. Lomperis rummaged through his pack and pulled out his camera to get a shot of the elephant.

Bibbi stood stock still for a few more seconds, and then backed away a few steps. The elephant stamped its feet and its tail and trunk shot straight up into the air.

"Run! Bob, run over here!" yelled John.

Bibbi let out an incoherent yell and then turned and hot-footed it to the shelter of the tree. The elephant hadn't moved after its threatening display, and watched Bibbi run off. Then it bobbed its head a few times, as if to say "You better watch out!", and calmly watched the hikers for a few more seconds.

Thus having asserted its supremacy over the invaders, the elephant turned and moved sedately and silently away. Mr. Lomperis emerged from behind the tree and ran after the elephant with his camera to take its picture. Unfortunately, he couldn't get the shot in the waning light.

For a few minutes nobody else moved from behind the tree. The elephant had disappeared, and they never saw it again. Mr. Lomperis gave the "all clear", and the group was able to continue on down the river.

Since this had all occurred so late in the afternoon, the group had already been talking about looking for a place to set up camp. With the elephant still on their minds, they decided that they would need a spot that offered them protection from an unwanted incursion.

Mr. Lomperis recalled that there was an old British Forestry bungalow nearby that had an elephant-proof ditch around it where they could safely spend the night. It wouldn't be as much fun as camping by the stream, but at least they could rest easy.

The bungalow was a small concrete hut with barely enough space for them to all stretch out, but they could have a small fire to warm their supper. Once they settled in, John and Tim stood outside the hut on the safe side of the ditch and challenged the elephant with shouts and laughter to come and try and get them now.

In addition to the Manjampatti hike, John and Tim had also hiked to Kookal Caves, which were situated on the highlands overlooking Manjampatti Valley from the east. The caves were really just a rock overhang that gave hikers a place to shelter from rain and wind and build a fire for the night. It was about a twenty-two mile hike from the School, but not as arduous as the hike to Manjampatti since the elevation was only about 800 feet lower than that of Kodai School, and followed roads most of the way. Only the last few miles followed trails. The caves overlooked a lush green grassy valley on one side, and the steep decline to Manjampatti on the other. John and his buddies thought that it would be quite an adventure to trek down from Kookal to Manjampatti, blazing a new trail for School hikers.

The following morning, the group left the bungalow and followed the stream deeper into Manjampatti Valley, looking for a good-sized pool where they could go for a swim and rest for a while before heading out to a road where they hoped to hitch a ride on a passing lorry back up the hill to Kodai. When they came to a clearing, John directed Bibbi's attention up the steep hills.

"That's where Kookal Caves are" he said. "That's the ridge you would come down from the caves, I think, and you would hit the stream right about here."

One of his regrets was that he never got to do it, but he had passed the idea on to Bibbi, and Bibbi was determined to show that it could be done.

***

"So now, here's what we need to decide," said Bibbi. "Do we want to camp by the stream of should we look for the forestry bungalow?"

"I vote we camp by the stream," Dave declared. "Elephants, that is, wild ones, will usually leave people alone. Plus, if there are any around, they may keep tigers and dholes away."

"What are dholes?" I asked.

"They're wild dogs, sort of like jackals, and they can probably cross an elephant ditch anyway." Dave replied.

We all agreed to camp by the stream, so shortly we set off again.

Linwood Gets Wet   Bibbi was still in the lead, and I was bringing up the rear. Had I not been behind Linwood, and seen him slip, we probably wouldn't have heard his first shout over the din of the water. Luckily, he slid feet-first into a small pool before losing his balance completely and sprawling into it. He made a wild grab for his glasses, which had been thrown off his face as he jerked to keep his balance, and rolled onto his back to hold them out of harm's way. His backpack was now underwater.

The stream was shallow, and he was in no danger of being swept away, but he was having trouble trying to get to his feet with the weight of his backpack holding him down. I dropped my backpack on the bank and shouted to the others before clambering over the rocks to help him. I managed to get close enough to give him my hand to steady him and pull him to his feet. He was standing thigh deep in the pool, and seemed to be okay. Bibbi and Dave reached us then, and Bibbi pulled Linwood's dripping backpack off his shoulders.

We stood there looking at each other for a moment, and then Linwood started to laugh. We all joined in, in relief, and pulled him out of the pool. We gathered on the bank next to my discarded pack

Linwood Saves his Glasses

. Dave, in his laconic southern drawl, allowed as how if Linwood wanted to test the water, he should have told us and we would have joined him for a swim. Linwood was soaked and embarrassed, and his sense of humor abandoned him for a moment. I could see that he was about to make a sharp retort, when Bibbi laughed his infectious belly laugh, and Linwood took the joke.   Bibbi upended Linwood's backpack and a stream of water poured out. He hugged the pack, and more water squeezed out. All of Linwood's gear was wet, and the backpack now weighed quite a bit more than it had. We had a dilemma as to whether to stop now and wring out the clothes and things Linwood was carrying, or forge ahead and take care of it at the camp.

After a short discussion, Bibbi pointed out that we would have more time to spread things out on rocks if we went on now, and that unpacking, wringing, and repacking could take us an hour or more. He voted for moving on. We all agreed, but the problem was that now Linwood's backpack was several pounds heavier. We compared it to mine, which was sitting next to it, and indeed, it was a lot heavier. Linwood was probably the slightest of the four of us, and, it seemed, would be carrying the heaviest pack over treacherous terrain. I knew that I was already struggling with mine, and wasn't eager to trade with

Linwood. So, as usual, Bibbi solved the issue. He gave me his pack, Linwood took my pack, and he carried Linwood's wet pack.

Thus laden, we headed off down the river again.

Either we made better time than we had thought we would, or the twists and turns of the stream were not as bad as Bibbi had feared. In a short time, we came around a long leftward curve in the stream, and it straightened up and leveled out to a gentle flow. Bibbi consulted the map and declared that we were now only about a mile from our objective. We were looking for the main Manjampatti stream that would flow into ours from the west. When we got there, we should be able to find the spot where he and John had found to camp on a previous trip.

This news refreshed me, as I was struggling with Bibbi's pack, which, although only about four pounds heavier than mine, had narrower straps that dug into my shoulders. Bibbi seemed to be impervious to the water-logged pack he was carrying, which must have been five or ten pounds more than his. He did complain about the cooking pot digging into the small of his back, though, and wondered how Linwood had been able to put up with it this far without complaining.

The air was much warmer and the afternoon sun much hotter than was comfortable. There were rain clouds above the peaks around us, but we were walking in bright, hot sunlight. I had taken a T-shirt out of my pack and wet it in the stream. This I draped over my head and shoulders like a Bedouin kufiyah, and felt great relief. Soon both Bibbi and Dave had followed suit. Linwood was still damp from his dunking, so didn't need the cooling off.

Reaching Manjampatti   We reached the influx of the Manjampatti stream known as the 'Ten Ar' just after three thirty in the afternoon. We had been traveling northwesterly from Mannavanur, and the Manjampatti stream flowed in from the southwest, meeting our branch at almost a perfect right angle, which made for quite a bit of turbulence at the juncture. From atop some high boulders, we could look up along the famous Manjampatti Valley, home to tigers, panthers, sloth bears, wild boar, Malabar squirrels, elephants and thousands of birds and insects. According to the topo map, the mountain peaks we could see were in the state of Kerala, and we were within a very few miles of the border.

We were now at about 2200 feet above sea level, about 4500 feet lower than Kodai. We were well within the heat of the lowlands. There were a lot of bedrock outcroppings near the confluence of the streams, and boulders and outcroppings provided us many options for organizing a camp. A short way down stream we soon found the outcropping that Bibbi had been looking for which showed signs of recent occupation by campers, with ashes on the ground and a smoke-blackened overhang. We were below the fork in the two streams, so the water was running fast, which we felt would give us a better chance at finding relatively clean water for cooking. There was a Jacuzzi-sized pool of water ideal for soaking nearby. We all agreed that this was the place to set up camp for the night and got to work.

Linwood set about emptying his pack and laying his wet clothes out on warm rocks. Dave went down to the water to gather rocks to build a fire pit. Bibbi and I walked into the brush and trees that grew along the river to collect firewood. Most of the brush around the area was lush and green, and would create way too much smoke, especially since we had promised to keep the fire going all night long to ward off critters. Some smoke would be okay, since it would discourage mosquitoes, but too much would chase us out of our shelter.

An Elephant Lends a Trunk   We walked about twenty yards up the bank away from the river to see if we could find drier fuel. Since it was the rainy season, almost everything was too green for our purpose. We found occasional branches or twigs that we began to gather into a pile, and kept working our way up the slope, away from the stream. I worked my way around a stand of trees, and suddenly came upon an uprooted tree. I called Bibbi over. It appeared to have been down long enough for the wood to dry out, so we began breaking branches off it. The trunk was too thick to break and too heavy to carry, so we broke off what we could. We would come back with Dave's hatchet to harvest some of the larger branches later.

As I worked, I noticed some scars on the trunk of the tree.

"Hey, Bibbi," I called. "Come take a look at these scrapes on the trunk."

Bibbi stood up and came over to where I was standing.

"You think those could be tiger claw marks?" I asked.

Bibbi poked his thumb into one of the gashes. "Nah, it's too wide. I think it was more likely an elephant sharpening his tusks. Maybe that's what knocked the tree down."

"Wow, I bet you're right!" I agreed. "What else could explain a random uprooted tree?"

We gathered up what we had collected and headed back to camp, marking the path so that we could find the uprooted tree again. There we found Linwood in a state. Having walked the last few miles with wet feet, he had developed some large blisters on the balls of his feet that were now filled with liquid. It also seemed that once he had gotten everything out of his pack, he found that the pot in the bottom of his pack had retained a good deal of water, and all the toilet paper he had brought had been reduced to soggy pulp.

But what really had him upset more than his feet or the toilet paper, was that his Bible had also been in the pot, and was soaked through.

We were much more bothered by the loss of the toilet paper, but Bibbi, having known Linwood all his life, knew that the Bible was going to be a big issue with him, and immediately began to see if there was some way to help. He got his towel out of his pack and began to turn page by page, patting each one carefully. Linwood asked him if he thought it could be saved, and Bibbi tried to be encouraging.

Meanwhile, I remembered that Dave had been carrying the bulk of our supply of toilet paper since we had only been able to come up with remnants. Thank goodness we hadn't redistributed it!

My mind set to rest on that front, I went in search of Dave to borrow his hatchet and make sure that his share of the toilet paper was safe. I found him in the cave with a fire pit well under way, and gave him the bundle of firewood and kindling we had brought. Taking his hatchet, I left him to it, passing Linwood and Bibbi working on the Bible, and went back up the slope to the fallen tree.

I noticed that, now that I knew the way to the tree, it seemed much closer to camp than the first time we had come up. In fact, I could hear Bibbi's and Linwood's voices over the murmur of the water. That encouraged me, and I began to chop some of the larger branches off of the trunk, so that I could drag them back down to the river. I soon had a good pile, more than I could carry in one trip, and so I sat for a moment to rest on the newly cleared section of the trunk.

Sitting there with my butt hanging off the back of the log, I realized that this would be a good place to put the latrine, and that the trunk would make a better seat than squatting over an open pit. It was far enough away from the stream so that we wouldn't be polluting our water supply or smelling up the area around camp. It might be a little far for a night session, but so far I had observed that we were all "morning people", so that would probably not be an issue.

I grabbed what I could carry of the branches I had cut and went back down to the camp. Linwood's Bible was propped upright and open, with its pages exposed to the sun and the breeze. Bibbi and Dave were working on starting the fire, and Linwood was turning over his damp clothes to hasten their drying before the sun went down. I dropped my load by the shelter and asked Dave if I could borrow his shovel to dig a trench for the latrine. Bibbi asked where I was thinking of putting it, and I said that I had found a spot that seemed good up by the toppled tree, holding back my idea of a seat on the log as a surprise. He said that sounded fine, and turned back to his fire building.

Back at the log, I dug a trench below where I thought our poop would fall, which I calculated by sitting on the log with my butt hanging off and dropping a stone from underneath me. I made it about 18 inches long and a foot across, and 8 inches deep. I piled the dirt to one side so that we could scrape a little over each of our deposits to hold down the stench. There was a branch stub handy where one could hang the toilet paper roll while one took care of business. I was quite proud of my arrangements, and couldn't wait to show them off to my companions. I bundled up another load of branches and walked back down the hill to camp.

Things had moved along at camp, and there was a nice fire going, and Linwood had propped his Bible near enough to the warmth to dry, but far enough away not to be in danger of charring. The pages were curling a little, but appeared to be readable. Dave and Bibbi were arranging our stores to get ready for cooking our evening meal, and the pot was sitting on a flat stone near the flame preparing to boil. I told them that I had prepared the latrine, and that they should come and take a look so they would know where to go in time of need.

I guess something in my demeanor let them know that something was up. That, as well as the fact that we would soon be losing the daylight, got them to follow me up the hill. I pointed out the trail markers I had left so they could find their way, and we soon came to the toppled tree toilet. They all thought that I had come up with a great idea, and for a few moments, I was quite proud of myself. Soon, however, Bibbi, in his attention to detail spotted a flaw.

"Hey, Charlie, how come you made the hole so close to the trunk?" he asked me.

"Well, this is what I did to spot it," I said. Smugly, I sat on the trunk with my butt hanging over, and dropped a stone, which fell nicely into the pit. Linwood and Dave were impressed.

"Oh, okay, let me try it," he said.

He positioned himself on the trunk as I had, but scooted farther back than I had. He dropped a stone and it hit the back edge of the pit and bounced away.

"That's what I thought," he said.

"Yeah, well, you stuck your butt way out!" I observed.

"I know," he replied. "When I pooh, I usually have to pee as well. If I sat how you were sitting, it would splatter on the trunk."

After a second of thought, I saw what he meant. One would have to scoot back another several inches to successfully pee behind the trunk.

Latrine with a View

I repeated the experiment with the stone again, positioning myself so as to be able to pee successfully. Not only did I find that the stone missed the pit, but I almost toppled over backwards, having to grab on to the trunk to keep my balance. That would make using toilet paper a risky operation.

"I think we're gonna need something to hang on to," I remarked. "I almost fell into the hole myself!"

Ever the engineer, Bibbi went to work on solving the balance problem while I went back to work with the shovel to widen the trench I had dug. Bibbi found some reasonably strong vines hanging from a large tree, and soon had them anchored to nearby tree with a loop that came over to the log. He tested the contraption by sitting on the toilet trunk again and held the vine in one hand, leaning his weight against it. Soon, he was satisfied that we could now safely use the bathroom I had devised, and we all went back to the camp to prepare our evening meal.

It was now about 5 in the afternoon, and the sun had gone behind the clouds over the peaks to the west of us, but we figured we still had about two hours of daylight. The sky above us was clear, and we were hopeful that the night would be dry. Monsoon rains usually come in the afternoon, from two or so until around five, so our hopes were based on that. We could see some lightning activity in the mountains, and we were on the lee side. The temperature was still in the eighties, and the air fairly dripped with humidity.

Time for a Swim   Dave had volunteered to cook the lentils and the rice, so he put the lentils to soak in the pan, and set the pot with water to heat up by the fire. It was time for a swim.

We stripped and left our clothes in the camp and scrambled over the rocks to the pool we had selected, barefoot and naked and as free as we could be. There was a soft breeze that came from the west where the rainclouds were that caressed us as we went. We slid into the cool water of the pool and sat on submerged rocks letting the current wash past us as we talked about the events of the day. We agreed that this dip in the river made all the effort of walking for miles with heavy packs worth it. We had hiked almost 20 miles that day, and had descended nearly 5,000 feet from the hilltop above Mannavanur. We had done it with 40 pound packs.

As we sat there luxuriating, Bibbi sighed in contentment and said "Boy, this sure beats skinny dipping in Kodai Lake!"

"When did you ever go skinny dipping in the lake?" Dave asked. "You'd get caught and suspended for indecent exposure, or something. We only ever went swimming nude in Tope or other spots when there were no girls or anyone else around."

"Yeah, well, we did it when there was nobody else around. You're prob'ly the only one in school who doesn't know about it," I said. "We did it last year, and, while this is ten times better, it was a fun adventure. It was one of those things we did following in Bibbi's brother's footsteps, like this hike. It all began from John Coleman's tale…" I began.

Skinny Dipping   One tale Bibbi had heard from John was how liberating it was to sneak out of the dorm on a moonlit night and go skinny-dipping in the lake. We never considered what would happen if we were seen by local townspeople or caught by School staff. Probably we could have been expelled, or at least given detention to last the whole semester. The thought that we might run into real trouble with cramps or drowning never entered our heads.

In my second year at Kodai I became a lifeguard for Saturday morning swim dates. There were about three months of the second semester, as well as the May break, when the water and weather were warm enough for us to want to go swimming in the lake. For those of us who tried out to be lifeguards, that meant going out to the lake about a month before the swim season to try out and improve our life-saving skills.

Although I was tall, I was a skinny, not-very-athletic kid. As such, I was usually cut from school teams whenever I tried out, picked last in pick-up games, and not involved in any of the Field Day sports. Bibbi, on the other hand, excelled in most sports and was a member of the school basketball team and volleyball team every year, as well as competing in several Field Day events.

I was, however, a fairly competent swimmer, having learned by falling into the lake and nearly drowning behind our house in Rangoon. I hoped that becoming a lifeguard would give me a bit more status among the guys, and especially with the girls.

The temperature of the lake water was somewhere in the mid-50 degrees Fahrenheit when we began our lifeguard course. Nearly half of the boys and all but one of the girls who had signed up dropped out after that first day due to the water temperature. It would warm up into the mid-60s by the time swim season started, but during our training period it would be consistently chilly.

We who remained were given the Red Cross CPR training; we had to swim a mile, across the lake and back, pulling a weighted inner tube; we had to "rescue" each other to sharpen our technique. All this was under the stern gaze of Mr. Root with his Navy training.

Seven of us made it through the four-week training, six boys and one girl, Rani. We called ourselves 'The Magnificent Seven' at Mike's insistence. We boys each got a chance to "rescue" Rani so that we would know the proper way to grab onto a girl and pull her to safety. I think the fantasy of having the opportunity to rescue one of the girls I was secretly attracted to gave me the strength and determination to persevere and make it through the program. The seven were Rani VandeBerg, Mike Aungthwin, Narain Mahtani, Keith Johnson, Jerry Haley, and John Brewer and me.

The Magnificent Seven
from left: Kieth, Narain, Rani, John, Jerry, Me and Mike

Each Saturday morning we would cover the swimming time in teams of two or three. Bibbi was a regular swimmer and showed up every Saturday whenever he was not involved in practice or tournaments for his other sports. If he came when I was on duty, he would frolic in the water with the other swimmers. If I was off duty when he came, I joined in the fun. We would joke with the others about skinny-dipping and invite the girls to join us, which they appeared to think was hilarious.

It was during this period that Bibbi told me about John's story of skinny-dipping at night.

"I think it would be so cool!" he exclaimed. "It would be an adventure we would never forget."

"Yeah, but what if we get caught?" I asked. "I'm the one who will get in trouble since I'm a lifeguard. They'll kick me out of the program."

"We won't get caught, but if we did it's actually better that you're a lifeguard! We can say you wouldn't let us go without you so that we could be safe. Come on! It'll be a blast!"

"Well, maybe you can get some girls to join us", I laughed. "Try to get Bonnie and Margie to come. They love to swim."

"Yeah, right!" he retorted. "Good luck with that!" He went on, "The Roots have just gone back to the States for the rest of the semester and there's nobody staying in their house. We can even use the dock."

So, we just went for it one weeknight at full moon with two other intrepid souls when circumstances fell into place for us. Mr. Root, the Vice Principal, whose staff cottage had a clear view of the School's swimming dock, had gone back to the States on a teacher recruiting mission for the semester, so we figured that we could get away with swimming in known waters, which would be safer than going in near the boat house.

After lights-out we met with Dale and Tim, who had signed on to join us, in the bathroom of Wissy, which is on the farthest corner away from the houseparents' apartment. We waited until all the talking and murmuring from the dorm rooms had quieted down. Like movie ninjas, we all had on our darkest outfits and quietest sneakers.

Bibbi had warned us, "Don't wear your *chappals* (flip-flop sandals). They can slap at the most inopportune moments, and if we have to run for it, we should be wearing sneakers."

Bibbi led the way out of the bathroom and down the covered hallway to the end of the dorm. Our white towels were tucked under our shirts, and our sneakers made no noise on the concrete walkway. The wall around the compound was easy to hop over from the inside, but dropped six or seven feet on the outside, which would make getting back in a little harder. After we climbed over it, we skirted the lake to the swimming dock below the Root's staff cottage and Bendy Field.

Quietly, we stripped and eased off the end of the dock into the chilly water, being careful not to create too much splash. There were quiet gasps as we lowered our crotches into the lake, and more than one whispered curse. "Oh, shit, that's cold!" exclaimed one of the guys and we all agreed.

It was, indeed, liberating and fun… and cold. We dog-paddled a little way out into the lake in order to avoid splashes. The water by our feet was much colder than the water near the surface, which still held some of the sun's warmth, though not much. The cold water had its effect, and most of us, if not all, held still as we peed into the lake. There were a few seconds of warmth until we kicked our legs again.

After about ten minutes, our teeth began to chatter, and we had all had enough. There was a light breeze blowing over the lake that raised goosebumps on our bare skin as we climbed back onto the dock. We were all shockingly white in the moonlight, and if anyone had been in the

Root cottage, they would surely have seen us, not to mention if anyone had happened to be passing by on the lake road. So we hurriedly grabbed our towels to dry off, and laughing at each other's tiny, shriveled private parts, dressed quickly.

Skinny Dipping in Kodai Lake in the Moonlight

"It's a good thing none of the girls joined us." I remarked to Bibbi. "They would have been so disappointed in your dingus!"

"Hah!" he barked. "Speak for yourself."

Feeling liberated and victorious, we headed back around the lake to Wissy. At the wall below the dorm, Bibbi made a stirrup out of his hands and lifted us up to grab the top of the stone wall. There was no easy place to grip, so he pushed us up further until we could bend our waists over the top of the wall. Once up, we tied two towels together and anchored them with our weight so Bibbi could pull himself up and over the wall. We felt just like prisoners making a jail break, except that we were climbing in, not out.

We successfully snuck back into our rooms and were in our beds before eleven. I slept soundly and dreamlessly until the wake-up monitor came around at six the next morning.

***

"…and so, that's the story of skinny-dipping in Kodai Lake," I concluded

After a short while, Dave got out of the pool and left us to go and tend to his cooking chores. Bibbi, Linwood and I sat in weightless splendor, enjoying the feeling of the water running over our naked bodies and soaking in the peace of the valley. The birds were settling down for the night, and there was a buzz of insects, crickets and katydids, mostly, taking over the dusk. Bibbi started singing camp songs, and we joined in. We heard a strange, mournful call answering our singing from higher up the valley, and repeated from farther away. We didn't know what animal made the cry, though later in life I heard a peacock call, and I believe that was what we heard. That evening, though, in our imagination, it was a strange and hungry wild animal, maybe even a tiger.

We stepped out of the water after a while, and were immediately set upon by mosquitoes. Our clothes were at camp, and we had no protection, so we set off slapping ourselves like penitents, and hurrying toward the smoke of our fire as quickly as we could. We were all up to date on our malaria vaccines, but none of us wanted to spend the night in itchy agony.

Hot Chai and Supper   After we dressed we found that Dave had been busy, and he surprised us with cups of hot chai. He had learned how to make pukka chai in his childhood, and we were delighted and grateful. The pot was now being repurposed for cooking rice, so there were no seconds to be had. There was dahl with sambar simmering in the frying pan, and chapattis were being laid out on hot rocks to warm. I guess we all suddenly realized how hungry we were, and after fetching our plates from our gear, sat around, noses quivering and mouths watering, waiting anxiously for supper to be ready, and watching while Dave busied himself with final preparations.

A comfortable silence settled over us. We watched the fire crackling and the smoke drifting up to the roof of the overhang. Every once in a while, a stray zephyr would chase a wisp of the smoke towards us keeping mosquitoes at bay and making us cough. The smell of curry and smoke filled the space, and the warmth of the plains worked its magic on the evening. The sky above our camp turned deep indigo and filled with stars, while a few miles away the mountain peaks were still topped by monsoon clouds.

The spell was broken by Dave, announcing that the rice was ready and we could eat. We each took a good scoop of steaming rice and several spoons-full of dahl and a warm chapatti, and found stones to perch on while we ate. With a flourish, Dave reached into his pack and brought out a Mason jar full of a white substance with green and brown flecks in it. Bibbi let out a whoop. It was coconut chutney! What a fine addition to a great meal! Dave scooped out a generous portion onto each of our plates. Linwood said grace and we dug in.

We ate with our fingers, Indian style, carefully folding each bite of chutney, rice and dahl into a piece of chapatti, using only our right (unsullied) hand to eat with. Bibbi was the most skilled, or at least the fastest, of us at this form of eating, but Dave and Linwood had eaten this way since childhood, and were much more adept at it than I was. I soldiered on, but all three of them were well into their second serving by the time I finished my first.

The chutney and the dahl were spicy and delicious, but, in my case, called for frequent sips of water, which slowed me down as well. Both Bibbi and Linwood had grown up in the Indian state of Andhra Pradesh, which boasts some of the hottest curries in the world. They had no trouble with the spicy heat of the dahl. By the time I went to get seconds, both of them were getting ready for thirds. We ate all of the coconut chutney, lentils and chapattis, leaving only a little rice stuck in the bottom of the pot. Dave insisted that the pot scrapings would make a fine addition to our breakfast oatmeal, so we should just loosen it and leave it in the pot until morning. We congratulated Dave on the 'Nala' ('goodness' in Tamil) Best Supper. Dessert was a couple of Britannia biscuits and an apple apiece, which we thanked Jackie and Cruz aloud for.

After supper we went down to the stream to wash our tin plates and our hands. The mosquitoes had calmed down, so we sat by the river with our feet in the water. Dave broke out a packet of bidis and offered us each one. Linwood was shocked, and turned him down flat. Smoking was definitely against the rules at Kodai. But, on the spurious grounds that bidis were made from pear leaves and cow dung, not tobacco, Bibbi and I both accepted one, and were soon puffing away on them. I didn't inhale, and I don't think Bibbi did either, but at least the smoke kept any mosquitoes that were still around after dark at bay.

We sat talking through the events of the day. Linwood and I had visible bruises on our collar bones from the straps of our packs, and Bibbi felt a bruise in the small of his back where the pot in Linwood's pack had hit him. He asked Linwood how it was that he didn't have a bruise there, and Linwood said that his bruise was about four inches lower down, as he was at least that much shorter than Bibbi. Linwood's feet were feeling better, and his blisters had popped. I retold the scene of Linwood sliding into the pool and lunging for his glasses with some exaggeration, and we all had a good laugh, even Linwood.

Talk turned to our plans for the next day. Bibbi told us how he hoped to be able to identify the point that we should head up to Kookal. We were looking for a point due northeast of the place where the Manjampatti stream intersected the one we had followed. There we would see two hills rising fairly steeply, and we could head up the valley between them or scale the hill to the east of the valley.

According to his topo map, that ridge ran straight up towards Kookal, and gave us the more direct path to the caves. About three miles into the longer, valley route there would be a place where we could cut over to the right and follow another valley that would be a longer, gentler climb to our objective. Which way we went would depend on how the terrain looked when we got into it, but Bibbi made it clear that he favored the shorter, albeit steeper path. He figured that we would be climbing about thirty-five hundred feet over the course of about 11or 12 miles, which meant a fairly steep climb a lot of the way either way we went. That said, he pointed out, we had traveled twenty miles, nearly twice as far, today from Poombari, so we could take our time.

It had been a long day, so soon we decided that it was time to head to bed. We got our toothbrushes and cleaned our teeth. We consolidated our clean water into two canteens and filled the other two from the stream, adding halazone tablets that would dissolve and purify the water by morning.

I blew up my air mattress to about three quarters full, and stretched it out on bedrock, making a joke about 'a rocking bed'. Bibbi, Linwood and Dave found some sand-filled hollows to unroll their ground sheets and sleeping bags in. My air mattress had a pillow built in, but the other three found some flat rocks that they folded their towels on to serve as pillows.

Night Watch   Since we were away from civilization, and in an area known to have tigers, panthers, wild dogs, boar and elephants, we had promised Mr. Root and our parents that we would a fire burning all night long and keep watch. We drew straws for fire watch, two hours each and I got the midnight-to-two shift. Bibbi got the eight-to-ten, Linwood the ten-to-midnight, and Dave the two-to-four. At that time, before going back to sleep, Dave would build up the fire enough to last till daylight, as we planned to rise at first light to breakfast and get ready to head out.

We must have all fallen asleep as soon as we lay down. There was neither chit-chat nor any fart jokes that would often take place as we settled down for the night. I heard Linwood muttering his usual evening prayer, but that was the last thing I remember until he shook me awake at midnight. I thought, at first, that he was still saying his prayer until I realized that he was talking to me in a whisper so as not to wake the others. He was telling me to go easy on the firewood so that it would last until morning. The fire was low, but had a good bed of coals, and seemed to be doing fine. I moved to the front of the cave and sat leaning against a rock, trying not to nod off back to sleep. Bibbi and Dave were both snoring softly, and Linwood soon joined the chorus.

My seat at the mouth of the overhang gave me a clear line of sight down to the stream. The sky was filled with clouds, but there must have been a moon above them which gave me enough light to see shadows. I soon became used to the sounds of the stream in front and the snores behind so that I could discern other noises that came to me. Most of the noises were very subtle, like rustling branches or grasses being shifted. In my imagination, I heard padded feet on soft dirt, breathing of large animals, and occasional coughs. Once, I was sure I heard snuffling and snorting that could have come from a wild boar. Something splashed in a nearby pool, maybe a fish. I added another log on the fire.

I never admitted it to the guys, but I may have fallen asleep for a moment. Something brought me upright, and my auditory memory told me that it was a scream of some sort. I couldn't tell if it had been part of a dream or real. I sat very still with my ears straining for any repetition of the sound, but none came.

The fire had burned quite low, so I added another log to it and used the light from a resulting flame that came up to look at my watch. Somehow an hour and a half of my sentry duty had gone by. Rather than risk falling asleep again and missing my handoff to Dave, I stood up and cautiously made my way down to the stream to splash some water in my face. The scream was still echoing in my brain, so I kept a nervous eye out for any movement. I had heard that tigers often attacked their prey when it came to the water to drink.

Now fully awake, I returned to my post by the fire to await the hour to wake Dave up for his shift. Our pile of wood was seriously reduced, and judging by the amount I had used during my shift to keep the fire going, Dave might well run out before the end of his. There was nothing I could do about it other than to conserve as well as I could, so I used a stick to push the coals together and slid the rocks of the fire pit together to make the space more compact in the hopes that a smaller fire would use less wood.

Eventually my watch told me that it was time to wake Dave up. I had made sure to note which position he had chosen to sleep in so that I wouldn't be waking up the wrong person, and soon had him out of his sandy hollow. I explained what I had done about the fire, and that we were running low on wood. He rubbed his eyes and said he thought it would be okay and that we could go up to the dead tree and get some more before breakfast. I also told him about the scream I thought I had heard, and he promised to keep awake until the end of his shift, and leave the fire burning when it ended at four o'clock. I crawled back onto my air mattress and was soon sound asleep again.

I was awakened by voices about three hours later. Linwood and Bibbi were up and standing over the fireplace. The fire had gone out, although there was still a small curl of smoke indicating that there were still some live coals. Dave was still asleep in his hollow, and the sky was beginning to lighten towards dawn. Bibbi seemed to be arguing that they should head up to the firewood tree right away to bring back wood for cooking breakfast, and Linwood was saying that they should wait a while longer for the light to get stronger. I pulled myself out of bed to join them.

Breakfast at River Camp   The light came up pretty quickly, and soon Bibbi and I went up the hill to harvest some more wood, and Linwood took the pot with the rice stuck in the bottom down to the stream to get some water to cook the oatmeal in. In order not to disturb our toilet seat, we worked on chopping roots that stuck up off the base of the tree. Bibbi thought that these would actually burn better and longer than the branches, and we had already cleared most of the branches off the top of the log. The ones that were left were holding it off the ground at a comfortable height. We soon had two good armloads, and I knocked the dirt off the roots with the back of the hatchet. We figured that would be enough for breakfast and boiling water to take with us on our climb.

Dave was up when we got back, and was working the rice off the bottom of the pot. He said he would make the oatmeal with crispy rice in the frying pan so that he could boil water for chai in the pot. Linwood took a couple of pieces of wood from us, placed them on the remnants of the fire, and began to fan the ashes to bring the coals to life. Bibbi mixed up some powdered milk with water in a cup to pour on the cereal when it was ready, and I took the opportunity to let the air out of my mattress and flatten it out. I took some flak about being a softy, and about not helping with breakfast preparations because I had to deflate my cushy mattress.

When I had rolled the last bit of air out of the mattress, I took the now-empty pot to the stream and washed it with sand, rinsed it out, and filled it with about a quart-and-a-half of water. This I hung over the fire that Linwood had mustered up, and stirred in a cup of powdered milk, a cup of sugar, and a good scoop of tea leaves. Dave would later perform the magic with special spices to make our breakfast chai.

Waiting for the oatmeal, I picked up a stick with a charred end and wrote "Charlie- Class of '66" on one of the sides of the overhang. Bibbi watched me, and soon had added his name. Both Linwood and Dave followed, and Dave added "July 1965" at the end. We heard from a later class at one of the annual Kodai School reunions years later, that they had seen our names still on the rock where we had left them.

While breakfast was getting ready, Linwood reminded us that it was Sunday, and that he had promised to lead us in devotions since we weren't going to be at church.

"We have to let the oatmeal cool a bit, anyway," said Dave, "and I can watch it while we have devotions."

"Yeah, better to take care of it now," said Bibbi. "We'll be in more of a hurry after breakfast."

So Linwood took out his wrinkled Bible and found the passage from Psalm 104 that he had prepared for us. It had to do with the wilderness revealing the glory and purpose of God, as I recall.

Each of us took a turn at saying something about the scripture and what it meant to us, and giving thanks that we were able to enjoy the beauty of the wilderness we were in. Bibbi started singing 'For the Beauty of the Earth' and Linwood and I joined in, harmonizing on the chorus and second verse. Dave held back.

When the oatmeal was ready and Linwood had said grace, Bibbi asked hopefully if there was any more coconut chutney, even though he had been the one to scrape the last bit out of the jar. Since there wasn't any, he, like the rest of us, ate his oatmeal with milk and sugar. By the time we finished, the chai was ready and we sat back sipping the hot, sweet elixir. We again commented that camp meals could be much better than cafeteria meals.

We ate and drank everything, knowing that lunch would be squashed bread with peanut butter and jam somewhere along the trail. As soon as the pot was empty, Bibbi ran it down to the stream to wash it out with sand, rinse it clean, and fill it with fresh water to be boiled before we set out so that we could fill our canteens with water that didn't taste like halazone.

Once breakfast was over, we started breaking down the camp and repacking our gear. One by one we visited the fallen tree to "lighten the load", so to speak. Unfortunately for the rest of us, Bibbi was the first to go, and we each complained about the stink when we came back from our turn. As the architect of the toilet, it somehow fell to me to be the last one to go, and to finish filling in the trench.

Bibbi's jury-rigged handle worked well, and the log, though rough on the backs of my thighs, performed well as well. Linwood, who had preceded me, had scraped enough of the loose dirt into the pit to lessen the stench to a bearable level. He had left the spade leaning nearby, and I used it to shovel the rest of the loose dirt over the poop in the trench and pack it down. Within a day or two, no one would be able to tell where it had been.

As I neared the camp I saw Bibbi, Linwood and Dave squatting around the topo maps spread out on a boulder. Bibbi was tracing his finger along the possible routes we could follow to find our way through the hills to Kookal. Dave and Linwood seemed to have no trouble translating the map representation to terrain, and were discussing the advantages of one route over another. Although we would have to reach the same elevation whichever route we took, one route was very steep to the top of a ridge at the beginning followed by a somewhat gentler climb along the ridge, while the other possible route followed along a valley, starting out more gently and avoiding much of the steepness. I heard Bibbi say that the valley route was longer by at least four or five miles.

Predictably, Bibbi wanted to take the more direct route. He loved to challenge himself to be the best and fastest. Dave seemed prepared to go along with him, but Linwood was apparently the voice of reason. When they looked up from the maps and saw me approaching, they fell silent suddenly, and I realized that they had identified me as a limiting factor in taking the more aggressive route. My instinct was to immediately deny that I was less capable of powering up the slopes than they were, but deep down I knew that I was the least fit of the four of us. So I pretended not to have heard what they had been talking about.

Bibbi seemed to fall for my pretense, and invited me to join them as they were discussing which route out of the valley we should follow. He went over the advantages and challenges of the two obvious routes. I felt that he emphasized the extra miles we would have to go on the valley route, while minimizing the steepness of the shorter route. I asked how much longer the valley route would take us than the ridge route, and Bibbi estimated that it would take us about two hours longer. He figured that the ridge route would take about six hours, and the valley route would take at least seven and a half or eight.

"Well, the valley route will be shadier, and there might be water in the stream, don't you think?" I pointed out.

"Yeah, it'll be shadier, and there might be water, but there will also probably be more obstacles, so it could be longer than eight hours," Bibbi replied.

Bibbi was hoping to reach the caves by at least four in the afternoon, because he had heard that Mr. Reimer was leading a hike to Kookal, starting out right after church, and he wanted to get there before the other group to stake out the better sleeping cave. If we took the longer route we would have to leave real soon. But if we agreed to take the steeper, shorter route, it would take at least an hour and a half less, which meant that we could hang out by the stream longer if we were going to follow the ridge.

"There are two or three caves that are okay, but the one I'm hoping to get is much nicer."

Not wanting to be the one to make the decision, I said that I would defer to the rest of the group. I guess I was hoping the Linwood would speak up and that I could side with him. And he did say that because of the loads we were carrying, the valley route might be the more prudent way. But Bibbi, who had been to Kookal, spoke about the fun we could have if we got to the caves early enough to see the bison and deer that were common in the area. So, despite any qualms they may have felt about my ability to make the climb, it was decided that we would take the shorter, steeper route.

Decision made, Bibbi declared that we had time for a final splash in the pool before we headed out. It was now around half past eight, and the morning was still cool, but, at that altitude, not too cool for swimming. We were accustomed to much colder temperatures. The sun was beginning to break through the clouds, so we happily stripped and climbed gingerly because of our bare feet, since our chappals were packed, down the rocks and into our pool.

We talked about how sad we would be to leave this spot, and how we hoped we could come back to it one day. I said that we should wait a few years before we thought about opening the latrine pit, as it would probably take that long for the smell to die down. That got quite a laugh, and Dave and Linwood chimed in about how awful it had reeked after Bibbi had been there.

We engaged in some more good-natured heckling for a while, and then Bibbi declared that he was getting water logged, which meant it was time to get ready to leave. We had packed our towels, so we sat around on the rocks letting the air dry us off.

We were semi-dry when we dressed, but the day was humid, and we wouldn't get any drier by waiting longer. Dave had dressed in shorts, even though Bibbi advised us that we should wear long pants for the climb since we would be encountering elephant grass after we left the river, which could slice into bare skin like a razor blade. Dave said it was too hot for long pants, and that he would push the grass aside with a walking stick that he had fashioned for himself. Bibbi asked him if he had dealt with elephant grass before. He said he hadn't, but he would take his chances.

8. The Hike - Part 2: Blazing a New Path

Elephant Grass

After a last look around the campsite, Bibbi checked the fire pit to make sure the coals had been properly doused, and, with groans and grunts, we lifted our packs onto our backs. They were a bit lighter than before, with fewer apples, oranges, and a pound or so less rice and dahl, but still well over 30 pounds each. Bibbi, as usual, took the lead, followed by Dave, then me, and Linwood took up the rear. We made our way back along the stream to where the Ten Ar river, the Manjampatti stream, had joined the one we had followed the day before. Bibbi had his compass out, and headed us out due northeast from the confluence.

The trees thinned out as we left the stream behind us, giving way to waving stands of elephant grass. The grass was patchy at first, and we were able to make our way through it fairly smoothly, skirting the thicker patches. It was up to our waists, and any number of tigers or boars could have been lying in wait for us. At one point, we came upon a trail that seemed to cut through the grass in the direction we were heading and followed it for a while. When we came upon a fairly fresh pile of elephant dung, we understood how the trail had come to be. We pricked up our ears and peeled our eyes, looking for the author of the pile. Unfortunately, or maybe fortunately, we never saw it.

Also unfortunately, the elephant trail veered off from our northeasterly objective, going more easterly, parallel to the stream, and we soon had to abandon it. The ground was rising gently, and by then we could see the ridge we were making for less than a mile ahead. In his zeal to shorten the route as much as possible, Bibbi aimed straight towards it, leading us right through some large patches of elephant grass. Dave, ahead of me, was flailing away at the grass with his stick, trying to keep it away from his bare legs. I could tell that he wasn't totally successful.

Soon I could see trickles of blood, and the tops of his socks were turning pink. I was glad that I had heeded Bibbi's advice even though my legs were drenched in sweat. I had my own cuts on my arms where I had neglected to keep them away from the lethal grass, so I knew that Dave must be having a tough time. The sweat on my arms was causing the cuts to sting furiously.

We came to an opening in the grass and Dave called out for a halt.

"Hey, guys!" he shouted so that Bibbi in the lead would hear. "I think I need to take a minute and put on my long pants."

Bibbi came back to us and looked at Dave's legs with an 'I-told-you-so' expression on his face, but, kindly, didn't say it.

Dave Vs the Elephant Grass

"I think you need to clean up some of that blood," said Linwood. "Those cuts could get infected. Who has the first aid kit?"

"I do," I replied, shrugging off my backpack.

We paused there while I took the first aid kit out of the pocket of my backpack, and Linwood wiped alcohol on Dave's cuts with a cotton ball. There was no point in trying to bandage all of them up; we didn't have enough Band-Aids for that. So Dave got his long pants out of his pack and pulled them on over top of his shorts. Bibbi was champing at the bit to resume our hike by the time we were ready to move on.

Dave apologized sheepishly for the delay. "Sorry, guys. I guess I underestimated the power of elephant grass."

Despite the fact that the rise had been fairly gentle, the tramp through the elephant grass had been fairly grueling in its own right. One had to step around the thicker clumps, which meant that we had followed a crooked path, changing direction often. Pushing through the thinner sections was also a chore as the grass dragged at our pant-legs requiring extra effort with each step. The day was humid, and the sun was out. We were all sweating freely. My metabolism, however, wasn't used to sweating so much. I was famous among my classmates for being the least sweaty after P.E. or sports, and it was always assumed that I didn't put as much effort out as the others. I chalked my current dampness up to the humidity and the fact that we had been still slightly damp from our swim when we donned our clothes.

We had covered just about a mile on the topo map when we reached the base of the ridge, but it had taken us more than 45 minutes, what with Dave's pause and the crooked track we followed. We had probably walked closer to two miles in all. Bibbi was not happy with our progress. We should have left earlier! We would have to pick up the pace! As usual, once he made a plan, he liked to stick to it.

Up the Ridge Line　There were no trails heading up the hill in front of us. We would have to pick one step at a time. There were few shrubs or trees to hang onto, but thankfully the elephant grass didn't seem to grow up the slope either. The sun was well up, and there were few shadows to shelter in. Bibbi walked back and forth at the base of the hill looking for a route that would give us good purchase. It seemed to me that he picked the steepest point to start up at, but I soon realized that he had been looking for the firmest footing. Loose sand and gravel tended to cluster on the easier pitches, so we would find firmer footing on the steep part. Using both hands and feet we started up the mountain.

For those first few hundred feet it seemed that we had to climb a foot for each foot of forward progress. Lift your foot to a solid foothold, lean forward, lunge upwards and try to grab something to hold yourself steady. Repeat. Again, and again, and over again. Even my hike up from Tope hadn't prepared me for this! I was soon soaked in sweat and gasping for breath after each lunge.

We Take the Hard Road

I could hear Dave in front of me and Linwood behind me panting as well, which let me know that it wasn't just me struggling with the climb. I couldn't spare a glance to see how Bibbi was doing in the lead, but I couldn't hear him panting, either.

By the time the slope eased up a little, we were probably eight hundred to a thousand feet above the stream bed. We were on the backbone of the ridge, and could see down both sides. Down to our left, according to Bibbi, was the other route we could have taken. It looked a long way down from our vantage, and there were a lot of trees. The shade would have been nice, but the going could have been tough through any undergrowth.

It was almost noon, and Bibbi wanted to keep on until we got to the next steep part, which he reckoned was another mile or so ahead. There we could stop, rest a little, and eat our lunch before tackling the steeper portion. My legs were trembling from the strain of the first climb, and I wasn't at all confident about making a second one. But the idea of a combined lunch and a rest sounded good to me, so I agreed we should push on a bit more.

There weren't many trees on the top of the ridge where we were walking, but as luck would have it, a nice one had found purchase on a level-ish spot as we were approaching the next steep climb. It was a good sign, and the shade it gave us was very welcome. We stopped on the level ground near the base of the tree and took off our packs. We all took drinks from our canteens. Bibbi had used the halazone water from mine to put out the campfire, and I had refilled it with water that we had boiled after breakfast. For that reason, the water in mine was still warm, as it hadn't had time to cool much after being boiled, and the insulation of the canteen case had held some of the heat in. It wasn't very refreshing, so I didn't drink very much.

I also didn't feel much like eating, but forced myself to have a few bites of a peanut butter and jam sandwich and a few sections of orange that Bibbi shared with me. My face felt flushed and now in the shade, I felt a little chilled. I leaned back against my backpack and fell asleep.

It felt like no time at all till Bibbi tapped on my boot with his toe and said it was time to get going. My watch said that it had been more than twenty minutes, and it was now after half past noon. We had been on the trail for two and a half hours, and if Bibbi's estimate about the time it would take was accurate, we still had about four hours more to go. I wasn't sure that I would be able to make it that far if we were to face another climb like the one we had just come through. My legs and back had stiffened up during our rest, and I was feeling a little feverish. I shouldered my pack and stood up, waiting for the spell to pass.

I Falter   Once we were all on our feet, Bibbi took out his map and compass to check where we were, and, satisfied, headed off up the ridge towards the next steep part. This time Linwood followed Bibbi, Dave went next and I brought up the rear. The rise, when we came to it, didn't seem to be as steep as the first one had been, but it was still steep enough so that it was like climbing a steep set of stairs. There was a lot of loose material underfoot, so one had to be careful to find good purchase with each step.

For the first hundred to two hundred feet of rise, I kept up with the group fairly well, though I was falling further behind little by little. I could see that Dave was struggling as well, but he seemed to be closer to Linwood than I was to him. He wasn't paying much attention to me as he had his own problems to deal with.

The sun was directly overhead, and in spite of the clear sky, the day was monsoon heavy with moisture. I began to watch my feet stepping out and up, out and up. I heard some kind of a roar, like river water pouring into a pool, and everything seemed to go dark.

I didn't remember falling down, but I came to lying with my face in the dirt. I was breathing heavily, and dust flew up every time I exhaled. It took me a minute to realize where I was and guess what had happened. I lay still and couldn't raise the energy to move.

The weight of my backpack pressed my chest against the ground. I thought I heard feet pounding on the trail as someone ran back down to see what had happened to me. I closed my eyes, and the pounding continued unabated. It dawned on me when the pounding kept on and never drew nearer that I was hearing my own heartbeat, and not someone hurrying to my rescue.

I may have just fallen asleep, or maybe I passed out again, for the next I knew, Bibbi was standing over me calling my name and asking me what had happened. Hearing him, I summoned a little strength and pushed myself over onto my side to look up at him. The weight of the backpack came off me, and I found I could breathe more easily.

"What happened, Charlie?" he repeated in an anxious tone.

"I don't know." I mumbled. "I was walking along, and suddenly I was just lying here."

With his help I got up to a sitting position. My heart had settled down at some point from its racing, and I was able to think. Even though the sun was still burning down, I felt a chill. My skin was now dry and a little clammy.

Linwood and Dave came upon us then. They had left their backpacks along with Bibbi's on the trail ahead and come back to see what had happened. Bibbi explained what he had found and Dave, whose parents were doctors, said he thought I was dehydrated and might be getting heat exhaustion or stroke. Together they helped me into some nearby shade and got me to drink some water. Bibbi fished an orange out of my backpack and peeled it. They waited while I ate it, one section at a time

Bibbi Finds Me on the Trail

Then Dave told me to lie down with my head pointed downhill so that it would be lower than my feet. He took a tee shirt out of my pack and wet it and wrapped it around my neck. They fussed over me for a few more minutes, until I felt totally embarrassed, and said that I was feeling much better. Dave said that, nevertheless, I should take it easy for a while.

After a few more minutes, Bibbi proposed that he and Dave should head back up to where their packs were, taking my pack with them. Linwood would stay with me, and we would follow them at our own pace.

Bibbi felt that, according to the map, the worst of the climb was behind us.

"Dave and I will head up the ridge and you guys can follow at a slower pace," he said. "We'll take Charlie's pack with us, so you'll only have yours, Linwood."

"I don't know the way, though," said Linwood. "Are you going to leave us the map?"

"No, but we'll leave markers every fifty to a hundred yards for you to follow." Bibbi replied. "They'll be on the ground… sticks and stones formed like an arrow pointing the way."

This sounded reasonable to me, though Linwood wasn't sure that was how we were supposed to proceed when one of the hikers in a group got injured or became ill.

"Do you think it's okay for us to split up like that?" he asked. "Aren't we supposed to stick together? What are we supposed to do when one of us is ill or injured?"

"Hey! I'm not ill or injured!" I protested. "Just give me a few minutes and I'll be fine!"

"The reason they make us have four hikers minimum is so that two can go for help and one stay with the injured person," Bibbi explained. "In this case, Charlie's not injured or really ill, but Dave and I can forge ahead and set up camp so you can rest when you get there."

"I guess that's okay," said Linwood. "Just make sure the markers you leave are visible."

"Don't worry, we will," Bibbi promised. Looking at the map, he added, "Just follow the ridge till it gets to that shoulder you see up there, and then follow around to the right. We're only four or five miles from the caves. You won't get lost."

"I hope not," Linwood replied.

Splitting the Group So Dave and Bibbi waited until I was on my feet, then they headed back up the trail taking my backpack with them. Linwood and I followed along more slowly. Without my backpack, I found that the trail wasn't all that bad. We moved along at a steady clip, but nowhere nearly as fast as Bibbi and Dave did. A couple of hundred yards farther on, we came upon Linwood's backpack, which he shouldered. I offered to spell him with it from time to time, and he said we would see. Bibbi had left a few stones forming an arrow pointing the direction he and Dave had set off in, and Linwood and I headed after them. Fifty yards farther on, a small branch had been broken off a tree and was pointing along the ridge.

We were still climbing fairly steeply, and although I was still a little wobbly from my collapse, without a pack I could match pace with Linwood easily enough. The markers Bibbi and Dave left were fairly easy to follow, and even when we were between the trail markers, we often were able to see their boot prints in the dust.

After about a mile or so, the slope eased a little, so I said, "Let me carry the backpack for a while."

"Are you sure?" Linwood asked. "I'm used to it."

"Yeah, but I don't want you to have all the fun," I joked.

"Okay," he replied. "Just let me know when you want to give it back."

He shrugged out of the straps and helped me position it on my back.

I began to realize very quickly how much more difficult it was to hike with a heavy pack versus without one. Not that I hadn't known it already, but the immediate contrast was very dramatic. My watch told me that it was about two o'clock, meaning that we had at least two more hours to go if we went at Bibbi's pace.

Out of sheer will power, I trudged on with the backpack for about 45 minutes. Linwood asked me a few times if I was okay, and if I wanted to transfer the pack back to him, but that only made me more determined to keep on with it.

As we climbed slowly up the hill, clouds began to pile up in the sky, covering the sun. This seemed to give me a great relief, and helped me find a reserve of strength to keep me going. Finally, though, I realized that either we were moving very slowly, or that Bibbi's markers were being spaced farther and farther apart.

"I think I'm slowing down a bit," I said.

"Yeah, but that's okay," Linwood replied.

"Maybe," I allowed, "but those clouds look like rain. I'd prefer to get to the caves before it hits, no?"

"You're right," he replied.

So we stopped and took a water break while transferring the pack back to Linwood.

I was feeling a little dizzy and light headed when we went on, and still felt my heart racing more than usual as we continued to climb. We pushed ahead, and eventually came to a marker that Bibbi had placed so as to indicate a curve to the left. This curve took us along the slope, instead of up it, and walking became much more bearable. We followed along to the next marker that had us continue along the slope at the same altitude as we seemed to be rounding a peak on our right. As we continued around, we saw that we were indeed headed to the back of the hill we had been climbing, and a wide valley fell away to our right now. There were large brown shapes moving on the slopes too far away to be properly identified, and Linwood thought that they must be bison, or maybe deer.

The sky had clouded over completely, and I could tell that rain was on the way. I was glad we seemed to have made the top of our climb and wouldn't have to climb in a downpour. The markers were taking us around the lip of the valley. A roll of thunder echoed around us, the first we had heard. We picked up the pace, hoping to get as far along the way as we could before the rain started. Linwood said he wasn't at all interested in having to dry out his gear again.

The wind came up from behind us and began to rustle the trees and grasses. The clouds grew darker and angrier with each passing furlong. When the first drops hit us, they gave me a burst of adrenaline that seemed to counter the weakness I had felt earlier and I picked up my pace.

The drops were large blobs of water that splattered when they struck, and began to fall harder and faster with every second. There was a flash, and a second, louder clap of thunder shook the sky. We were in for it.

It wasn't a good idea to be out in the open during a thunderstorm, so we made for a stand of trees in one of the clefts. There, Linwood pulled a poncho out of his pack and covered the pack to keep it as dry as he could. We huddled under the thickest branches we could find, but the rain found paths through the branches and we were soon soaked.

The good thing about tropical thunderstorms is that they usually don't last very long. This one lasted only about fifteen minutes before moving off across the valley.

We climbed back up to the trail we had been on, and moved forward looking for Bibbi's next marker. We found it around a curve of the hill, though it had been partially destroyed by the rain. Luckily, enough of the stones had stayed together that we could tell what it was. Linwood worried that the next one might have been wiped out entirely. We didn't have the map with us, and neither of us had been to the caves before, so we would be traveling blind.

Our luck held, as we found the next marker mostly intact, so we figured we were on the right path, and took our bearings from it in case we missed the next one or two. I picked out a tree that seemed to be in line with the last two markers, and we continued on.

The afternoon had cooled down, whether from the rain or the altitude I couldn't be sure, and the soaking had done me some good. It was approaching five o'clock, so I really hoped we were getting close to our destination.

After a few more furlongs, I suddenly realized that I could no longer see the tree we had picked as a marker. I asked Linwood if he knew when we had lost sight of it, but he, too hadn't been keeping his eye on it. I said I thought we would have to retrace our steps until we caught sight of it again to make sure we hadn't lost our bearings. We stood there for a few moments trying to decide what to do.

Last Mile to the Cave   As we were standing still, we heard a distant shout, and looking across the valley we saw Bibbi, standing on top of a large boulder a few hundred yards away, waving his shirt. We whooped and hollered in reply, and he scrambled down from the boulder and began to run toward us around the edge of the valley. We set off on a track to meet him as fast as we could. Soon we reached each other and celebrated with hugs and back slaps. Bibbi took Linwood's backpack and led us for what turned out to be the last mile or so of our journey.

Bibbi had started back down the trail when the rain storm passed. He had realized that his markers could be washed away, and that we might get lost. He and Dave had reached the cave well before the storm and had been working to set up camp when the clouds burst. Based on where he found us, he figured that we had only been about three quarters of an hour behind him and Dave. They had made it to the caves at about four o'clock, which meant that he had kept to his schedule, even with my slowing them down.

The caves were not caves in the traditional sense if you are thinking about traditional limestone formations or volcanic lava-tube caves. They are actually overhanging slabs of granulite, a metamorphic rock from deep in the earth's crust, thrust upwards eons before in some tectonic upheaval, such as when the Indian subcontinent smashed into the Asian landmass. There were several caves in the area, but the one Bibbi had chosen was apparently the one that was most often used by Kodai campers. In fact, previous campers had left a supply of firewood and a well-constructed fire pit for us to use. There was a small spring nearby that gave us clean running water that Bibbi swore was okay to drink.

With Bibbi carrying Linwood's backpack, our pace picked up considerably, and we covered the last mile to the cave in less than twenty minutes, even though we were following no discernable trail and dodging bushes and boulders that were scattered randomly in our path.

We smelled smoke before we saw the cave, because Dave had lit a fire and was making chai to welcome us in, making use of the nice pile of firewood already in the cave, which was more than enough to last us through the night, and which made our camping chores that much easier. In addition to the firewood, there was also a latrine site already prepared, although nothing as elaborate as we had enjoyed in Manjampatti.

For me, the chai Dave made for us was a potent restorative; hot, spicy, strong and sweet. When I finally sat down with a large cup of it and allowed my muscles to relax, I realized just how beat I was. My legs felt like jelly and my back ached. My feet were throbbing, and my ankles were sore and swollen. My head felt like it weighed 40 pounds. As I drank the tea, however, these ills slowly drained from my system, to be replaced with a wave of contentment.

I was leaning back against my pack with my legs stretched out in front of me along the floor of the cave. Beyond the toes of my boots, the mouth of the cave opened out onto a stunning view of the valley. The sun, coming from over the hill behind the cave, had sunk beneath the clouds just before setting, and was lighting up the far side of the valley with its last rays.

"Well, it looks like we're going to have the caves to ourselves," said Bibbi. "I doubt that the other group would try to get through Leech Shola in the dark, and they woulda been here by now."

Even though we still had nearly twenty miles to walk the following day, I knew the hardest part of the trek was behind us. And even though I had faltered on the trail, I had, with the help of my buddies, made it through. I leaned my head back against my pack and closed my eyes.

Cave Interlude   I awoke abruptly, not having been aware of falling asleep. The cave was filled with the smell of smoke, rice and sambar, and the evening light had faded to black. I was still looking out of the mouth of the cave, but now it was a black curtain framed by the flicker of the fire dancing off the roof and walls of the cave. There was a murmur of voices behind me.

I struggled up a little groggily and twisted around to see Dave, Linwood and Bibbi sitting on rocks around the fire. Dave saw me moving first, and announced that the sleeping beauty had awakened, so we could eat. My nap seemed to have lasted all through camp set-up and dinner preparation. Embarrassed, I asked why I hadn't been awakened to lend a hand.

My View from the Cave Mouth

Dave told me that he had convinced Bibbi and Linwood to let me sleep. He thought that I had had a close brush with heat stroke and that the sleep would do me good. He said that his parents, both medical people, had often had to deal with patients suffering from heat exhaustion or heat stroke, and that rest was one of the most important prescriptions. He also thought that my condition had included some dehydration, and that I should drink as much water as I could over the next few hours. I followed his advice with another cup of tea, even though he told me that tea wasn't exactly the right thing to drink, and that I needed to drink plain water.

So, with a little good-natured ribbing, about my laziness, we prepared to eat our evening meal. Unfortunately, there wasn't any more coconut chutney to go along with it, but as Dave began serving up plates I remembered that I had brought some canned sardines and a can of peas and carrots with me, so I dug them out of my pack. With that addition to the meal, I was forgiven for not having assisted with the rest of the work. Linwood reminded us to say grace before we started.

We each got a good helping of the fish, which actually went very well with the rice and sambar, adding a delicious salty accent, especially when each bite was wrapped in a piece of warm chapatti. Every bit was eaten, as we shared another memorably good meal.

We left our dishes to soak under the drip from the spring rather than trying to wash up in the dark. I hadn't discovered where the latrine was before dark, so Bibbi took me out with a flashlight to show me. With all the water I was drinking, I wanted to be sure I was able to find it in case I needed to go during the night. The appointed spot was to the right out of the cave, the opposite direction from the spring, and about twenty paces out. When we got there, I suddenly realized that I hadn't peed since after breakfast that morning, and was happy to feel the urge come over me, which told me that my body was stabilizing itself.

Bibbi and I stood companionably peeing into the dark and looking up at a cloudy sky. Bibbi wrecked the peace of the moment by releasing a loud, stinky fart.

"Boy, I wish you'da had a match to burn that one with!" I exclaimed, holding my nose.

Laughing and holding our noses we stumbled our way back to the cave.

"What are you guys laughing about?" Linwood asked as we entered.

"Bibbi could've lit up the whole sky if we'd had a match," I replied
"Oh, you mean 'Blue Flame'? Glad he was outside!"

***

The Blue Flame Club   Another famous tale that John had imparted to Bibbi, and that we were able to duplicate, was about his membership in the Blue Flame Club. Since that time, I have discovered that this is a world-wide organization with chapters in every boarding school and college dormitory, and not a very secret one. However, up until I heard about it from Bibbi, I wasn't aware of it at all. To become a member, one has to hold a flame close enough to one's anus to light a fart as it comes out. The fart, being methane, when lit, burns with a blue flame.

Our discussion of this phenomenon took place one evening when Bibbi and Kris and I had come down to the dorm after study hall. Bibbi was in a desperately flatulent state, and we had banished him to the half-wall by the walkway outside the door of our room, where he sat reading a book in the dim hallway light. Unfortunately, it seemed that the breeze kept wafting the stench into the room, so we finally had to close the door on him. After a few minutes with the door closed, however, the smell occurred again.

"Oh, Jeez!" I exclaimed. "That's awful!"

"Bibbi, what's *wrong* with you?" Kris was too quick to blame Bibbi, claiming that the smell must have come in under the door. However, he had a look on his face that gave him away. He, too, was silently breaking wind every few minutes.

It wasn't long before whatever we had eaten for dinner began to affect me as well, so we gave up trying to clear the air, let Bibbi back in, and were soon gagging and guffawing with each new emanation. That was when Bibbi chose to tell us about the Blue Flame Club.

He explained the process. One would lean back and raise one's knees to one's chest, and hold a lit match close to ones' lower exit and let it rip. He had never tried it or seen it done, but said that John had sworn that it was real.

So we found some matches and tried it, with disappointing results. There may have been a tiny ripple of flame on one of the tries, but we couldn't swear to it. Kris, thoughtfully, suggested that our jeans were too thick, and that we had to do it in the nude. There followed a discussion of how dangerous it might be if the flame traveled up into the bowel. Kris then opined that it was just a matter of expelling the gas as forcefully as possible so that everything was projected outward, like a fire eater blowing alcohol out of his mouth. As long as the gas was exiting, nothing would go the wrong way.

"It's like a Bunsen burner in the Chem Lab," he posited. "The flame never goes down into the tube. And, anyway, if anyone had ever had their bowels singed, we would have heard about it before."

"Just make sure you're pushing it out," he recommended. "The gas needs to be moving faster than the flame."

The theory seemed sound, but none of us was eager to be the first to try it. Finally, since it was Kris' argument, he agreed to go first, but only if we swore that we would do it after him. We agreed that if he was successful in creating a blue flame, we would follow him. Swear to God.

"You guys better not be messing with me. If I do it both of you need to do it too." He said.

"Yeah, if it works we will," said Bibbi.

"Yeah, but if it doesn't work or if you blow up or something, we won't," I chimed in.

"No 'ifs'! If I do it you guys gotta try to do it, even if mine isn't perfect." Kris gave us a baleful look. "Just watch carefully and try to do it better if my try doesn't work out just right."

So, after waiting a few minutes for the urge to build, Bibbi and I stood back and watched as Kris leaned back on the bed and exposed his buttocks. He drew in a breath and held it, reached around his legs, and lit a match. The result was quite impressive. A small jet of blue flame leapt out from the yellow flame of the match.

We were ridiculously excited. I was surprised that the trick had worked, and I think that Bibbi was, too. Who knew that farts could explode?

The aftermath was also informative. First, the burning of the gas seemed to counteract the smell that usually accompanied it. However, the second thing I thought I noticed was the smell of burning hair. All of us had sprouted pubic hair by then, but Kris was not exceptionally hairy, and Bibbi was much less so. I, on the other hand, had been blessed with abundant hair in the area, so the smell of burning hair gave me pause.

Now it was time for Bibbi and me to live up to our part of the bargain. To be honest, our objective had only been to prove whether or not the stories were true, and now we had firsthand knowledge that they were. Neither Bibbi nor I was that eager to continue the experiment.

Kris, seeing our reluctance, began to get quite heated, reminding us that we had sworn that we would.

"And besides," he said, "I want to see it more clearly than I could with my butt in the air."

I hoped that Bibbi would somehow get us out of it, but being the straight arrow that he was, he agreed that a deal was a deal, and proceeded to fulfill his duty.

"It'll take me a couple of minutes, but I guess I'll go next." He sat on the edge of the bed with a look of concentration on his face. "It's coming."

We had to wait for a few minutes for him to build up a little pressure. It was getting close to lights-out, but soon enough, Bibbi was ready and got into the position pioneered by Kris. The match was lit, and Bibbi's face turned red as he powered up. The results were spectacular when he released. Kris and I estimated the resulting flame to be nearly a foot long, and it lasted twice as long as Kris' had.

Bibbi was exultant. "That's how you do it!" he exclaimed. He grinned and exchanged high-fives with Kris.

Both of them then turned to me. It was my time to perform.

I asked Bibbi "Did you smell burning hair when Kris lit his fart? I'm sure I did."

Bibbi agreed "Yeah, I think so, but maybe Kris was holding the match too close or something."

"Well," I said, "I've got much more hair in danger than Kris. The last thing I want is to have to explain to Putzy (referring to Mrs. Putz, the school nurse) how I burned my butt and have her smear some cream on it."

"Stop being such a chicken!" said Kris. "Nothing bad is gonna happen. A few hairs aren't gonna be a problem."

Just at that moment, the lights-out gong rang, and Linwood, who was the current lights-out-monitor, began his rounds to make sure everyone was ready for bed and complied. We had so far neglected to get ready for bed, so we quickly changed into our pajamas and flicked off the light before he reached our room. We would have to sneak out to brush our teeth and pee after Linwood had completed his rounds and gone back to his room. I thought I was off the hook, at least for the time being.

Linwood knocked and opened our door and turned on the light to make sure we were all in the room. His nose wrinkled and he asked, "What on earth have you been burning? The room smells foul!"

We tried unsuccessfully to control our laughter. Kris said, "We've been burning matches to try to neutralize Bibbi's farts."

As if on cue, Bibbi let a loud one. "Oh, my!" said Linwood, which was about as strong an expletive as he ever used, as he flicked off our light and quickly closed the door, suddenly eager to be on his way.

"Okay, Charlie," Bibbi said. "No more excuses or delay."

"Hey, guys!" I said. "The lights are out. Let's try again tomorrow."

"Heck, no, man. You promised, and anyway, we'll be able to see it better in the dark." Bibbi pointed out.

"Yeah, that'll make it cool!" said Kris.

"Well, what if I set my hair down there on fire because I can't see?" I asked.

But Bibbi said, "Don't worry, Charlie, I've got my towel ready. I'll smother it out. Just don't fart again till I take it away. I've got to use this one until dhobi day."

"Aw, jeez, guys. I don't think I have any more farts, anyway." I said, even though I could feel another one building.

"No problem. We can wait." Kris said with finality. "You're not getting out of this."

It seemed that I had run out of excuses.

All too quickly, I felt the pressure building up in my gut, and I said "Hey, Kris, hand me the matches."

Following Bibbi's example, I leaned back, held my breath, and put pressure on my bowel while I lit the match.

By the light of the match, I brought it towards my butt, but I was afraid to bring it very close

"That's too far away, Charlie," Bibbi said. "If it doesn't work, you'll have to try again."

"Okay, okay!" I exclaimed.

The match went out and I lit another. This time I brought it closer and, pushing hard, released my fart. From my vantage, I saw the room light up and a blue glow reflected off Kris and Bibbi's faces. They were grinning. I had succeeded, and I didn't seem to have burned anything.

"Wow! That was cool!" Bibbi declared "The whole room lit up!"

"Good job, Charlie!" said Kris. "I was afraid you were going to weasel out of it."

"Yeah, I was hoping to," I admitted. "But it was actually kinda fun! With a bit of practice, we should be able to burn all our farts. Heck, it might even be a way to warm up our room on cold nights.

"So, now I pronounce that we are all official charter members of the Wissy Blue Flame Club of the Class of '66." Bibbi declared in an official tone. "We need to recruit and initiate as many members as we can."

Laughing, we grabbed our toothbrushes and then quietly snuck off to the bathroom to finish getting ready for bed. I felt that I had passed a test of some sort and become more part of the group.

I Create a Blue Flame

Over the next few weeks, we initiated several more members of our class into the club. Sam Turner and Stan Bissel both joined, as did Phil Koszarek and Curtis Johnson and Bob Hammond, all from our dormitory. Narain thought it was hilarious, but refused to try, and Linwood refused on ethical grounds. We even got Lyn, the principal's son, to join the club, although he performed his initiation rite wearing underwear, claiming that he was too "high-standards" a fellow to be completely naked in front of others.

***

Cave Interlude (continued) Back in the cave we spent some time going over the events of the day, with Bibbi recounting how he had found me out cold on the hillside, much to my chagrin. He told us how he and Dave had fared, sharing my backpack by passing it back and forth to each other every five hundred steps or so. The counting of the steps had been a fine distraction that kept their minds off the toil, and a typical Bibbi strategy to make work fun and keep one's mind off the pain. It gave them interim goals to reach. Whoever was carrying the extra pack would hang it in front of them, on their chest, to balance the weight of their own backpack.

Essentially they were each carrying some sixty-five or seventy pounds, five hundred steps at a time. While the extra burden was terrible, knowing that it was for just five hundred steps seemed to give them the strength to carry on. They even began to compete to see who could get through their five hundred steps the fastest. In that way, they kept up the pace, much to Bibbi's delight, and made it to the cave by Bibbi's self-imposed deadline.

Linwood told how I had insisted on spelling him with his backpack and had carried it for forty-five minutes, which was almost a third of the way. He kindly didn't mention that our pace had slowed to a crawl while I was carrying it.

With all the talk of backpacks and their weight, Bibbi suggested that we try to redistribute the weight in the packs now that we had eaten all of the sardines, chapattis, rice and dahl, as well as almost all of the fruit. We would finish the tea, spices, sugar, powdered milk and oatmeal in the morning, and would only have the last of the bread, peanut butter and jam and the last of the oranges to carry forward as far as food. So we took out all the contents of our packs and spread them out. We each kept our personal items, and the pile of shared items seemed quite manageable: pot and pan, bread, peanut butter, jam, toilet paper (now down to about three-quarters of a roll).

My pile of personal belongings was the biggest, primarily because of the size of Doug's sleeping bag and my air mattress. Linwood's pile was almost Spartan, but because of the dimension of the pot, he would have to take that, and would have to wait until after breakfast to pack, since the pot had to go in first. His Bible was now fatter than it had been, since the now-dry pages had curled and rippled. Bibbi's and Dave's piles were somewhere in the middle, size wise.

Bibbi, Dave and I repacked our personal belongings, and Bibbi said he would redistribute the rest of the things in the morning after breakfast. Linwood stacked his meager belongings by the wall of the cave. Bibbi declared that it would soon be lights out, so we should prepare our beds for the night.

Once again, I blew up my air mattress and stretched my sleeping bag out on it. It was still fairly pleasant in the cave, but we could tell that the night would be cold. Since I had the mattress and fat sleeping bag, I encouraged Linwood, Dave and Bibbi to spread out nearer the fire. We decided to take the same fire watches that we had been assigned in Manjampatti, with Bibbi taking the first, Linwood second, me third and Dave fourth.

Since we were going to bed a little later than we had in Manjampatti, Bibbi's watch started at nine o'clock, and Dave's watch ended at five. Bibbi took out his topo maps and sat down by the fire. Dave, Linwood and I crawled into our sleeping bags, and I was soon asleep...

I found myself walking along a path at the edge of a steep hill. The path made a turn straight down the hill towards a wooded valley far below. I began to follow the path downward, but every step I took seemed to take me upwards, but I was still on a downwards path into the valley. I watched my feet, and by focusing on them, I could see that as my foot moved forward, the path seemed to rise until I had to raise my foot to meet it. The wonderful thing was that it was easy, effortless. I felt the pack on my shoulders, but it weighed nothing. The problem was that I was making no progress. Bibbi was suddenly right in front of me. I could see his back as he moved down the trail. I tried to ask him where we were going, but no sound came out. So I tried again, and my words were garbled. I tried once more, and Linwood bumped my shoulder...

...and I awoke, with Linwood's hand on my shoulder, remembering that it was my turn to watch the fire.

Linwood told me that he hadn't been going to wake me up, but that I had been talking in my sleep and he thought I might be having a nightmare. He said that Bibbi had sat up for an extra hour, till midnight, and that he had also taken a three hour watch, and it was now three o'clock, time for Dave's shift. They had decided among themselves that I needed to have a good night's sleep so that I could recover from my episode as much as possible because we had a pretty long walk ahead of us.

I didn't quite know how to react to that. I wanted to be angry and insist that I was fine and could carry my weight, but I was also embarrassed and a little grateful that they were looking out for me.

Additionally, I could tell that I was stiff in every joint, and that my muscles were going to complain in the morning. I said that now that I was awake, why didn't I just take Dave's watch and let him get the extra sleep. Linwood insisted that I was the one that needed it, and that if I faltered again he wouldn't forgive me. I saw the logic, and agreed to go back to sleep. It took me a while, though, to fall asleep again.

As I had been lying nearest the entrance to the cave, I was the first to wake up as the light began to creep in. I got up quietly and made my way around to the latrine to pee. I stood by the latrine and stretched, feeling my muscles complain.

The morning was overcast, but still. My watch said that it was a quarter to six, so sunrise was still a few minutes away. I finished my business, and turned to see Bibbi standing outside the entrance to the cave stretching and yawning. We waved at each other, but didn't speak so as not to wake the others. He came over to use the latrine, and asked me how I was doing. I told him I was stiff and sore, which he took as an off-color joke, even though it was a fairly accurate description of my state. I added that I thought I would be fine once we got underway and my muscles and joints loosened up. He grinned and patted me on the back in an "atta-boy" way.

Linwood was up and awake when we returned, and Dave was stirring. He had been up with the fire till five, and so had only just gone back to sleep. As it was our third morning on the trail, our breakfast chores were now routine, and we were fairly efficient at it. We soon had the last of the oatmeal cooked up and the milk powder stirred into some warm water, and were ready to eat. Linwood said grace, as usual, and we all dug in. The great thing was that we weren't going to have to carry the supplies around with us anymore.

As I was getting ready to pack my things away in preparation for the day's hike, it occurred to me that this had probably been the last time I would ever need my air mattress. I was planning to take a hammock with me to Senior Camp at Lake Berijam, and would only need my ground sheet at Senior Sneak in Mandapam, since we would be sleeping at a guest house, or, if the weather was good, on the beach outside the guest house. So, I asked aloud what everyone would think if I left my mattress here in the cave for the next group. They all thought it was a great idea, and joked that it could be reserved for the hiker who had the hardest time. Since it was made of a heavy rubberized canvas material, it weighed about six pounds, which I was glad to get rid of. So I folded it and placed it beside remains of the stack of firewood, where the next group of campers could find it.

One by one we headed off to take care of our morning business at the latrine, and to the other side of the cave to wash off and brush our teeth in the spring. The water from the spring was bracingly cold, so none of us did more than wash our faces, hands and feet. After this, Bibbi called us to him to plan for the day's hike. We would start out on a trail that would take us through Leech Shola and from there we would eventually hit the road from the town of Kookal to Poombari. That would be about eleven and a half miles. We could have lunch at our old camp site, if we left by about half past eight.

By now we were used to Bibbi's obsession with setting and following a schedule. We knew better than to try to argue with him about it up front, and that if things came up that threw us off the schedule he had set, he might get impatient, but he would never get angry or irritable. He would simply adjust to a new schedule. So we each went about getting ready to leave by the appointed time, getting our gear together, lacing up our boots, checking around for items left out inadvertently, and sealing off the latest layer of the latrine. We had each fallen into a routine for breaking camp, just as we had for preparing breakfast, and went about the tasks that had fallen to us. Unfortunately, because of my enterprise in Manjampatti, sealing off the latrine fell to me, so, as my last task before departure, I borrowed Dave's shovel and went off to take care of it.

When I got back from filling in the latrine, I found that Bibbi, Dave and Linwood were all ready to go with their backpacks on their shoulders. Bibbi had the topo map out and was going over it with them. I thought that they were sharing some kind of a joke, and when I asked, Bibbi gave Linwood and Dave a "let me handle this" look. Then he chuckled and asked me if I had heard anything about Leech Shola.

Sholas One of the features of the Western Ghats that make them so fascinating to hike in is the abundance of sholas. Originally and actually, Sholas are a species of tree native to the Western Ghats that grows at elevations of between 4,000 to 6,500 feet in the clefts between hills, where they are sheltered from the cold mountain wind and fog. Water tends to collect in these low points between hills and run along the cleft during seasonal rains, creating a lush valley, while leaving the crests dry and treeless. Shola trees are a slow growing species that take years to establish themselves. Unfortunately, they are very susceptible to being displaced by faster-growing species.

The forests between two hills are still called sholas, even though many of the actual shola trees have been replaced by invasive species. The predominant trees in the sholas around Kodai in the 1960's were wattle trees, an invasive acacia introduced by the British to supply India with their bark, used for the tanning of leather, and their wood, used in producing paper pulp. Wattle grows quickly and thickly, so thickly that even wild animals can become trapped in wattle thickets, and have been found starved to death, apparently unable to find their way out.

Many sholas are in clefts and valleys that are fed by watershed and water running at the bottom of the cleft while the treetops themselves are in the open sun. In some cases, however, sholas are positioned in valleys that are often cloudy or misty so that the moisture permeates the upper foliage as well. These sholas are dark and dank, and a perfect environment for leeches.

While sholas aren't necessarily marked on topo maps, it is easy to see the valleys where they would grow. Mr. Root had told Bibbi a harrowing tale of following a deer into a shola and getting lost and disoriented. He spent an hour walking in circles. When he finally got out into a cloudy day, he couldn't tell which side he was on and spent an hour walking in the wrong direction until he saw a landmark he recognized and corrected his course.

Our next obstacle was well marked on our topo maps.

Leech Shola I had heard the name and seen it marked on our topo maps, but other than that it was just a place on our road for me.

"Well, Bibbi said, "Leech Shola is more than just a name, it's a description. We'll be walking through a shola that, due to local conditions, is infested with leeches. They're waiting on leaves and branches everywhere."

The leeches would transfer to a hiker who brushed by, or fall on them from the trees as they passed underneath. He warned me that we would have to run through the shola one by one, and that the shola was about three hundred yards across. He showed me again where it was on the map, telling me that it was about two miles up the road from here. We would stop before entering it and get ready.

Although I was not sure that I had learned what had been going on among my friends upon my approach, I allowed myself to be distracted by the revelations of what we were about to encounter. I shouldered my pack, and was pleased to find that it felt a good deal lighter now. I attributed this to the fact that I had ditched my air mattress and we had finished off almost all of the supplies.

Bibbi helped me adjust the straps, and asked me how I was feeling about the trek ahead. I replied that I was feeling much better than I had the day before, and that I seemed to be adjusting to carrying a pack, especially now that it was lighter than the forty pounds I had started out with. Bibbi was pleased with my answer, and said that I should follow him, with Dave and Linwood bringing up the rear.

As we set out, the trail was wide enough for us to walk two abreast, and sometimes even all four of us could walk together. The trail rose and fell gently, and was much easier going than any we had encountered since we left the Forty-mile Round. All of us were feeling well, and chatted away as we walked along.

We made good time, and soon enough were approaching the infamous Leech Shola. The edge of the forest was well defined partway down a lengthy slope in the path. The trees grew thickly on either side of the trail, which disappeared into its darkened depths. As we drew nearer, the ground grew damp and slippery, and Bibbi called a halt.

It was time to take some preventive measures before crossing the border into the realm of the leech hordes. We had all donned long-sleeved shirts, and now rolled down and buttoned the sleeves around our wrists. We also buttoned our collars and wrapped bandanas around our necks. We were wearing long pants, which we tucked into the tops of our boots. Then we took a bar of soap which Bibbi produced and rubbed it on our boots, leaving a film of soap. We sprinkled salt on the soap and rubbed it in so that it stuck. Finally, Dave broke out his pack of bidis and lit one for each of us to carry. The smoke would discourage the leeches, and if one fell on us, we could burn it with the lit end of the bidi. Even Linwood took one.

Bibbi then went over the final instructions on how we would negotiate our passage. We would enter the shola singly at intervals of about ten yards. Leeches reacted to the passage of animals and hikers through the shaking of the ground around the base of the trees. If we followed too closely, leeches disturbed by one of us could fall on the one behind.

"Whatever you do, stay on the trail. It's pretty well marked, I think, but if you get off it, you'll be in trouble pretty quickly. Charlie, you follow me, then Dave, then Linwood," Bibbi instructed.

His instructions continued: The shola was about three hundred yards wide, and we needed to cross as quickly as possible, so we should run, but be careful not to crowd too closely to the person ahead.

Entrance to Leech Shola

The trail inside was wet and slippery with mud and leaves and leeches, so we would have to watch our step. If we fell, we should get up as quickly as we could and keep running, and not try to brush ourselves off until we were out the other side. Once through, we should continue up the slope until the trail had become dry again and then strip off all our clothes and shake them out. Before dressing, we would check each other for leeches, removing any that we found, and disinfect any bites.

These elaborate instructions did more to frighten me than any of the stories I had heard about snakes and tigers ever had. I asked Bibbi what the worst that could happen might be.

Dave answered, telling a story about a man his parents had encountered who had gone into a leech infested shola to gather wood, and had lost so much blood that he had needed a transfusion. Additionally, he said, the man had pulled the leeches off himself roughly, which left their mouth parts under his skin, and the bites became infected.

"Whatever you do," he told us, "you shouldn't try to yank the leech off. Once the leech is attached to your skin, you need to remove both ends by scraping them off with your fingernail and flick them away. Don't burn or salt a leech that is on your skin, either."

With these dire warnings echoing in my head, we lined up to run through the shola. Bibbi would go first, I would count slowly to ten and follow, then Dave, and finally Linwood. Bibbi looked at us and said, "Remember! You gotta run!" and he was off. It took me a couple of seconds to remember that I was supposed to be counting, so I started at three, and set off when I reached ten.

Plunging into the trees was like diving into a well. Within a few feet of the entrance I had lost almost all light and was jogging into the twilight. It took my eyes a few seconds to adjust, and it was fortunate that the trail was straight for a hundred feet or so, or I might have run straight into a leech-filled bush or tree.

Thinking about it later, I realized that the forest was beautiful and lush. There were trees of many varieties, vines, bushes and shrubs, some with flowers. At the time, though, everything looked threatening and evil and dark.

I could hear Bibbi ahead of me, and shortly picked up the sounds of Dave jogging behind me. Other than that, there were a few bird calls and small rustlings, but mostly silence. I got the impression that if I stood quietly, I would be able to hear water drops and leeches falling from the leaves of the trees. Bibbi's footfalls were getting fainter, and Dave's were getting louder, so I upped my pace, trying to keep the distance between us even. The trail did curve to the left at one point, and began to rise, telling me that I had reached the halfway point of the transit, the bottom of the shola.

Leech Check   When I exited the other side of the shola, I saw Bibbi twenty yards further up the trail. He had already dropped his pack and removed his shirt, and was taking off his boots. I ran up towards him and he motioned me to a spot off to one side a couple of yards away.

"Post up over there," he ordered. "If we're too close to each other we might get our leeches on each other. You're gonna want to shake out your clothes after you take them off. Don't shake yours onto me!"

As I dropped my pack, Dave plunged out of the shola and Bibbi repeated his instructions of keeping his distance, directing him to another spot.

I watched Bibbi and copied his actions. I checked my backpack and found a leech on one of the flaps, which I burned with my bidi. I shook my shirt away from where Bibbi and Dave were working as Linwood ran out of the trees. Bibbi pointed him to the fourth corner of the square we now made and he began to follow our lead.

My boots rendered the greatest number of leeches. There were at least a dozen or so wiggling around on them below the line of soap and salt, and where it had been wiped off by the grass as I ran.   There were a couple on my pant legs, and one had made it up to my belt. I brushed them off and stomped them or burnt them as soon as I found them so they couldn't attach themselves to any exposed skin. I heard yelps and curses to match my own coming from the others, but couldn't take my eyes off my own endeavors long enough to see what was happening.

Soon we were all standing in our underpants with our clothes in a small pile beside us, and searching our torsos, legs, arms and the ground around us for any escaped leeches. Other than one on my arm, I didn't find any that had made it onto the parts of my skin that I could see. Dave had found three, and won the prize for the most. Bibbi didn't find any, and Linwood also found only one.

Once our separate checks were accomplished, we converged in the center of the square. There Dave showed us how to safely remove our unwanted passengers without leaving any of their mouthparts under our skin. We then checked each other from scalp to toes for any leeches that might have made it past our defenses and initial scrutiny. Thankfully, we were all now clear, even inside our underpants. We congratulated ourselves on our successful passage through the infamous Leech Shola.

We vigorously shook our clothes off and got dressed again, and headed up the trail towards the ridge line ahead. From there, we could see the drop down to Kookal Lake, although only a glimpse of it, and its dam, and the road that would take us back to Poombari.

Once we reached the road, Bibbi estimated that we would have about ten more miles to our Poombari camp site. We should be there before one o'clock if we made it through the rugged terrain between us and the road in about half an hour. It was just past nine in the morning, so Bibbi thought we were in good time. He thought we might even be able to make it back to campus in time for tea. Since all we had left to eat with us was bread, peanut butter and jam, we agreed that we should try to make it, even though it meant that we would have to forgo a possible swim in Kookal Lake. That wasn't too much of a concession, since at about 6,000 feet altitude on an overcast morning, the temperature was around sixty degrees Fahrenheit, and the idea wasn't that inviting.

Back to Poombari   We soon reached the road, and were climbing more gently towards the town of Poombari. We could now walk four abreast, and Bibbi turned it into a contest of keeping up with him. We were back on his schedule, and all of us wanted to get to Kodai in time for tea, so we went along. Bibbi told us that when we reached the top of the rise we were climbing, most of the rest of the way would be downhill or level until we reached Poombari.

The road followed the contours of the hills so that dips and rises were gentle. I seemed to have become more accustomed to the weight of my pack, which was in fact somewhat lighter, so the going was much easier than any we had encountered up till now. We talked and laughed in the level or downslope sections, but saved our breath in the uphill parts.

Bibbi and Linwood were each other's closest neighbors in the off-season. They lived in the neighboring state of Andhra Pradesh about a two and a half hour train ride from each other, and could get together from time to time. They had been in India since early childhood, Bibbi having been born in Kodai, and had many tales of their adventures together. Dave had also been born in India, but had spent part of his childhood in the States, North Carolina, I think, and had retained his Southern accent and laconic speech patterns.

As we walked along, I reflected on the fact that these three boys were much more to my liking and had more in common with me than any of the fellows I had met in my freshman year of high school in the U.S. My own background involved more countries and continents than theirs did, but I realized that there was something important about being exposed to more than one culture, something that gave them an attitude and outlook that was more in tune with my own than any I had found at Andrew Lewis High School in Salem, Virginia.

As these thoughts came, I realized that in six short months we would be heading back to the U.S. for college, and I would again be subjected to people with more provincial outlooks on life. I wasn't sure that I would be able to adjust to a small college town, but was unlikely to have the grades to qualify for any of the more cosmopolitan schools. Bibbi asked me why I was looking so sad.

When I answered him, our conversation turned to our plans for college. We had all been reading about several and were awaiting the results of our SAT's to send off our applications, based on their required qualifications. I commented that Bibbi would have his pick of colleges, since he carried an A average in almost every class. Linwood was also a good student and confident that he would get into his chosen school. He was Canadian, and would be attending college in Canada. Dave was determined to go to medical school to follow his parents' profession. We all agreed that we would keep in touch, wherever we ended up going.

The country we were walking through was beautiful, and mostly wild. There were fairly thick forests on both sides, but through occasional breaks in the trees, we could catch a glimpse of terraced rice paddies. We met a few local people walking along the road in the other direction. Once or twice a lorry passed us in one direction or the other. We were greeted and salaamed by everyone we passed and acknowledged the greetings happily. These were the first people we had seen since descending into Manjampatti, which seemed like a long time before, although only two days had passed.

After about five miles we reached the turn from Kookal Road onto the Forty-Mile Round, formally called Kodaikanal Road. We turned left to retrace our steps of two mornings before, heading back to Poombari. Bibbi speculated that if we turned right, we could reach Mannavanur by lunch time, and be back at our Manjampatti camp site by dusk. We all contemplated how wonderful that would be, if only we didn't have to cover the miles between, and if we weren't already thinking about tea time and supper at Kodai. As soon as he realized that we wouldn't have the wonderful dahl, sambar, rice, and coconut chutney supper, Bibbi quickly gave up the idea, and we picked up the pace toward Poombari and home.

We reached the Poombari rest house shortly after noon. The sky was still overcast and the cloud cover was getting thicker. The rest house was once more locked, the attendant supposedly having gone home for lunch. There was evidence that other Kodai kids had been there at some point during the weekend, as the trash cans were full of the kind of trash that came with school-packed lunches. We climbed up onto the porch and took off our packs. Dave pulled the remnants of the bread out of his backpack, and Linwood produced the peanut butter and jelly out of his. This would be our last meal on this hike.

I decided that since we would be on the road for the rest of the hike, I might as well take off my hiking boots and wear my sneakers the rest of the way. I took off my boots and socks and walked off the porch onto the grass. My bare feet loved the feel of the grass. They had been pounded and blistered and wrapped up wet for three days. I walked through the grass, avoiding bare and stony patches, and let them soak up the sensations. I was in no hurry to put my shoes on.

'Hey, guys!" I called out. "Check this out! This grass feels great on bare feet!" I shifted from foot to foot with a huge smile on my face.

Soon enough, they had removed their boots as well and were also sighing with pleasure.

In just a few minutes, though, Bibbi looked at his watch and put a stop to the foot party. We had to eat our lunch and be on our way shortly. He thought we should be ready to leave by a quarter to one so we wouldn't have to rush to make tea time at four o'clock. So we went back to the porch and used up the rest of our bread, peanut butter and jam. We each got three sandwiches. Linwood and I each ate only two and a half sandwiches. We gave our extra half sandwiches to Bibbi, who happily ate them. When we were done, I threw the empty jars and bread wrapper into the trash can.

"Okay, guys," said Bibbi. "We need to be ready to head out in about ten minutes so we make it back in time for tea."

9. The Hike - Part 3: Back to School

I Discover a Ruse   I grabbed my boots and took them over to my backpack. I meant to pull out my sneakers and stuff my boots in their place. Except that when I looked in my pack, I couldn't find my sneakers. In fact, there were very few of my belongings in the pack, just some underwear and tee-shirts all bunched up. I cursed, and Bibbi asked me what was wrong. I told him that I must have left my sneakers and some of my clothes in the cave along with my air mattress. He looked puzzled for a second, and then burst out laughing. He went over to his pack and rummaged around and pulled out my sneakers. My jacket fell out as well.

He, Linwood and Dave had conspired to lighten my pack as much as possible by sharing out most of my gear amongst them. Bibbi had taken my sneakers and jacket, Linwood had my flashlight and extra socks, and Dave had two of my shirts. No wonder my backpack had been so comfortable. It wasn't that I had gotten used to it, nor because we had eaten all of the supplies. It was because my pals had decided to lighten my load. I was angry and I felt humiliated. I'm afraid I said some things that I didn't mean, but I felt that I would be made a laughing stock when it came out that I hadn't pulled my weight.

Bibbi tried to tell me that it had been for my own good, but I didn't want to listen to him. So Dave took over. He said that I had probably suffered from heat exhaustion, and hopefully not from heat stroke. Full recovery could actually take several days, and even though I had felt better by that morning, they had wanted to avoid a possible repeat and having to carry me out on a stretcher. So they had decided that since our overall load had been reduced by what we had consumed, they would reduce the weight of my pack as much as they could by removing the heavier items and carrying them in their packs. I was little mollified by this explanation, and asked them to please give me back all my stuff.

I took my time repacking my backpack, shooting dark looks at the three of them as I carefully folded and rolled my gear. Once I was packed, I hefted the pack and realized fully how much the lighter pack had helped. They must have taken more than ten pounds of stuff off me. I realized that instead of being angry, I should be proud to have friends who would look out for me. As quickly as it had flared, my anger cooled, and I thanked them all for their good intentions.

It was almost one o'clock when we left the Poombari rest house. The attendant hadn't returned, if he was even going to. I was determined not to be the reason we didn't make it to Kodai in time for tea, especially since it was arguably my fault that it had taken us more time to get underway than Bibbi had planned. Although my backpack was noticeably heavier now, I set off in the lead at a brisk pace. The first two miles or so was a fairly gentle uphill walk, which was followed by two miles of gentle decline. I started timing the furlong markers, and was concerned to see that we were doing about three and a half miles per hour, which meant that we would cover the eleven mile distance to the school in three and a quarter hours. That would make us late for tea.

I told Bibbi that I thought we should pick up the pace so as not to be late, but he said that we were doing fine. When I explained the math to him, he agreed that if we followed the road all the way as we had when we came out, we wouldn't make it. However, now, since we were traveling in daylight, there were a number of shortcuts that he knew that would take more than a mile off the distance. It wasn't something we could have tried in the dark on our way out, but in daylight they were easy enough to follow. Nevertheless, when we reached a downhill part, I picked up my pace a little, and if the others noticed, they said nothing.

Little by little, the tension caused by my discovery of their deception eased, and we began to chatter again. We were seeing more people and traffic out on the road now. The sky was darkening with clouds piling up, promising an afternoon shower or storm. Bibbi came up and walked beside me, and after a few minutes of silence, said he was sorry. I told him he had nothing to be sorry about, and that I understood he had just been trying to help me. I said that I was actually angry with myself for not having held up my end. This he poo-pooed, saying that it could happen to anyone, and that if it had happened to him, he was sure that I would have given him the same treatment. The idea that it could happen to him struck me as hilarious, and we had a good laugh about it.

Shortcuts   At the end of a long straight stretch we came to a waterfall beside the road and stopped for a short rest and to splash our faces with the cold mountain water. With so much civilization around, it was never safe to drink the water, but we drank from our canteens and refilled one of them after consolidating our purified water into the other three, and dropped a halazone tablet into it. It would be safe to drink in about an hour.

After this, the road made several switchbacks, and Bibbi kept looking for a landmark to tell him where the shortcut he had spoken of started. For a while, though, the road was bordered by fairly thick forest, with no sign of a trail. Soon, though, after another stretch of straight road, we came to a place where the road doubled back sharply to avoid a fairly steep drop. Looking over the edge at the apex of the curve, Bibbi gave a whoop. He had found his first shortcut. There were some rough stairs cut into the slope below the road that led towards a well-defined break in the woods.

We clambered over the stone wall that lined the curve in the road and made our way down the steps to the trail below. The trail ran straight, falling gently to a stream bed. After crossing the stream we came to some fields that were being worked, although no one was in them as we crossed them. Beyond the fields was a collection of huts, and there were several people sitting around and some children playing under a tree. They waved to us and salaamed, greeting us with the usual "Namaskaram". They were apparently used to having Kodai School hikers traipse across their land.

Leaving the huts behind, we climbed back onto the road, having cut off at least three furlongs to half a mile of the distance to Kodai. We were on the road for only a few hundred feet when we left it again to cut off another pair of switchbacks. This time we were walking through fairly dense forest, but there was a well-traveled path that we could follow. We met the road again and dove straight across it and back onto our trail. These two dips into the trees saved us another few furlongs, so we had already cut a good mile off the trip.

Bibbi had one more shortcut in mind, which he said we would reach in about a kilometer (five furlongs) that would take at least another three quarters of a mile off the distance and land us on the Ten-Mile Round. From there into school should take us only about an hour and a half, so he wanted to reach it by two-thirty if we could. However, he told us, if it started to rain before we got there, he didn't want to take the shortcut. The trail could become very treacherous when it was wet. So we all prayed for the rain to hold off for another hour or so.

It was still dry when we came to the next and final shortcut, but the sky was getting darker. The air was still and heavy. We knew that once the wind came up, the rain would start, so we stood for a moment at the edge of the road where the trail took off, trying to decide if we should risk it or not. We were all up for the adventure, and none of us wanted to miss Tea Time. Bibbi, always looking for a challenge, agreed. So we climbed over the wall again, and made our way down the steep bank and onto the trail.

Washout   The shortcut was only about five furlongs from start to finish, so we hurried as much as the terrain would allow. We made it three quarters of the way before the wind, and then the rain, hit hard. We were among the trees, and somewhat sheltered, so the full force of the thunderstorm wasn't apparent to us, but we could hear the wind in the trees, and the rain quickly began to penetrate the layers above us. Within the next hundred feet we were soaked.

It was fortunate that we were almost at the end of the shortcut, and by now could see the side of the road ahead of us. However, the water had turned the slope up the road muddy and slick. Getting up to it, especially since we had changed from our hiking boots into our sneakers, was going to be a problem. There were few shrubs or trees to hang on to, and the top of the wall was about ten feet above us. There were some rough stairs that travelers along the trail used, but the water sluicing down them made them look treacherous and unstable.

If we couldn't somehow clamber up that embankment, we would have to wait out the storm where we were and probably lose all the time advantage we had gained by taking all the shortcuts. We would not be back at school in time for tea. It also occurred to me, though I didn't mention it then or ever, that if we had left Poombari ten minutes earlier, we would have made it up to the road just before the rain came. I would be the reason we hadn't made it back in time. I felt I couldn't carry that burden, so I desperately looked for a way to get us up to the road.

I walked back and forth along the embankment, watching the water spill over and rush down from the road. The wall along the road had drainage sluices through which the water spilled. There were a few feet between the sluices, so I could see a space where the only water coming down was from the rain that fell on it. I saw some rocks that looked stable and might give me purchase to get a grip or a foothold.

I consulted with Bibbi, explaining my thoughts to him. I was a good climber, and had a longer reach than either Dave or Linwood, and didn't weigh as much as Bibbi, so I volunteered to try to scale the embankment up to the road. Once there, they could hand me up the backpacks, and we could use the straps of one of the packs to help them climb.

By this time we were entirely soaked through, so I had no problems getting muddy as well. I went to the wall and reached up to grab the first handhold I had seen.

Bibbi made a stirrup of his hands and gave me a push up to where I could grab on and then find a foothold to push myself up further. My chest and belly were pressed against the hillside, and mud and water were coursing down under my shirt. I tried to look for the next hold, but when I raised my face, I got hit by a splash of muddy water that blinded me.

Up the Embankment

I shouted down that I couldn't see, and to tell me where the next handhold was. Bibbi talked me up to the next one, and then guided me as to where to place my foot. I pushed myself up, and asked for the next hold. Bibbi told me that I could probably feel the wall, which was just above my head, and that I could hopefully find a space for my fingers. I felt along the wall, and sure enough, found a crack that was big enough to get my fingers into. I moved my free foot up to where my lower hand was, and settled it there.

With a hearty shove, I pulled myself up. Reaching up, I found the top of the wall and was soon sitting on top of it trying to wash the mud out of my eyes. The guys were cheering.

A few minutes later, we were all at the top. The rain was still falling, but the worst of the downpour seemed to have passed on, or maybe it just seemed that way since we weren't looking up into it.

I took off my shirt and let the rain wash all the mud I had collected away. I got backslaps and grins from all of them, and was feeling pretty good about myself. I wrung out my shirt and put it on, and shouldered my backpack, which was now somewhat waterlogged, even though it was supposed to be waterproof.

We were back on the road and had made it by Bibbi's two-thirty target.

Back to Campus   We had emerged from our shortcut onto the Ten-Mile Round. We were about four miles from school and would be walking on the road the rest of the way. At this point, the road ran along a ridge at an altitude of some 7,500 feet, and had reached the highest point of our trek. The Kodaikanal Solar Observatory was a mile or two ahead, and after passing it, the road descended into the Kodai Lake basin. We hiked along in great spirits, feeling that we had overcome great obstacles to make it through our hike. We now had our goal in sight and it served to wash away any fatigue that the efforts of the past few days had laid on us.

There was more traffic on the Ten-Mile Round, so we had to walk single-file along the shoulder of the road. Bibbi led the way and began to sing one of the many songs we had learned for camp and class outings, and Linwood and I joined in. Dave claimed not to be able to carry a tune, and had proved it on several occasions, so he kept silent. At some point we moved on to Peter, Paul and Mary, which I could harmonize with. Ladies in saris and men in dhotis waved and smiled and wagged their heads at us as we marched along singing.

A mile or so past the Observatory the rain had tapered off, and we had made it to Upper Lake Road. There we got our first glimpse of Kodai Lake.

From here our way was all downhill. We were approaching the lake from the north, and could pick out the Boathouse and the Carlton Hotel across the lake. In the distance, almost straight ahead of us, Mount Perumal was in sunshine, even though we were still under clouds. The lightened mood and the singing had carried us along at a good clip, and Bibbi, looking at his watch as usual, said that we would be getting to campus a good ten minutes before tea time. That meant that we could at least drop our backpacks at the dorm before running up the hill to the cafeteria.

Dave decided that he would head back to his compound, where he could get high tea and more whenever he wanted. So he left us when we got to Lake Road and headed off in the other direction. He was looking forward to a hot shower and a delicious meal.

Bibbi, Linwood and I followed the Lake Road around the arm of the lake and entered campus by the gate below the dorm, which we called the Phelps gate. Since it was a holiday, however, the gate was locked and unmanned, so we ended up throwing our packs over the wall and climbing in. Most of the kids were already on their way up to the cafeteria for tea, so we made it to Wissy almost unobserved. Only a few grade-schoolers saw us, and they were used to the antics of upperclassmen.

We were soaked and muddy, but there was no time to do more than pee and wash our hands after we dropped our wet backpacks in our dorm rooms. I did manage to put a clean jacket over my scruffy shirt before we walked up the walkway towards the cafeteria. Others were also heading that way, since holiday weekend tea was usually fairly decent. Of course everyone had heard about what we were planning, and our disreputable appearance probably confirmed that we had indeed accomplished what we set out to do. We happily confirmed it to all who asked, and were the center of attention as we crossed the Quad.

A couple of the girls came over to greet us, mainly because of Bibbi, since neither Linwood nor I held any great attraction for them. However, as soon as they got close enough to see our muddy clothes and catch a whiff of our so-far unwashed bodies, they wrinkled their noses and backed away. Linwood and I thought it was hilarious, but Bibbi said he wished we had arrived early enough to clean up a bit before going to tea.

We discovered that Mrs. Henderson had taken the weekend off, so rather than the cinnamon rolls that we had been craving, tea consisted of a biscuit with some butter and a cup of weak chai. Cruz and Jackie brought us extra biscuits and some fruit, so we got some of our energy back, but our appetites were anything but satisfied. We were even more disappointed when Cruz told us that there would only be soup for supper: the kind of vegetable soup we called "mystery soup". After nothing but peanut butter and jam sandwiches for lunch, we were after much more substantial sustenance. I knew that we were all thinking about going down to the Budge for a good meal.

While we were sitting there thinking about how we could sustain ourselves, Mr. Root came into the cafeteria and walked over to our table. He was checking up on us to make sure that we had made it safely back, and that he wouldn't have to send out a search party, or worse, tragic news to any of our parents. We assured him that we were all back with no permanent damage, and that Dave had gone back to his compound. We glossed over any of the troubles we had encountered and told him that we had had a great time. He asked a couple of questions, the purpose of which seemed to be to verify that we had indeed gone where we said we were going, and not just disappeared into the countryside for a few days. He seemed satisfied, but he made us nervous when he asked us to stop by his office after classes the next day.

A few of our friends had come over to our table during our conversation with Mr. Root to listen in on our replies, and when he had gone, they asked us to go into more detail about the hike. I was concerned that the main topic would be my collapse on the trail, but Bibbi and Linwood both downplayed the story, making it sound like just another bend in the road. They emphasized that Bibbi and Dave had made it to the caves as scheduled, and that Bibbi had come back to me and Linwood and found us just a mile down the trail. At the same time, they celebrated my climbing of the embankment during the storm and getting us back on the road. I came off very well in the retelling, better than I felt I deserved, but I would take it. No mention of them lightening my load was made.

Kris and Lyn were sitting at a nearby table with their respective girlfriends, and were listening to the retellings of our adventures with one ear. Lyn was "slumming", in that, since he lived with his parents he got anything he wanted for tea, and usually didn't take it in the cafeteria.

I was glad that I didn't come off as the weak sister in the story, which would have been very embarrassing and damaging to my fragile teenage ego, especially since the girls would have spread such a juicy tale to all of the other girls. Some of the details might come out later when we were together in the dorm, but as a rule, things we shared in private usually stayed private.

A Hot Shower   After tea, and after a few more girls had made comments about our appearance and smell, we went back down to the dorm. We desperately needed to have a shower, but hot water was only provided on Wednesdays and Saturdays. A cold shower after spending hours in damp clothes and especially with a chilly evening coming on held no appeal to any of us. We desperately wanted a nice, hot shower more than anything.

Bibbi was one of our class' stellar math students and was expected to raise the school's average in the overall SAT scores. He was one of Mr. Amstutz' pets in calculous class. The previous year, Mr. and Mrs. Amstutz had replaced Mrs. Gibbs, who had retired, as our house parents. So, making himself look as bedraggled as possible by sticking his head under a drip falling off the roof, he went over to their cottage and asked if it would be possible for us to stoke the boiler for some hot water. He may have sniffled or sneezed as well. As a result, he was given the key to the boiler room. Mr. Amstutz didn't want to risk the health of his star student.

We all went through the hall past Room 11 and out the door to the back of the dorm behind the bathroom. There we unlocked the door to the small boiler room. It was warm inside, so we crowded in. There was kindling and wood and newspaper and matches all stacked neatly at the ready. We soon had a fine fire going in the box under the giant steel tank, and slid in a couple of the fatter logs onto it to make sure the fire lasted for a while. We knew from experience, we had about forty-five minutes before the water in the tank would be hot enough to give us the water temperature we craved. After soaking up the warmth of the boiler room for a few more minutes, we all went back to Bibbi's and my room, Room 11, to wait.

In the room, I had my reel-to-reel tape recorder, and Bibbi and I enjoyed Peter, Paul and Mary, so I turned it on and loaded the tape with their "In the Wind" album which I had acquired last Christmas. We listened and sang, thoroughly enjoying ourselves. We stripped off our damp and dirty clothes and stuffed them into our dhobi bags that would be picked up for washing on Wednesday. Then we sat around in our underwear, whiling away the time till the water heated.

After about half an hour, Linwood put on his dhoti and said he was going to check on the water temperature. He headed down the hall to the bathroom and quickly came running back a moment later

"Hey, guys!" he was almost shouting. "There are three freshmen in the showers using up our hot water! What should I do?"

"No way!" exclaimed Bibbi, jumping off the bed and heading out the door.

I followed right behind him. When we got to the bathroom, sure enough, there were three naked freshmen using up the warm water that was building in the tank. We yelled at them and asked them what the hell they thought they were doing. We were filled with righteous anger. These were lowly freshmen! Who did they think they were?

Seeing three upper classmen, two of us in our underwear, the younger boys looked thoroughly frightened. They rinsed off their soap and turned off the water quickly and grabbed their towels and covered themselves, confused and not knowing what they had done to offend us. They stood there cowering under our furious glares.

One of them, I think it was George Caldwell, stammered "I just came in to wash my hands and face. I guess I opened the hot water tap out of habit, and when the water came out warm, I decided I could have a shower."

"So you went and got your buddies? To use up OUR hot water? Just who do you think you are?" Bibbi yelled at them.

"We're sorry. We didn't know. We just thought that because it was a holiday... you know... We just wanted a hot shower," George stammered. Monday showers were apparently a luxury they couldn't pass up.

Our anger had crested, and now we felt sorry for these younger boys. However, we kept our pity to ourselves. As freshmen they needed to be kept in line. So we told them that we had been given special permission to have showers, which they had not. We sent them back to their rooms and told them that we would let them know when we were done, and if there was any hot water left, they were welcome to have showers then. We also warned them to keep it to themselves or we would make sure to use up all the hot water ourselves.

We went back to our room, but left the door open and kept an eye out for anyone headed towards the bathroom.

Fifteen minutes later we took our towels and soap dishes and filed back in ourselves. The water coming out of the sink faucet was scalding hot by then, so we jumped into the showers and let the hot water run over us. Since we were the only ones using the water at the time, unlike Wednesdays and Saturdays when everyone was cleaning up, the water pressure was high and the spray massaged our tired backs, shoulders and arms. After soaping off the grime of the weekend and rinsing, we stood in the spray for a good ten minutes, hanging onto the shower heads, letting the hot water run down our bodies and restore us to life.

Supper in the Budge   It was now getting close to supper time, and Bibbi lamented the fact that there would be nothing but mystery soup for supper, which he would only eat if he were starving. I laughed at that, because Bibbi was always starving. I suggested that we should skip school supper and head to the budge. We could get some mutton biriyani at Hotel State and celebrate our successful hike. Bibbi loved the idea, but confessed that he had used up all of his allowance buying the supplies for the hike and couldn't afford it. I said that I had a few rupees stashed away which we could use, but maybe not enough. As we had learned earlier, mutton biriyani cost two rupees fifty paise with mutton or one rupee twenty-five without mutton.

Linwood said he had a rupee, and if I lent him 25 paise, he would get the biriyani without mutton. We scrounged around, looking in pockets of pants we had worn and into drawers and came up with another half rupee in annas and naye paisa. We even checked a pair of Kris' jeans that were lying on the floor under his bunk, and found one rupee crumpled up in the bottom. I only looked because I thought they might be mine or Bibbi's.

"He'll never miss it," I said, hopefully.

"Well, if he does, we'll pay him back later," said Bibbi.

"I don't know…" said Linwood, "we should pay him back even if he doesn't notice… no?'

"You're right, Linwood," Bibbi laughed. "Otherwise it would be like stealing. We'll pay him back for sure."

Pooling it all together, we had just over five rupees (about $1.25 US in those days). That would buy two orders of mutton biriyani, which we could divvy up into three shares. I asked Linwood if he thought he could get the manager of the Hotel State to give us hot chai with our biriyanis. The manager had been to Andhra Pradesh, and could speak a little Telegu, which he enjoyed speaking with Bibbi and Linwood, who were fairly fluent, and so might be amenable to giving us chai.

When the dinner bell rang we exercised our senior prerogative to leave campus, and headed off to the Budge to celebrate and fill our bellies with fine Indian cuisine. As explained before, Hotel State was really just an eatery. The word "Hotel" in its name was an Indian application of the word, and would have been "Restaurant" in most other parts of the world.

As one of our favorite off-campus haunts, we knew we could get a tasty meal to supplement our boarding school diet. We walked down Budge Road to the dingy looking storefront half way down the hill of the main bazaar street with its big blue and white sign out front. As usual, we got the manager to seat us in the small back "family" room which we could have all to ourselves.

Bibbi and Linwood chatted away with the manager in Telegu to his great delight. He loved to show off to any customers who happened to be there that he had good relations with Kodai kids, and especially that some of them spoke his language, showcasing even more intimacy. When they explained our dilemma about money, he immediately agreed not only to give us free chai with our dinner, but that he would give us two and a half portions of mutton biriyani to share. The meal came with unlimited chutneys and gravy, called mutton juice, as well.

The meal arrived quickly, since mutton biriyani was a house specialty and a large pot of it was always at the ready. The 'boy' brought in a large tray with a clay pot of biriyani, three banana leaves and containers of chutneys and raita and cups of "mutton juice" (gravy). He laid a banana leaf in front of each of us and set the other containers down on the table. This was special service, since the portions were usually measured out onto each one's leaf. In truth, the manager didn't know which one of us would get the "half portion", so rather than let the boy know that we were getting a deal, he opted for the "family style" service.

Bibbi carefully spooned out a third of the biriyani onto each of our leaves, making sure that no one got less than the others. For the chutneys and the mutton juice, however, it was every man for himself. That was okay, since if we ran out, we could ask for more.

The biriyani was delicious, flavored "Dindigul" style. There were several nice chunks of mutton mixed in, and the spices were bracingly hot. We, of course, dug in with our fingers, and were soon silently engaged in stuffing our mouths. The coconut chutney was creamy and very hot. The coriander leaf chutney was tangy and hot. The lime chutney was sour and hot. The mutton juice was steaming and hot. We had to order two more rounds of chutneys and mutton juice before we were done. Then we sat back sipping the hot, sweet milky chai and just smiled at each other. This had indeed been a fine celebratory feast.

Our bellies happy, we strolled back to school, enjoying the fresh evening and the unhurried pace we could take now that we were done hiking. The sky was still cloudy, so the day's warmth wasn't escaping too quickly. We were comfortable in our windbreakers and jeans. It felt good to have clean, dry socks on my feet.

Bibbi wondered aloud what Mr. Root wanted to see us about after school the next day. I said I didn't think it could be anything too dire, or he would have marched us up to his office right then. He probably just wanted to hear about the climb from Manjampatti to Kookal which had never been done before. Anyway, there was no use worrying about it. We arrived back at campus and went straight to the dorm. The day, the meal and the idea of our own lumpy beds overcame us. By lights out at ten we were all sound asleep.

Mr. Root Raises a Question   The next day at breakfast and between classes, more and more details of our hike were elicited by other students and staff who knew either or both Manjampatti and Kookal, and who were vying for top point status over the hiking season. My jury-rigged toilet seat was given good reviews. The black turd in Mannavanur grew into a pile and created a stir. Dave's struggles with elephant grass were reenacted, with Bibbi demonstrating how Dave cut at the grass with his stick. My collapse on the trail got me some unwelcome sympathy from the girls. Dave's cooking skills made it into the top ten. Bibbi's pace-setting and his schedule imposition were laughed at. My scramble up the flooded embankment was exaggerated to epic proportions. Linwood's soaked Bible earned a mention.

In subsequent renditions, the toilet got better, the turd got bigger and blacker, my collapse became epic, Dave's cooking rivaled the meals at Hotel State, Bibbi was made out to be a slave driver, and the embankment grew taller and wetter. Fortunately for me, there was no discussion of my pack being lightened, or even that Dave and Bibbi had carried it up to the caves for me after my collapse on the trail. As far as anyone knew, I had carried my weight the whole way and contributed to the success of the hike.

After our last class of the day, Linwood, Dave, Bibbi and I made our way to Mr. Root's office. As well as being the head of the hiking committee, Mr. Root was also in charge of discipline for the school, so the fact that we had been summoned generated a good bit of curiosity among our fellow students. They asked if we had done anything that we could be sanctioned for, but we couldn't think of anything.

We knocked on Mr. Root's office door and he called us in. He had brought in a couple of extra folding chairs and told us to sit. When we were seated, he fixed us with his Navy Commander stare, looking at each of us in turn. I was totally intimidated, and so too, it seemed, were Linwood and Dave. Bibbi seemed impervious and was smiling happily at him. They had had several meetings while Bibbi was planning for the hike, so he was used to 'the Treatment'. The last time I had been in Mr. Root's office was for cheating on a biology test, and I was still smarting from the dressing down I had taken nearly two years before. Linwood and Dave had had no occasion to be disciplined, but were cowed anyway.

In his gruff way, Mr. Root began to question us about the hike. He wanted to know if we had hitched a ride on any part of the trip. He was interested in the shortcuts we took. He asked Bibbi to show him our route on the topo map. He studied the path we took out of Manjampatti and asked why we hadn't taken the longer, less steep route to Kookal. He delved in to how we had handled my collapse on the trail and what symptoms I had had. He got into our schedule for each day; what time we had started out, where and for how long we had stopped, and what time we had reached our destination. He penciled our route onto a topo map.

When he was finished questioning us he told us that he was going to discuss our hike with the hiking committee and they would decide how many points we had earned. Each destination, Manjampatti and Kookal, was considered a "D" hike. The round trip to Manjampatti was worth twenty-four points, and the round trip to Kookal Caves was worth eighteen points. We were expecting to be awarded a total of forty-two points. Mr. Root explained that we had only gone one-way from Kodai to Manjampatti and one-way from Kookal Caves to Kodai. Therefore we would only earn half the points for each of those hikes. The committee was going to determine how many points the climb from Manjampatti to Kookal Caves was worth. He would let us know.

We had foolishly been banking on getting full points for both hikes to give us the clear point-lead over the other hiking contenders. It now looked as though we were going to get a lot fewer points. We would be awarded only 21 points for the first and last legs and some yet-to-be-determined number for the climb from Manjampatti up to Kookal. Since we had taken the shorter route, the distance covered had only been about eleven miles. If we had taken the easier route, the distance would have been closer to fifteen or sixteen miles. The rule of thumb, as we understood it, was one point per mile, with additional points given for elevation change and other less-defined factors. Eleven points for the mileage, if they approved it, would give us only 32 points total, and we didn't know how many more points we would get for the climb.

Disappointed, we resigned ourselves to getting only around thirty to thirty-five points. We could probably have gotten as many points by climbing Mount Perumal three times over the three day weekend and eaten most of our meals in the dining room.

"But…" Bibbi reminded us, "…we wouldn't have gotten to swim in that stream."

He was right.

Bibbi Confronts the Committee   During hiking season, the Hiking Committee met on Wednesday evenings while we campus boarding students were enjoying Canteen. The Committee included the Hiking Coordinator along with an ad hoc group of hike leaders, mostly staff members. There they would review which students had signed up for which hikes on the coming weekend, and create a list of packed lunches that would be needed. They reviewed which hikes had been completed by whom on the previous weekend. They awarded and tallied points for hikes completed, and published the point rankings in the Quad on Thursday morning. As a hike leader in the case of our trek to Manjampatti, Bibbi was eligible to attend.

That night, Tuesday, at study hall, Bibbi again brought the topo maps and spent a good hour or so going over every step of the route we had taken. He studied the steepness of the climb we had made out of the valley, calculating the slope and comparing it to the longer, alternative route we could have taken. He also compared the distance from Kodai to Poombari with and without the shortcuts we had taken on the way back. He even factored in the weight of our packs for a three day hike versus what packs would weigh for three one day hikes, such as climbing Mount Perumal three successive times. When I asked him what he was thinking, he told me that he planned to attend the Hiking Committee meeting and argue our case for more points.

Bibbi was one of the most popular boys on campus and heartily enjoyed Canteen night. So to give up going to Canteen his first Wednesday back to attend the Hiking Committee meeting was a big sacrifice. His decision to attend the meeting told me how seriously he wanted to win the bragging rights that came with having the highest point total at the Hiking Season Awards Assembly.

Linwood rarely attended Canteen, and Kris and Lyn were both occupied in their relationships with their girlfriends. I was of two minds about going since Bibbi would not be there. However, on Wednesday evening Narain came by my room after supper to ask if I was going so he could have someone to hang out with, and I agreed to go. Most of the evening, I stood with him and the other 'single' guys on one side of the room. I told stories about the hike, and listened to tales of what had happened around campus during the three day weekend. I did get a couple of dances in, one with Carol and two with Emmy, which were memorable. I tried to get 'last dance' with Chellie, but got beaten to the draw by another kid. I ended up heading back to the dorm to hide my disappointment.

Bibbi was already in our room when I got there. When I opened the door, he put on a sad face, making me believe that the news of our point totals would not be good. I steeled myself for another disappointment.

Bibbi saw my reaction and broke into a big grin. He had been punking me. "We did it!" he crowed.

"For real?" I asked. "How many points did we end up getting?"

"Exactly what we wanted: forty-two points."

He had triumphed at the meeting. The committee had consisted of Mr. Root, Mr. Neufeld, Mr. Sipantzi and Mrs. Hall. Bibbi had been the only student. He had carefully gone over our route with them and explained the decisions we had made and the hardships we had overcome. He explained that the distance on the topo map was misleading since we had to dodge around trees, clumps of elephant grass and other obstacles. He had exaggerated very little, he said. They were impressed by the weights of our packs, especially when he had brought out his pack which he had loaded with weights from Wissy and weighed at the dish to show them what a forty-pound pack actually felt like. He compared that to a pack with just a jacket and a packed lunch that one would take to climb Mount Perumal and return the same day.

In the end, they had awarded us twelve points for the leg down to Manjampatti, nine points for the leg from Kookal to Kodai, which was what Mr. Root had told us to expect. For the climb from Manjampatti to Kookal they awarded twelve points for the mileage, eight points for the altitude change and four points for blazing a new trail. The total came to forty-five points. However, Bibbi had told them about my collapse as a way of emphasizing how grueling the climb had been. They asked him how we had handled the emergency. When he explained that the group had split up, with him and Dave forging ahead and leaving me and Linwood to follow, Mr. Root turned serious. He scolded Bibbi for splitting the group. Since he and Dave had left us, and were not going to get help as the manual stated, we were in violation. Since the violation had only lasted for a three-mile stretch, the committee decided to deduct three points from each of us. The forty-two points left exactly matched the points that would be earned for the two separate hikes; one to Manjampatti and back and one to Kookal Caves and back. No one else had earned that many points over the three-day weekend, putting us solidly in the lead with only one weekend left in hiking season.

Hiking Season Champions The next morning at break we hurried to the Quad to look at the Point-Totals posting. There were a number of other avid hikers crowding around to see where they stood. A hush came over the group as we approached. Apparently they had been talking about us.

We pushed our way past lower classmen and looked at the list. Our names were at the top. We were ten points ahead of the nearest competitor. Ron Koepke and Tim Lutz, who had often had the highest point totals of anyone in our class every year up to now were there, and were very good-natured about it. Ron casually asked us which hike we planned to go on next weekend. Bibbi laughed and said we were thinking of doing the same hike again. We knew that Ron would try to catch up with us if he could, but that since it was a regular two-day weekend, and Sunday was not available for hiking for either Ron or Tim as a Loch End students, they would not be able to catch us. Bibbi and I had signed up for our regular Friday to Saturday assault on Mount Perumal, which would keep us well ahead of him no matter which hike he went on. Dave and Linwood were satisfied that they had qualified for Tahr pins and would be taking the weekend off.

The Perumal hike was anticlimactic in many ways. There was no full moon, so we couldn't repeat our glorious moonlight climb. It rained on us on the way down to Rest-a-bit, and even though we had ponchos and fairly light packs, it was miserable. When we reached the top of the mountain the next morning, a fog bank rolled in and obscured any view we might have had. To top it off, we missed a pancake breakfast and were late back for lunch and had to settle for some cold plates that Jackie and Cruz had saved for us. But we didn't care. We were going to be the top point-getters in our final hiking season.

This was the last of the John-inspired exploits that Bibbi had wanted to accomplish, and he had done it. When he mentioned this to me as we were waiting to be called up to receive our Tahr pins at the Awards Assembly, I thought back over all the other John-inspired exploits that we had shared over my three years at Kodai: skinny dipping in the lake;

"acquiring" orchids from Shembug for our prom dates; a moonlight hike up Mount Perumal; starting our own chapter of the "Blue Flame Club"; and, finally, the one that John hadn't realized, the combining of a hike to Manjampatti with a hike to Kookal Caves. I felt that fortune had really smiled on me the day I had arrived at Kodai and been met by a boy named Bibbi.

For some reason, after the Manjampatti/Kookal hike, my status on campus was enhanced and my self-confidence grew. I was accepted into more groups and conversations. My advice was sought on a variety of topics. Lyn ran for Student Council President, and chose me to manage his campaign, which was successful. My grades seemed to improve as the school work flowed more easily. I felt more self-confident and sure of myself.

Map of India

Map of Adventures

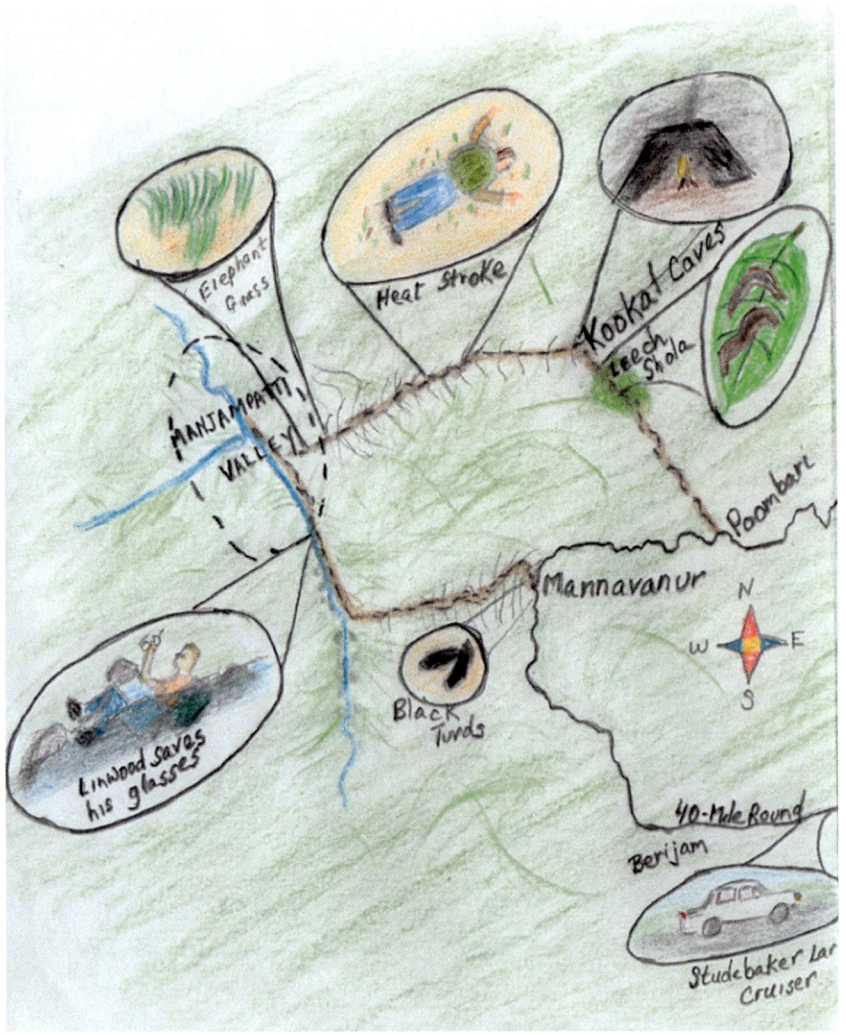

Elephant Grass

Heat Stroke

Kookal Caves

Leech Shola

MANJAMPATTI VALLEY

Poombari

Mannavanur

N
W   E
S

Linwood Saves his glasses

Black Turds

40-Mile Round

Berijam

Studebaker Lar Cruiser

Western Reaches

Map of Adventures

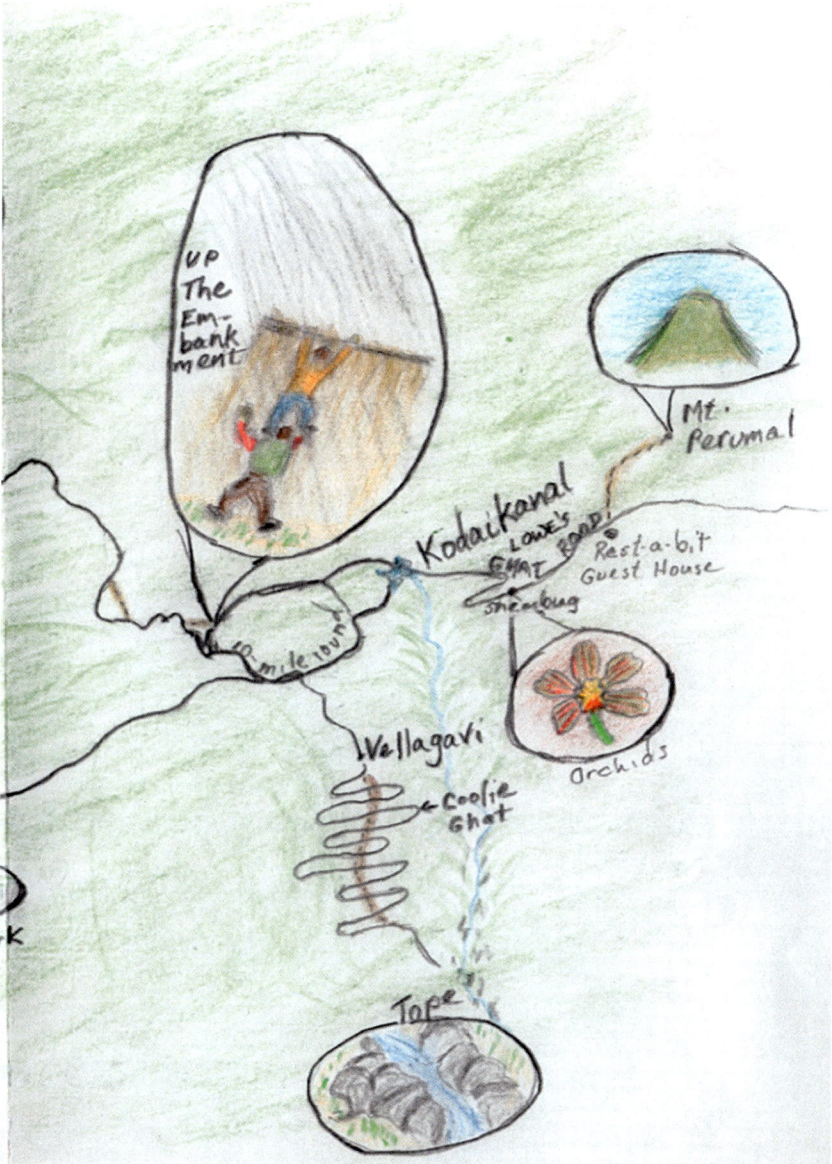

Eastern Reaches

Calcutta Misadventure

A Final Adventure   Our final semester of high school remained and we would soon be going our separate ways. I had experienced these shifts many times, every few years, throughout my life. I had had great friends in every country we stayed in. Jimmy Bowler and Prinnie Anderson in Rangoon; Gene Motley and the Burr boys in Herndon; Jane Kilgore in Jerusalem; Linda Matamoros, Glen Tilton and Tony Hansen in Tegucigalpa, were all dear friends that I rarely, if ever, heard from or about since. However, unlike previous pending departures, I was sure that I would take Kodai and my friends with me. Something had shifted inside me, some combination of coming of age and being among broad-minded, multi-cultural fellows. I felt I had a family that I would take with me.

At the end of our first semester of our senior year, Bibbi and Lyn traveled to Madras with the Kodai Basketball team to take part in the State Championship.   I had invited them to stay with me during the tournament, but Mr. Root, the coach of the team wanted them to stay with the team through the tournament. After that, Kris had invited us to visit him on the Tea Estate his dad managed in Assam during the winter break, and we were planning to travel together after the tournament.

So it was that on the final day of the tournament Krishnan drove me to the one of the Madras University Guest Houses where they had been staying and we picked them up.

There was a crowd of players standing outside the Guest House getting ready to depart with their duffle bags, surrounded by friends, family, fans and vendors. I spotted Bibbi's head above some shorter people gathered around.

"Hey, Bibbi!" I shouted from the front seat, trying to make myself heard over hubbub.

His head jerked in my direction and he saw me. He raised a hand in greeting and walked toward the car.

"How's it hangin', Charlie?" he greeted me, another one of our stock greetings, leaning in to the window.

"About the same as usual," I replied, with the stock answer. "How's yours?" I opened the door and stepped out onto the pavement. "Where's Krause?"

"I think he's still checking out at the front desk… prob'ly arguing with the clerk about his bill," Bibbi remarked.

"Yeah, they prob'ly charged him an extra eight annas on his breakfast tab," I laughed. Lyn was famous for being tight with money.

Just then Lyn came up carrying his duffle bag over his shoulder.

"Yenna, Charred-Lee?" another stock greeting. "Nice ride!"

"Hey, Lyngam," I answered, responding to his use of my off-color nickname with an equally dirty one. "Yeah, this is the old car. You should see the new one!"

Krishnan loaded their bags into the trunk while they said goodbye to their teammates and I said 'hi' to fellow Kodai-ites. Mr. Root came over to make sure that Bibbi and Kris weren't being kidnapped and said hello to Krishnan. Then we got into the car and rode back to my house.

We were planning to spend the next the next five days or so enjoying my parents' hospitality, before heading up the Assam. We spent a day at the beach, and two more at the gymkhana club, and another in the used books section of the central market. We went to the movies to see Cat Ballou with Jane Fonda and all fell in love with her.

Our plans were to travel to Calcutta by train, where we would take a small Jamair plane to Siliguri, in West Bengal, and then a train to Cooch Bihar, about 90 miles from Dhubri, Assam, near Kris' home. This was going to be our last chance to travel around India, to see a part of the country that few foreigners did. We were hoping to take a train up to Darjeeling at some point during our stay with Kris to get a view of Mount Everest from there. The planning we were putting into this adventure was on a par with our planning for the Manjampatti-to-Kookal hike, and I was very hopeful that this adventure would be just as seminal in my life.

There were other reasons I was tremendously excited to be making this trip. With my newfound confidence brimming and my love for all things Kodai at a new high, I was ready to spend a couple of weeks with Bibbi, Lyn and Kris. Best of all, for me, was the hope that I could spend a little of the time with Kris' sister, Emmy. I had developed quite a crush on her over the past semester, and I thought that I had picked up some signals that she would not reject any overture I might make outright, and that she might even welcome it. Of course, I was also very nervous about how things might develop.

So, late in the evening, the Friday before Thanksgiving, we boarded the Howrah Mail at the Madras Central Railway Station heading north up the coast to Calcutta. We had chosen the Howrah Mail because it was the cheapest train to Calcutta, and Lyn wanted to keep his expenses as low as possible. Unlike the Express trains, which stopped at 'only' 20 stations over the thousand mile route, the Howrah Mail stopped at thirty-four stations along the way. Most of the stops were scheduled for one minute, since the purpose was just to pick up and drop off mail bags, not to board passengers, but it still slowed the train down with every pause. There as one 20-minute stop at Visakhapatnam to add cars to the train, and another 15-minute stop at Khurda Road Junction. There were several 5-minute stops where we could pick up passengers and where we could buy tiffin from trackside vendors. The ride to Calcutta would take a little more than a day, arriving in Calcutta at around six o'clock on Sunday morning.

We had reserved seats in an air-conditioned second-class car to Visakhapatnam, where we upgraded to a second-class sleeper car that joined the train for the rest of the journey, and our second night on the train.

Train stations in India are boisterously busy at almost any time of day, and Central Station at Madras was one of the busiest. There are passengers and waiting for trains, others disembarking, all with baggage and possessions of every description. There were baskets and bundles, suitcases and duffle bags, trunks and crates. Many of these were carried upon heads giving the impression of a floating sea of bundles.

There is noise, of course. Train engines thundering, wheels squealing, valves hissing, and people shouting to be heard above the din. There are vendors hawking food and drinks, fruit and snacks. Beggars sat despondently around the sides of the hall with hands extended and well-rehearsed misery on their faces. As a through train arrives, vendors crowd around the windows of the cars shouting out their practiced refrains, offering passengers hot chai, pakoras, and many other delicacies.

Although I was used to them, there were also smells layered in the heavy air. The most intrusive were the diesel fumes from the engines arriving and leaving. But as you passed tea stalls and snack vendors, you could pick up their enticing aromas. Human sweat and filth would make their presence known, especially around the public lavatories, but also near groups or families of indigents who used the public space of the station as housing.

We arrived at the station just after eleven in the evening, and the crowds were still teeming. Krishnan, the driver, had driven us to the station, taking advantage of the trip to give me a driving lesson in our family Studebaker Lark Cruiser, which scared Bibbi and Lyn mightily. He offered to accompany us in to help us with our luggage (large backpacks) and to make sure we boarded the right train. I thanked him, but insisted that we could find our way, since both Bibbi and Lyn had boarded trains at Madras Central Station many times before and knew their way.

On trips to Kodai we had always taken the train from Egmore station, which was smaller and had fewer tracks. This time we would be traveling on a "meter-gauge" line pulled by a diesel engine. Egmore trains were narrow-gauge pulled by steam locomotives that burned coal. Meter-gauge trains with their diesel engines are wider than their narrow-gauge cousins, and can travel at higher speeds.

Rajahmundry Stop

Traveling to Kodai was a three-hundred-mile journey with coal smoke blowing back through the open windows of the cars, which were not air conditioned. One would arrive at Kodai Road Station with coal grit in one's hair, around one's neck and in one's teeth. The trip to

Calcutta would be over three times as far, a little more than one thousand miles. However, the car we would be traveling in would be air-conditioned.

The train had a 5-minute stop scheduled in Rajahmundry at around nine a.m. the following morning. We had purchased snacks along the way, but were starving by then. Lyn was still sleeping in his seat, so Bibbi and I got ready to find our breakfasts. Since he knew the food vendors in the station, Bibbi's parents had arranged for a full breakfast to be ready for us to pick up. He hopped off as soon as the train had slowed to a walking speed and ran off into the crowd.

While Bibbi headed off to collect our breakfasts, I flagged a chai-wallah and bought three cups of chai to take away, which cost a bit more, since it included the price of the paper cups.

As I paid the vendor, I kept scanning the crowd, wondering what I would do if our breakfasts didn't make it for some reason or if the train left before Bibbi returned. Lyn and I would have to get by without food for another 4 hours until the next passenger stop. I was greatly relieved when I saw Bibbi pushing his way back through the crowd of vendors hawking their goods outside the car with a large carry-out bag in his hand.

Train Ride   Except for his height and coloring, Bibbi could be taken for any random Indian traveler, and I almost missed him. He was wearing a brightly colored lungi shortened to his knees, with a plain grey t-shirt and chappals on his feet. He was looking along the cars to see which one was ours. I leaned out of my window and waved, calling his name.

"I'm starving!" I said. "What did you bring us?"

"We have masala dosai with all the fixings," he replied. "I ordered extra-large portions and extra chutneys. We also have bananas for later, and hard-boiled eggs."

"Excellent!" I exclaimed. "I was afraid you were going to bring peanut butter jelly sandwiches from home. We've only had a snack since supper last night."

He laughed. "I was going to buy some kind of sandwiches, but they already had the dosai ready, and it really smelled great," he said. For once I was glad of his voraciousness. Sandwiches would have sucked.

Lyn was finally waking up as the train began to pull away from the station. Bibbi pulled large twine-tied banana-leaf bundles out of the take-away bag and handed one to each of us. He pulled out another one for himself, and a smaller bundle with coconut chutney. We carefully untied and spread the meals bundles on our laps, exposing the fragrant contents, and began to eat as the train pulled out of the station.

A number of our fellow passengers in the car turned to stare at us, but since we were in a second-class car, there were no beggars around, so, enduring the stares, we ate our meals in relative peace. Perhaps they were just curious to see obvious Westerners eating with their fingers.

As usual, Bibbi was done with his before I was half finished with mine, and got up to dispose of his banana leaves and wash his hands in the lavatory at the end of the car. Lyn followed right after him. After a few more minutes, when I was done and sated, I copied their actions. We drank our tea, and settled in for the long haul to come.

We talked about our exploits over the three years that I had been at Kodai, regretting that we would soon be leaving to go to colleges as yet unknown. Bibbi was hoping to attend Lehigh University, in the Pennsylvania steel town of Bethlehem. He had also applied to Harvard on a lark. He felt that he had done pretty well on his SAT, and he was carrying a high grade-point average. Lyn was set on attending Tabor College, a Mennonite school in Hillsboro, Kansas. I was much less secure about where I would be able to attend college. My grade-point average was less than a 3.0, which was the cutoff for many of the more prestigious schools.

We had sent out preliminary applications to a number of schools, but weren't expecting replies until later in the following semester when the colleges had received the results of our SAT's. I had sent preliminary applications to Antioch and Cornell, but wasn't optimistic about either of them. I had also sent preliminary applications to University of Arizona and University of Hawaii, which were more appropriate to my academic status. However it turned out, we were going to be far away from each other.

Talk turned to our current journey. We would be arriving in Calcutta the next day, Sunday, at around six o'clock in the morning. We would walk from Howrah Junction Railway station to the Salvation Army Guest House about two or three miles across the Hooghly River. We were hoping to get to the Guest House in time for breakfast, which Lyn, who had stayed there before, said was pretty good.

On Monday we would go to the Indian Government Tourist office to apply for our permits to enter Assam. The Indian Government had declared that Assam and surrounding territories required foreigners to secure a Protected Area Permit (PAP) to enter these restricted areas due to political unrest. With these in hand, we could book our flight to Siliguri on Jamair for Wednesday morning.

"Hah!" I barked. "You guys need those permits, but I won't. I have a diplomatic passport. I could walk across the border between Israel and Jordan when we were in Jerusalem. All I had to do was show them my black passport and they waved me right through. And that was going between enemy countries, not just between provinces like this. The soldiers on the Israeli side would have me in their gunsights until I crossed the line, and then the Jordanian soldiers would point theirs at me until I entered the guard station. I'm sure I won't need a permit, but I'll go with you guys when you get yours."

"That's cool!" said Bibbi. "Let me see it."

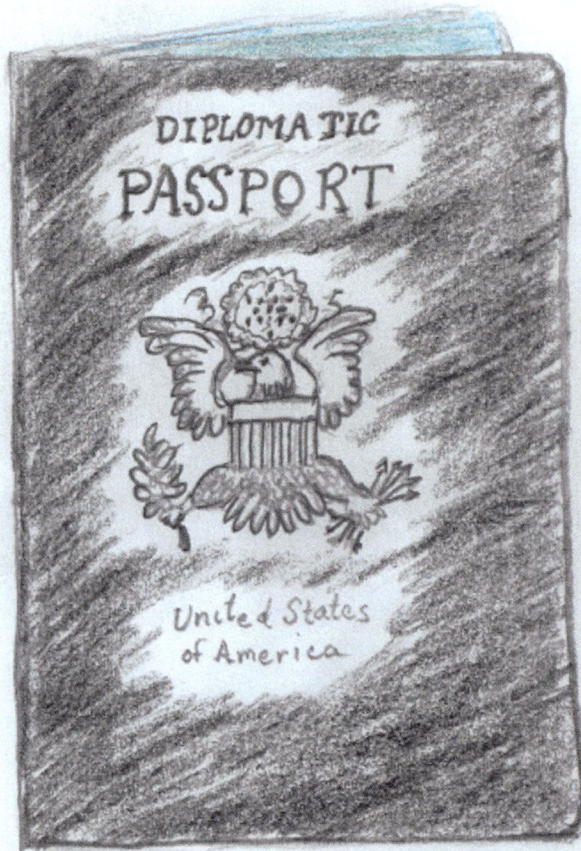

Diplomatic Passport

I dug my passport out and showed it to him. He was suitably impressed. He thumbed through it looking at all the stamps from my last year's trip through Europe with my dad and Johnny.

"Wow, look at all the places you've been!" he marveled. "We stopped in Europe on the way to the States when I was little, but I don't remember it much. Maybe we can travel through Europe on our way back to the States in June."

"That would be awesome! We should start planning something." I replied.

"Well, let me see this magic ticket. I've never seen one before." Lyn held out his hand expectantly, so Bibbi handed it over to him.

He remarked how cool it was, and like Bibbi, thumbed through the stamped pages that showed all my entrances and exits over the past eight years: our exit from Israel, our travels to the U.S. and Honduras with a home leave, and my travel to India and then through Europe the year before.

"Wow!" he marveled. "You've really been around!" He handed me back the passport. Bibbi returned to the idea of traveling back to the States together.

"We can go through some maps in the library when we get back to school," he said. "You've probably got some good ideas."

"Kris and I have already made some plans," said Lyn. "I think we're going to spend some time with his uncle in Denmark, but maybe we can meet up after that."

We settled back in our seats and let our full stomachs and the gentle swaying of the train lull us as the day outside brightened into full heat. Unlike the open cars of the narrow-gauge train to Kodai, we couldn't hang out in the entryway and watch the scenery flow, and the tinting on the windows making peering out a chore. In some ways, Bibbi would have preferred to ride in a third-class car with no air-conditioning. He always liked to stand in the open doorways, feeling the wind and watching the countryside slide by. We all did.

The previous winter break one of our schoolmates, Jerry Pofahl, had been killed when the train he was hanging out of went over a narrow bridge and he was hit by a pylon. It was a cautionary tale, but young boys rarely heed them.

After about three hours, the train slowed and stopped in Visakhapatnam, where it picked up the sleeper cars. We moved our gear to our new accommodations and purchased three curry meals from a trackside vendor.

We had three narrow plastic-covered bunks in an open carriage with about twenty other male passengers. I got dibs on a lower bunk, and Bibbi took the one above me. Lyn took a third bunk leaving one empty above him. We were hoping that the fourth bunk would remain empty, but soon enough we got a compartment-mate. There were partitions separating us and our compartment-mate from other passengers. We could draw a curtain to block some of the passageway light from our space, but no doors. There were six compartments in the car, and they all appeared to be full. There was a lavatory with a western toilet at one end of the car for all twenty-four of us to share.

We sat on my bunk, eating our curries and chatting for a while. We followed the curries with the bananas Bibbi had brought. Our companion was Bengali with limited command of English. We smiled a lot with him and wagged our heads, but not much information was exchanged.

"Well, guys," said Bibbi, "it's seven hours till our next meal stop according to the schedule. I hope we can make it!"

He was only half kidding. Seven hours was a long time to wait for our supper.

"I think you still have those hard-boiled eggs, Bibbi," I reminded him, "and we can pick up snacks at the 4:30 passenger stop I saw on the schedule."

"I've got some I.J. (Indian Junk = Spicy bits and crackers) I can share in my backpack," volunteered Lyn.

The afternoon rolled past with the countryside. At the 4:30 stop in Palasa we purchased 3 chai's and some fried pakoras to hold us over until the 8 o'clock stop in Khurda Road Junction, where the train would stop for fifteen minutes. There we picked up mutton biriyani from a vendor with a large steel bowl that he carried on his head, and more chai from another vendor pulling a brass urn on wheels.

After we had eaten, Bibbi said, "I think I'll go to the bathroom and brush my teeth. We should try to get some sleep."

"Good idea," I agreed. "I'll go right after you're back."

Bibbi pulled his toothbrush out of a side pocket of his backpack and headed off down the aisle. I rummaged around in mine till I found where it had sunk to, and waited for his return. Lyn had already stretched out on his bunk, seemingly ready for the night. Our compartment-mate seemed to be of similar mind, and began to spread out his bedding on his bunk above Lyn's.

Bibbi returned and I headed off with my toothbrush and toothpaste, to find that someone had beat me to the bathroom. I waited patiently in the passageway, keeping myself steady with one hand on the rail along the wall. After a few minutes a large man with a Sikh turban and beard exited the lavatory. He was apparently not feeling well, and was sweating despite the air-conditioning. Further evidence of his discomfort wafted out of the lavatory door with him, and almost made me gag. I considered letting someone else go ahead of me, as there were now two people waiting behind me, but decided that either one of them could foul the bathroom up just as badly, so I might as well brave it myself.

I hurriedly peed and brushed my teeth, breathing as shallowly as I could and headed back to my compartment, hoping that the next person in line would not ascribe the smell in the lavatory to me. I heard him cough as he entered.

Back in the compartment, Bibbi had already settled himself into the top bunk, and I realized the wisdom of his choice of clothing for the trip. His lungi was now wrapped around him like a sheet.

"That's so cool!" I commented. "I'm just gonna sleep in my clothes, I guess."

"What took you so long in the bathroom?" Bibbi asked.

He laughed when I told him the tale of the Sikh passenger. "I'm glad I went when I did. I think the bathroom had just been cleaned."

Bibbi always had good luck.

We settled in a little after ten o'clock, and the swaying of the train and clacking of the rails put us right to sleep. From time to time, I was distantly aware that we were stopping in stations. Lights would come on outside our compartment and voices would raise and lower, but the window above my head showed me it was still night time, so I would wait for a few minutes until the train started up again, and fall back to sleep.

Sometime before sunrise we pulled into a large station. I sat up and looked out of the window, which was away from the station. There was a sign that read "SANTRAGACHI", which meant that we were about an hour from Howrah Junction in Calcutta. There were lively sounds coming from the other side of the car, so I rose and went to check it out.

Bibbi's bunk was empty, and I found him outside the car on the platform negotiating with a chai vendor. The vendor poured a long stream of steaming liquid into a plastic cup from his large brass urn and handed it to Bibbi. I ordered another cup for myself and joined him. We stood quietly on the platform gently slurping our chai. It was very hot and very sweet. "Just how I like my women," joked Bibbi, trotting out another of our tired jokes.

The whistle blew a shrill blast announcing the proximate departure of our train, so we downed the rest of our chai and clambered back on board. We would be in Calcutta in about an hour according to the schedule Bibbi produced. There were no more stops before Howrah Junction in the center of Calcutta.

Lyn rolled over and looked at us with bleary eyes.

"What's going on?" he asked.

"We'll be there in about forty-five minutes," said Bibbi, looking at his watch. "You missed out on the chai Charlie and I just got at the last station, but I still have these hard-boiled eggs."

We were now some twenty or twenty-five miles from our destination, and the train would be traveling more slowly, passing through densely populated areas. We sat on my bunk and chatted, eating our hard boiled eggs and peering out the window, willing the train to get to the station quickly.

A Walk in Calcutta   Howrah Junction Station was even more crowded and noisy than Madras. We shouldered our backpacks and pushed our way through the crush on the platform and into the main hall. There were signs everywhere, mostly in Bengali, but enough in English to help us find our way out. We stopped at a shop next to the tourist police kiosk and purchased a map of Calcutta. Bibbi loved maps, and was soon absorbed in finding us on it and tracing a route to the Salvation Army Guest House. We crouched down next to a large column while he scanned the map.

As Bibbi studied the map, Lyn and I gazed at the milling crowds around the station hall. There were all castes, from "untouchable" Dalit to Brahmin, picking their ways through the throngs. There were beggars and sadhus, vendors and tourists, families and school groups. The primary colors were white and khaki, among the men and bright reds and golds among the women. There were pigeons flying in the rafters and swooping down on any errant scraps that happened to spill. Early morning light coming through high windows filtered through dust and smoke.

"The Salvation Army Red Shield Guest House is over here on Sudder Street." Bibbi interrupted my reverie. He poked his finger at the map. "And here's where we are." His finger poked again. "It looks pretty close. I think we could walk it, and it would help us get to see some of the city. We've got to cross the Hooghly River, either here [poke] or here [poke]."

"How far do you think it is?" I asked.

"Looks to me like less than three miles… a little more than two miles, I think. I don't know how long the blocks are and the map doesn't seem to have a scale. It's just seven o'clock, which gives us plenty of time to get there before breakfast and wash up a bit."

"You aren't thinking of walking at four miles an hour, are you?" I asked, warily.

Lyn chuckled, knowing Bibbi's love of stepping up the pace. "Only four miles per hour?"

Bibbi laughed. "No way! We'll take it nice and slow so we can see the sights."

"What sights?" I asked.

"I don't know. We'll just have to keep our eyes open," was the reply.

In 1965, Calcutta was a filthy city, and I hear it still is today. The air was sooty and, although there were reportedly gangs of cleaners who swept the city and gathered the trash every night, by six a.m. the streets were already getting quite littered. It was also crowded. As we left the railway station, we found ourselves in streets teeming with bicycles, pedestrians, taxis, carts and cars. We had to dodge our way along the sidewalk on our way down to the river.

We climbed up the stairs to the pedestrian walkway running beside the traffic lanes that crossed the river. The view across the river was impressive, even through the early morning haze. The Hooghly River was about a thousand yards wide, and the bridge afforded a spectacular view along the river and to the banks on either side. The view from the bridge was the high point of the walk.

We walked along for nearly an hour, with Bibbi consulting the map from time to time to make sure of the turns we were making. We consulted other pedestrians from time to time, with mostly blank stares as a result. At some point we passed a storefront that announced itself to be the Regional Passport Office, and Bibbi speculated that that was where we would need to go to get our permits to enter Assam.

Guest House I was happily surprised when Bibbi exclaimed, "There it is!" pointing to the Salvation Army shield hanging in an archway we were passing. It was nearly eight a.m. when we checked in and were given keys to our room.

"You are in time for breakfast if you hurry," said the clerk as he handed us the keys. "Did you walk over from the station?"

"Yes, we did," Bibbi replied.

"Oh, that's quite far. You must be quite tired" said the clerk, solicitously.

"Nah, it was a piece of cake." I said. "If we could hike out of Manjampatti, this was like a walk in the park... a very dirty park, mind you."

The clerk gave me a blank stare.

"Let's wash up a little so we can come down and have breakfast." Bibbi was always practical.

We would have liked an Indian breakfast, but the Guest House offered tea, toast and scrambled eggs. As Lyn had promised, it was pretty good anyway. There were also some fresh fruits, bananas, melons and mangos, so we were able to satisfy our hunger.

After breakfast we decided that we were tired from our travels and should take a nap before lunch. We all had showers first, and we were soon all racked out in our underwear with curtains drawn and the fan in the ceiling whirring away at its highest setting.

We rose from our nap around noon, and lazed around our room as the day's heat intensified. The air outside was stagnant and gritty, so we left the shades down, hoping to keep most of it outside. I decided that I needed another shower before heading out in search of lunch, so I grabbed a clean t-shirt, underwear, and a pair of shorts from my backpack and headed to the bathroom. The neck of the t-shirt I had worn on the train was black with soot, and there was still soot in my ears and nose as well, despite my earlier shower. I realized that I would have to do some laundry sooner than I had expected, as I had only brought three changes of underwear with me.

After my cool shower, Bibbi decided that he, too, would have one, so Lyn and I sat on our beds chatting while he took care of himself.

Bibbi came out of the bathroom in his towel, and was soon dressed and ready to go. Lyn decided he didn't need another shower, so we began to think about where we would have lunch. Neither Bibbi nor I wanted to eat in the dining room downstairs again, although Lyn pointed out that it was included in with our fare plan. Bibbi mentioned that he had seen a restaurant with a sign in Telegu, Hindi and Bengali when we walked from the train station. It had looked to be fairly inexpensive, which was one of the qualities we were looking for, and advertised South Indian meals. That struck a chord with us.

We asked the attendant in the front lobby if he knew any good South Indian eateries, and Bibbi described the one he was thinking about. The attendant wagged his head at us and gave us a gold-toothed smile. He knew the place, and said that the food was good. He pointed us in the right direction out the door and we headed off. We walked out into the noonday heat.

The restaurant was a hole in the wall with a limited number of seats, most of which were taken. We took it was a good sign that almost all the customers were locals. A waiter showed us to a rickety card table with hand-made stools in a back corner. The flow from the overhead fan was barely discernable back there, but the interior was not yet too warm. The menu was all vegetarian, so I ordered masala dosai, and Lyn copied me. Bibbi ordered a 'thali meals' with extra chapattis. We all had chai.

We discussed our plans for the following day. After breakfast we would go to the Government Tourist Office to apply for our travel permits to enter Assam. They would be ready the following day. Once we had those, we could purchase our airline tickets at the Thomas Cook office, as well as train tickets from Siliguri to Cooch Behar. Thomas Cook's would send Kris a telegram letting him know when we were arriving in Cooch Behar, where he and his dad would meet us to take us back to the Tea Estate.

We spent part of the afternoon at the Indian Museum which was very near to our Guest House, and which let us in for free as students. There were impressive displays of Hindu artifacts and a section that included prehistoric fossils and skeletons. Later we went back to our room for another shower and another nap before heading out for supper.

Diplomatic Passport The following morning we headed out to the Tourist Office shortly after nine o'clock in the morning. It was an easy walk from the guest house down past the Indian Museum and Fort William. Fort William, now the headquarters of the Eastern Command of the Indian Army, was built during the British Raj, and sits in the largest urban green space in the world with parade grounds, cricket fields, football (soccer) stadiums and a race course. Fort William was the site of the 'Black Hole of Calcutta', a small cell about the size of a two-car garage, with limited ventilation, where 146 British prisoners that included two women and several wounded men had been imprisoned during a sweltering June night in 1756 by the conquering Bengal army. In the suffocating heat and the crush to get near to the small window for air, or the small bucket of water left by the guards for a sip, many were trampled and died. In the morning, only twenty-three of the one hundred and forty-six were still alive. I had read about this tragedy in G.A. Henty's book, <u>With Clive in India</u> a couple of years before.

We passed the surrounding park, found the Government Tourist Office and went inside. There were a number of desks around the room with signs describing the function of the person behind it. We went to the one that advertised 'Travel Permits'. There was one customer ahead of us at the desk, so we waited while he finished his business. When he had departed, the official made some notes in his log, and then gave us a wave to call us forward.

Lyn explained that we wanted to travel to Assam to visit our school chum who lived there with his parents. The official wagged his head in understanding.

"You will please show me your passports for this travel," he said. "For this journey you must have passports. What country are you from?"

We all pulled out our passports. "We're from the United States," said Lyn, who had appointed himself our spokesman, and rightfully so, since he had made the trip several times before. He handed the official our passports, two teal green ones and one black one.

Starting with the teal green ones, he thumbed through them and pulled out a form from his desk which he tucked into the cover of the passport. When he got to my black one, he thumbed through it two, and then three times.

"Whose passport is this?" he asked.

"It's mine." I stated. "My father is the American Consul General in Madras."

"Oh, very good," he replied. "So he can give you the clearance from the U.S. to travel to the Protected Area. You must have that in order to secure a permit."

"But it's a diplomatic passport!" I exclaimed. "I should be able to travel freely wherever I need to with this." I felt my face turning red with embarrassment after all my bragging.

"Oh, yes, sir," he agreed. "However your government and mine do not want any 'diplomatic incidents', which would happen if a diplomat or the son of a diplomat, especially such an important one, were to be harmed while traveling in an area where unrest is common. You will just please go to the American Consulate and get the clearance, and then you can come back here to get your permit. Meanwhile, you other boys can fill out the form I have given you and we'll take care of you. Your passes will be ready first thing in the morning tomorrow"

Bibbi and Lyn filled out their forms and handed them to the official who handed them each a receipt. "With these chits you can make your travel reservations," he said.

Lyn was laughing. "Good thing you have a diplomatic passport, Charlie," he joked. "It'll get you into anywhere."

Bibbi was much more sympathetic. "Don't worry, Charlie. We still have the rest of the day and tomorrow to straighten this out. If you want I can go with you to the Consulate."

As it turned out, the U.S. Consulate was only a couple of blocks away from the Indian Government Tourist Office. By the time Bibbi and Lyn had filled out their forms and gotten their permits, it was about ten thirty in the morning, and we all three walked over.

The American Consulate The American Consulate General in Calcutta is one of the oldest American Consulate General Offices in the world. As we entered, we read a plaque that told us that the first American Consul to India, Benjamin Joy, was appointed by George Washington in 1792, and that the consulate had been operating continuously from this spot since he arrived in India in 1794. A marine guard stood at the gate and asked to see our passports and directed us to the consular section for visas.

There were a lot of people, mostly Indians, waiting in the consular visa section. I went over to the reception desk and explained to a clerk in western attire what I was there for. He wagged his head and clicked his tongue.

"Yes, sar," he said. "You will need to speak with the consul. There has been a recent travel advisory to diplomatic personnel about travel to Assam. Unfortunately, he is currently out of the building until later this afternoon. So could you please return after two o'clock?"

"Isn't there anyone else I could speak to now to clear this up?" I asked. "We are on our way to Thomas Cook's to purchase our tickets for the trip."

"I'm so sorry, sar," he replied. "The situation is quite delicate, and the consul has instructed that he should be advised directly of any diplomatic persons traveling to the area."

"Okay, I'll come back," I said. "In the meantime, we'll go ahead and book our travel."

"Well, sar," he said, "I wouldn't do that until you have spoken to the consul. One doesn't know what he might say, and I wouldn't want you to lose your fare in case you were not able to travel. Isn't it? Also, I am thinking that Cook's will not sell you a ticket without the permit."

"What about my friends?" I asked.

"They have no problem, as they already have permission and their permits from the Tourist Office will be available by tomorrow," he explained, unnecessarily. "So long as they have the chits from the Government Tourist Office, Cooks agency will sell them their tickets and they can travel." He wagged his head affirmatively to emphasize his point.

Lyn was cracking up so hard that tears were coming out of his eyes, and Bibbi was suppressing a grin and trying to look sympathetic. I was feeling totally humiliated. My vaunted diplomatic passport was proving to be a real problem. I was wishing that I had never said anything about it.

"Okay, guys," I said. "I guess I'll have to come back this afternoon. Let's go over to Cook's and get your tickets. And thank you, sir, for your help. I'll see you this afternoon."

The walk to Cook's Travel Agency was short, but very painful. Lyn cracked jokes about the advantages of having a diplomatic passport with all its privileges, and Bibbi couldn't help laughing at all of them. I tried to laugh along with them, but my efforts were obviously half-hearted.

"Come on, guys," I said after the fourth or fifth crack. "Give it a rest. I just hope I can get my permit and tickets this afternoon."

"I'm sure it'll be alright, Charlie," said Bibbi. "I'll come back with you, if you want. I'm glad everything is so close together. It makes it easy to walk around."

Thomas Cook Travel Agency   The Thomas Cook Agency on Lord Sinha Road was an opulent, well-appointed space with air-conditioning and marble countertops and floors. There were several employees standing behind the counter and one or two more in open offices to the side of the room. Bibbi unerringly led us to a beautiful young lady in a teal green sari with blue trim standing behind one of the counters.

She smiled encouragingly. "How may I help you?"

"We need to fly to Siliguri tomorrow and connect to a train to Cooch Behar," said Bibbi.

"Yes, sir, I can help you with that. Will it be one-way or round trip?"

"One-way," said Bibbi. "We aren't sure exactly when we will be returning."

"Oh, no problem, sir," she responded. "You can purchase an open return and use it any time. Or you can purchase one way now and one way after, but two one-way tickets are a little dearer than one round-trip."

"What would the difference be?" asked Lyn

"Sure, I can figure that for you," she said. "So will that be three passengers?" she asked, smiling at each of us in turn. "Please give me your passports and travel permits."

"No, only two for right now," said Bibbi, indicating himself and Lyn. "He," he pointed at me, "will come back this afternoon or tomorrow morning to purchase his tickets, but please reserve him a seat and have us seated together." He and Lyn handed her their passports.

"I'm sure I can do that for you. Please give me a moment."

She turned to her fare charts and worked out the fares for the one-way and round-trip options. The difference was not insubstantial, and Lyn could never resist finding a less expensive way to travel, so they went with the round-trip fare. She scheduled them for a flight on Jamair at 10:30, which she said was the first flight of the day. They would land in Bagdogra International Airport in Siliguri at 12 noon, and their train would depart from Jalpaiguri Junction, about ten miles away, at 1:25, which should be no problem unless their flight was seriously delayed. There were taxis at the airport that would get them to the station in about twenty minutes. She assured us that she could get me a seat next to them when I returned in the afternoon, as she had already reserved one on a temporary hold.

We walked back to the guest house, debating whether we should eat lunch there, since it was included with our room, or eat more appealing food at a restaurant. I was for eating at a restaurant, but this time we deferred to Lyn, who, as usual, didn't see any use in spending money if we didn't absolutely have to. The meal, when we got it, was fairly decent, consisting of a breaded cutlet of some kind with mashed potatoes and canned peas. The desert was canned peaches.

We went up to our room to relax for a little while. None of us felt like heading out into the heat. Lyn went back to making jokes about my diplomatic passport, but I ignored him, and Bibbi gave him a look that said "Lay off."

At about half past one, Bibbi and I set off for the consulate. Lyn had decided to hang out in the hostel, and maybe go for a walk back down to the Indian Museum for a look around. He said he would also send Kris a telegram letting him know when we expected to reach Cooch Behar since in the midst of setting up Bibbi and Lyn's travel plans, we had neglected to ask the lady at Cook's to do it.

So, Bibbi and I set off heading south down busy streets, past markets and restaurants. We were in a hotel district, but there were very few western foreigners in the crowds.

At the Consulate… Again   We arrived at the Consulate a little before two, but I wanted to get there as soon as possible so that we could get to the Government Tourist Office and then the Cook Agency to purchase my tickets.

The clerk at the desk recognized me when we approached him. "Oh, hello, sar," he greeted me. "I haven't seen the consul yet, but he should be along shortly. I will put a chit on his desk to let him know that there is someone here to see him. Please have a seat over there." He pointed to a seating area where there were several others waiting for their turns.

Bibbi and I went to the area indicated and sat on two plush chairs that were available. I took the one that allowed me to see the clerk so that I could jump up as soon as he called us. There were a number of pamphlets around on a nearby table, and I picked one up to look at while I waited.

The clerk waved at me about twenty minutes later, and I hopped up and walked hopefully over to his desk.

He smiled sadly at me. "I'm sorry, sar, but Consul has been delayed. He is hoping to be here in about half hour. Can you please wait?"

One thing I had learned in dealing with officials in various countries: there was no use in getting impatient or upset, and absolutely no percentage in trying to bully or intimidate them. So I smiled reassuringly, and agreed that I would wait, thank you. I went back to my seat and gave Bibbi the update. He sighed. He knew the drill as well as I did.

It wasn't until after three that the clerk waved me over again and told me that the consul would see me now. Bibbi stood up to join me, but the clerk said that only 'the interested party' could enter the inner sanctum. He called an attendant over and told him that I was here to see Mr. Lewis regarding a travel permit. I followed the new attendant past a rope chain into a suite of offices. The attendant led me to an open door and rapped respectfully on the door jamb.

Mr. Lewis was a trim man with a well-groomed mustache and a slightly receding hairline. He looked up from his desk and beckoned me in to his office. "Good afternoon," he said, "sorry to keep you waiting, but I was at a meeting that ran long. How can I be of service today?"

"Hi," I said. "I'm trying to get a permit to travel up to Assam with my school buddies, but since I have a diplomatic passport, it seems I need to get permission from you first in order to get a travel permit."

"Here," he reached out his hand, "let me see your passport."

I gave it to him and he looked through it briefly.

"Are you related to Albert Franklin in Madras?" he asked.

"Yes. He's my dad." I replied.

"Does he know you are planning to go to Assam?" he asked.

"Yes, of course. I told him I was going to visit my school roommate at the tea estate his dad manages in Assam. He bought me my train ticket here and gave me money to buy my tickets the rest of the way," I explained.

"I see. Well, it's a little complicated up there right now. Your father might have known. There was a riot and some work stoppage in the last few days, and there have been some border squabbles with the Chinese, so the situation is dicey. If you were the kid of a less prominent American officer, we might be able to grant you permission right away, but since you are the son of the Consul General, we can't just let you go up there. We'll need to get special dispensation from the Embassy in New Delhi, and they will probably need to contact your father. You understand, of course. I'll send a telex to the Embassy right away this afternoon, but these permits usually take several days." He smiled encouragingly at me.

"Should I wait here for a reply?" I asked. "My buddies have already purchased their tickets and the girl at Cook's is saving me a seat near them. I need to get this clearance from you to get my travel permit from the Tourist Office so that I can buy my tickets."

"I will mark my telex to the Embassy as 'urgent', but they will probably not act on it today. They will likely contact your father tomorrow morning." He sounded dubious. "You'll have to wait until morning. We open at eight, but I wouldn't expect a reply until tomorrow afternoon at the earliest. The following day, Wednesday, is the day before Thanksgiving, and we will only be open until noon." He handed me back my passport.

I walked despondently back out to the lobby. Bibbi saw me coming and knew that my news was not good.

"What's the story, Charlie?" he asked.

"They need to telex the Embassy, which will probably telex my dad to get his permission before they can give me the clearance I need. The Embassy prob'ly won't send a telex to my dad until tomorrow, but just possibly today… If they don't hear from him by five, I'll have to wait until tomorrow morning when they open at eight. Hopefully, my dad will get the telex right away and answer within the next hour so we can go get my travel permit," I explained.

"Well, I think we should go find a tea stall and have a cup of chai and some snacks. That way we won't be just sitting around here all afternoon," he said.

"Good idea," I replied, "my treat."

There was a tea stall around the corner and down the block from the Consulate where we could sit at a small table. We ordered chai and Bibbi ordered a serving of pakoras. I wasn't in the mood to eat anything.

"What should I do if I don't get the clearance?" I wondered aloud.

"Oh, don't worry!" said Bibbi. "I'm sure your dad will come through for you."

Just before five p.m. we swung back by the Consulate to check if there was any word yet. The clerk made a short call, and shook his head. No word yet.

Glum Dinner Back at the Guest House, we caught Lyn up on the situation and discussed how to proceed from here. Calcutta's Chandra Bose Airport was about a half hour taxi drive, and Bibbi and Lyn planned to get there by half past nine for their ten-thirty flight. That would give me an hour to retrieve any clearance that had come in overnight from the Consulate when it opened at eight, run to the Government Tourist office for my permit, back to Thomas Cook's for my tickets and back to the Guest House. It was going to be quite a scramble, all based on the assumption that my clearance would come through from Delhi and Madras during the night and be waiting for me when I got to the Consulate.

We went back to our South Indian restaurant for supper still discussing the problems and coming up with contingencies.

"In case you don't make it onto the ten-thirty flight, I think there was another one at one-thirty that you could take," said Bibbi.

"Yeah, but the next train to Cooch doesn't leave till after six in the evening and gets in the next morning. Remember? That would mean that

Kris would have to come back for me the next day or you guys would have to spend the night in Cooch," I said.

"Or you could take a taxi to Dhubri and we could come get you there," Lyn offered.

"Yeah, okay, that could work, but how do I let you know? They don't have a telephone." I reminded him.

"Just send us a telegram as soon as you know what you're doing. I'll give you Kris' address," said Lyn, pulling out his address book and a pen. He wrote the phone number on the back of an old receipt he found in his pocket and handed it to me.

Our suppers arrived. This time I was having a Thali meal, which had looked so delicious when Bibbi got it the day before, but now, to me, tasted bland. I'm sure it was my anxiety seasoning what should have been a wonderful meal.

I slept poorly, and the next morning I said goodbye to my pals and said I would meet them at the airport if I could. "But don't wait for me," I joked.

Lyn made another crack about diplomatic passports, which relieved some of my tension, but not much. They were still in their underwear and getting ready to go down for breakfast after packing their backpacks. I shouldered mine, which I was taking with me in case I had to grab a taxi straight from the Thomas Cook agency to the airport. I raised my hand in salute as I walked out the door.

"Good luck!" called Bibbi, as I left.

"See you soon, I hope," added Lyn.

Another Try   There was a line outside the Consulate when I got there a little before eight o'clock. I joined it and waited. At precisely eight o'clock, the marine guard opened the gate, and we began to stream into the reception area. My clerk was at his desk again, but there were two people ahead of me waiting to talk to him. He sorted them out fairly quickly, and by a quarter past the hour I was greeting him.

"Oh, good morning, sar," he greeted when he recognized me. "Let me call the dispatch officer to see if we have anything to tell you."

He picked up his phone and dialed a number. After a few seconds he spoke into it and I heard my name, which he repeated twice more. There was a wait, and a couple of minutes later he said "Thank you" into the phone. From his expression, I knew what his information would be before he spoke.

"I'm sorry, sar," he said. "Nothing has come over the wire as yet. The Consulate in Madras has just opened, so maybe we will receive something shortly. If you wish to wait over there, I will call you as soon as we hear anything."

I went back to the seat I had occupied before in a black mood. Why wasn't Dad responding? Surely he would have been advised of a telex from the Embassy in New Delhi about his son. I looked at the watch on my wrist. It was a Tissot that Dad had purchased for me on our way through Switzerland the year before. It told me that it was almost nine o'clock, and that Bibbi and Lyn would be catching their cab to the airport. I felt terribly sorry for myself, and felt all my old insecurities raising their ugly heads in my mind. I was really close to tears.

At nine thirty I went back to the clerk's desk to check and make sure that he hadn't forgotten about me. He made a show of calling the dispatch office again, although he said that they would surely call him the moment they received anything. Nothing had come through as yet.

At ten fifteen I figured that Bibbi and Lyn were on board their plane and strapping in to their seats. They had probably boarded at the last possible minute waiting for me. I caught the clerk's eye, and he sadly shook his head.

I waited through the morning, becoming more and more upset. At noon I went to the tea stall around the corner where Bibbi and I had gone the day before and had a cup of chai and some snacks. I resigned myself to the idea that even if my permission came through I wouldn't be able to fly out until the following day.

I went back to the Consulate and spent the afternoon with my eyes on the clerk, and dozing off from time to time. When the Marine guard came out at five to tell us that the Consulate was closing for the day, I went back to the clerk's desk as he was straightening up his papers and locking them in his desk.

"Are you sure there is no word yet?" I pleaded.

Seeing how desperate I appeared, he smiled sympathetically. "I don't believe so, but let me call to make sure for you." He dialed a three-digit number and had a short conversation with the person who answered

"I'm sorry, sar. Nothing yet," he shook his head sadly. "We will be open tomorrow only until noon, so please stop by in the morning to check back."

I walked sadly back to the Guest House. I sat in their dining room alone and ate whatever they served for supper, feeling very lonely and sorry for myself.

A Final Try   Hope is hard to kill, so the next morning I rose early, and after a breakfast of reconstituted orange juice, tea, toast and scrambled eggs, I went back to the Consulate for one last try.

The desk clerk greeted me like an old friend when I walked in to the lobby, and immediately picked up the phone and dialed the three-digit code. After a short conversation, he hung up and shook his head. "Sorry, sar, nothing has come in overnight. I will check later for you."

"Thank you," I said. "I'll walk around for a while and be back soon." I did not want to spend more hours sitting in the Lobby.

I wandered aimlessly through the streets, looking into shop windows and watching people. I found a spot on a park bench that overlooked the Hooghly River behind Fort William. I was feeling very small and very alone. After an hour or so I went back to the Consulate at around ten a.m.

The clerk was away from his desk when I came in, so I went back to my chair and sat down for a while. After about twenty minutes I saw him coming out of a small door in the back of the lobby wiping his mouth with a handkerchief. He walked to his desk and saw me. He smiled tightly, and waved me over.

"Sorry, I was just at a small celebration for a colleague who is retiring," he volunteered. "I haven't heard anything, but let me call again."

He repeated his three-digit dial and spoke briefly to the person at the other end. This time he seemed to wait for a reply. When it came, he asked a quiet question, looking at me as he spoke. He shook his head, sadly.

"I'm so sorry, sar," he said, hanging up his receiver. "Nothing has come in, and it seems that the Embassy in Delhi is going to be shutting down their operations for the holiday in about one hour. We will also be closing at noon, in just about ninety minutes time."

"What if a message comes in after you are closed? Is there any way I can get informed if the message comes in later?" I asked.

"I can leave a note for the duty officer to get in touch with you, sar," he said. "But as a rule, he only is responsible for messages marked 'Urgent' or above when the embassy is closed, so he may not read it. We will open again on Friday morning after Thanksgiving. Maybe you will have something by then." He must have read my expression because he added, "I am sorry, sar. Maybe something will come in before we close."

I sat in the waiting area until I saw the Marine Guard walking around to secure the lobby. I walked over to the clerk for one last try. He made his three-digit call as I was approaching, and was already hanging up when I got there. "Sorry, nothing has come in, sar," he said.

I walked out of the Consulate for the last time.

A Bad Decision   I returned to the Guest House in a very dark mood. I was feeling abandoned by my father, deserted by my friends, and stuck alone in a dirty city. All the excitement I had felt about this trip had been stripped away.

When I entered the reception area of the Guest House, I was greeted by the receptionist who asked me if I was planning to stay another night, as our room had already been cleaned. I dreaded the idea of spending two more nights there alone until I could return to the Consulate on Friday, with the possibility that even then I would face more bitter disappointment.

"I'm not sure, Miss," I said. "Do you have a train schedule I could look at?"

"Of course, sir," she replied. "What direction would you be traveling?"

"South to Madras," I said.

She handed me a timetable for southbound trains, and I saw that there was one leaving at around four in the afternoon that would get me back to Madras at around six in the evening the next day, Thanksgiving day.

I let my mood get the better of me and made one of the decisions I have most regretted in my life. "I won't be staying tonight," I said. "I'm going to take the train back to Madras this afternoon if there is space available."

I walked out of the Guest House with my backpack still on my shoulders shortly after one in the afternoon, and hailed a passing taxi, which took me to the train station. The cab dropped me off near the ticket windows, and I found the one that listed Madras among its destinations.

I approached the window in a short queue, and when I got to the front I asked for an air-conditioned second-class sleeper ticket on the four o'clock express train to Madras.

"We only have first class sleepers still available, sar. Sorry."

"How much is that?" I asked, checking the funds in my wallet. I still had the money I had been going to spend for the plane ticket and the train ticket, and my other expenses for the journey, so I was sure I had enough. Besides, at that moment I would have accepted a third class standing room only ticket to get out of Calcutta.

He named a price which was quite expensive, but I wasn't in a position to haggle.

"How many will be with me in my compartment?" I asked.

"Oh, that is a single compartment, sar. You will be quite private," he replied.

That suited me perfectly, so I handed him my money and he gave me my ticket telling me what time and which track to report to, to catch my train.

I walked around the station for a while and acquired a bottle of grape soda and some tea biscuits for an afternoon snack. I would pick up some supper along the way, probably at Balasore, which the schedule I picked up indicated that we would be reaching at around seven o'clock. Just before departure time I purchased a cup of take-away chai and walked to my platform. I found my first-class car and my compartment and settled in.

It Gets Worse   At that precise moment, just before four pm, a telex was rattling in to the U. S. Consulate in Calcutta clearing me to travel to Assam. The telex was marked urgent, so the officer-on-call read it and placed a call to the Salvation Army Red Shield Guest House. He was informed that I had already returned to Madras, so he let the matter drop, having done his due diligence. There were other, more important matters to occupy his time.

Oblivious to this, I sipped my chai and ate my tea biscuits as the train pulled out of Howrah Junction.

My self-pity accompanied me into the night, but at least I slept better than I had the night before and awoke feeling a little better about things. It was Thanksgiving Day. I would be back home by suppertime.

Just after eight in the morning, the train pulled in to Rajahmundry station, where Bibbi had picked up our lunches on our way up to Calcutta. The stop was programmed for twenty minutes, so I dashed out to get something for breakfast. I ordered an omelet with green chilies and a chai to go, and added a slice of toast with peanut butter and jam to round off my breakfast.

My mood lightened a little when I had eaten, but I was still very disheartened by my failure to join my friends in Assam. Had I known that the clearance had come through, I would probably have jumped off the moving train in despair.

There was an extended stop in Vijayawada Junction late in the morning where the sleeping cars were removed from the train and we were moved into regular first-class cars for the remainder of the journey. I took advantage of the time to find a restaurant that would sell me a large order of chicken biriyani with all the sides that I could take back to the train with me. This would be my Thanksgiving feast.

I Discover My Mistake   My parents were dismayed when I arrived home in a taxi while they were having their light supper. They had hosted a Thanksgiving dinner for a fairly large number of consular staff, and had eaten very little themselves, so they were making a meal of some of the leftovers.

"What happened?" they asked. "Why didn't you go up to Assam with your classmates?"

I started to explain about needing the clearance, but Dad interrupted.

"I sent it to the Consulate in Calcutta yesterday afternoon. They were supposed to contact you at the Guest House," he said

"Well, gee," I said, "I was at the Guest House until about two, and nobody contacted me. The clerk at the Consulate told me that only 'urgent' telexes would be read during the holiday, which meant that I wouldn't hear anything till Friday at the earliest. I didn't want to spend two days by myself in Calcutta. It's not a pretty city. I thought that the message from the consul hadn't got through to you and that you might not even find out about it till after the weekend."

"Oh, I'm so sorry!" said my Dad. "I sent it as soon as I got the message, but there was some delay in that because we had a new officer handling messages and he didn't recognize that that one was meant for me and involved my family."

If only I had waited! To this day, I regret taking that train.

I had neglected to send Kris a telegram letting him know what had happened, so I asked my dad to send one, but not to mention that I had missed getting my clearance by a few minutes. It took me a week or more to get over my disappointment.

I spent the rest of that vacation practicing driving with Krishnan, and by mid-December I had received my 'India Motor Driving Licence' [sic], a fifty page book with pages for fines and renewals, and a section dedicated to laws and regulations and rules for good driving.

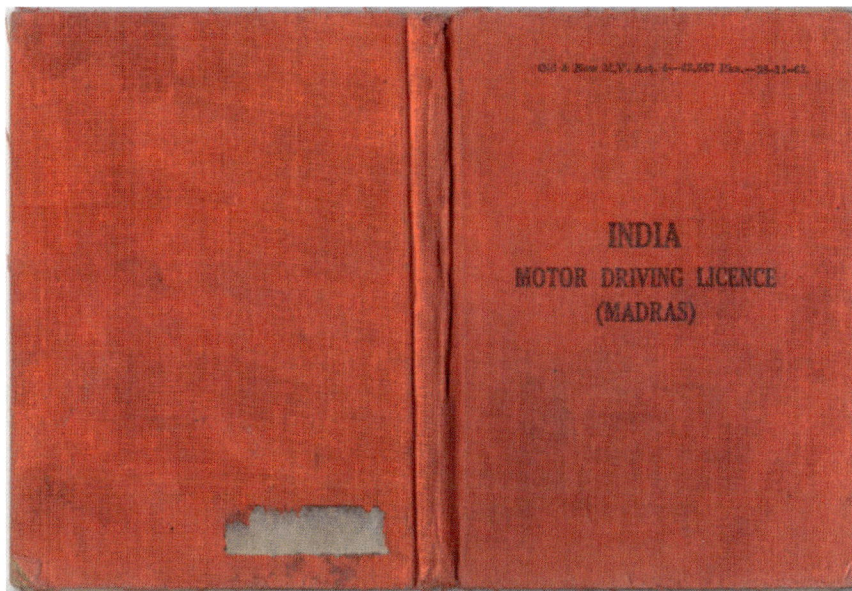

My Indian Driver's License from 1965

The achievement went a long way towards restoring my self-esteem. As far as I knew, since I had turned eighteen ahead of my classmates, I would be the only kid in our class to have a license to drive a motor vehicle. I knew a couple of my classmates were getting their motor cycle licenses, and Lyn rode a motor scooter around Kodai, but I would be the only one with a motor vehicle license

With my new license I spent many evenings driving around the quieter neighborhoods of Madras. Boulevards which teemed during the day were mostly empty after nine, and I could drive our left-hand-drive Studebaker at forty miles an hour, with the tropical sea air flowing through the open windows. My father never had a radio in any of his cars or I would have been playing a local radio station with Indian music at maximum volume as I drove around, and probably picked up a ticket or two. This freedom proved cathartic, and I rebounded from the depression induced by my failed trip with my pals.

10. Preparing to Move On

Final Semester   Johnny, my brother, George Caldwell, another diplobrat, a ninth-grader just starting his second semester at Kodai, and I took the train from Madras to Kodai Road shortly after the festivities of Christmas and New Year had faded away. We occupied a first-class sleeper compartment for the overnight trip, and emerged from the train at ten in the morning covered with the soot and grit that had been flowing through our un-air-conditioned coach throughout the night. There we took a bus that took us up the Ghat to Kodai, arriving too late for lunch and too early for dinner.

So, after depositing our gear in Wissy, the three of us headed down to the Budge for a meal, ending up, as usual, at the Hotel State. We were ushered into the back room where Bibbi, Kris and Lyn were already occupying a table and enjoying a cup of hot chai. There were greasy banana leaves on the table in front of them, evidence of a recent repast.

"Yenna, Charred-Lee!" shouted Bibbi and Lyn together. Bibbi stood and gave me an enthusiastic hug. They shifted their chairs and made room for us at the table, which was a family-sized round table. Johnny and George sat on one side, and I moved in between Bibbi and Kris.

"I heard all about your diplomatic passport," said Kris. "It can get you anywhere!" He chuckled and Lyn joined him.

"Come on, guys," said Bibbi. "It's not like you guys never had anything go wrong for you. Ease up!"

We settled down and ordered our meals while Bibbi, Lyn and Kris told me all about their adventures in Assam that I had missed. Lyn's parents and Maureen Aung Thwin had traveled by different means, and were there as well. The whole group had hung around the tea estate waiting to hear from me, and had finally received my dad's telegram on Saturday. They had visited a game reserve and ridden elephants and seen a rhino, Sambar deer and other smaller deer. Kris had driven them around in his dad's jeep with his younger brother Karl, to visit various parts of the estate. They had driven along the Brahmaputra River. I hoped to hear mention of where Kris' sister Emmy had fit into their activities, but other than a mention of them all sitting around the table at Thanksgiving, and joining their outings, her name never came up until Bibbi mentioned that he was 'dating' her. I felt deflated.

On their way back after their week or so, they had gone a day early to Siliguri and taken the train up to Darjeeling where they caught glimpses of Mount Everest and rode an elephant across the River Rangeet so they could say they had been in Sikkim.

Bibbi, Kris and I moved back into our three-man room in Wissy and began our final semester at Kodai.

The second semester of your senior year at Kodai is full of prescribed activities designed to keep you engaged in your school life. There are activities to plan like Senior Sneak, the Senior Prom, the Class Camping trip to Berijam Lake, graduation ceremonies, and others. There are the usual school activities that include Field Day and Spring Concerts, and the School Play. Seniors are encouraged to step up to be Dorm President, Student Court judges and attorneys, and are usually heavily involved in Student Council.

Additionally, we were all on tenterhooks waiting for our acceptance/rejection letters from the colleges we had applied to. Those were supposed to arrive sometime in March. We joked about who would receive the most letters of rejection as we compared our Grade Point Averages. Mine was the lowest of the four of us, sitting at around a 2.2, or "C" average, so I regularly was expected to get the most.

Fairly early in the semester, Bibbi let me know that he and Emmy had 'broken up', sort of... but that they had already agreed to go to the next Formal. My crush on Emmy, Kris' sister, persisted, but I was too shy to do much about it. By the time I got up the courage to ask her to a dance coming up, I found out that she was already seeing another boy. The story of my life, I guessed. I kicked myself all over again for not waiting for a few more hours in Calcutta for my clearance to come through. Maybe if I had, I could have made an advance with Emmy while in Assam that would have given me the confidence to start dating her.

The year rolled on as if on tracks, with everything happening as planned. Sports teams were formed and entered tournaments; students signed up for various field day events and began their training; swimming season in the lake started and I helped out with life-guarding; Field Day came with the Blue team triumphing over the Orange team, and several records broken.

Our class went off to our Senior Sneak destination, Mandapam Beach at the beginning of March. It was just about our last chance to have fun before our acceptance-rejection letters began arriving. My fickle fantasies about girls had shifted back to Cathy, Bonnie and Chellie for the duration of our trip. In my underdeveloped way, I showed them my feelings by squirting them with sea cucumbers that lived in the shallow waters in front of our beach resort. Needless to say, I made no headway with any of them.

The Senior Formal was held, and as usual, I had trouble psyching myself up to ask someone, especially someone that I had feelings for. Emmy was only a sophomore, anyway, and we were encouraged to choose among juniors and seniors. In the end, I made a safe choice. I chose Barbie Ford, who accepted my invitation graciously and was shy and sweet. Again I had a wonderful time, and was glad that I had invited her.

Letters from Colleges   Letters from colleges began arriving the week after we got back from our Senior Sneak at Mandampam. Bibbi got two, both nice fat acceptances, and Kris got the one he wanted from Augustana. I got a letter from Cornell. My envelope was much thinner than Bibbi's or Kris', so I knew before I opened it that in was a rejection letter. Over the next week, Bibbi got two more acceptance letters, and Kris and I each got one. Mine was from the University of Arizona, one of my back-ups. I thumbed through the enclosed catalogue included and studied the information about the dormitories and the tuition, both of which concerned me more than the academics. The tuition was modest enough, but the dormitories looked huge and impersonal, and the kids walking around in the color pictures all looked like they came out of a Sears catalogue.

Over the next week I got replies from the only two other schools I had applied to, and they were both acceptances. One was from Antioch College, and the other was from the University of Hawai'i. The tuition at Antioch concerned me. My dad had shared his concerns about funding my college education and then Johnny's a year later, and I didn't want to be a burden. The University of Hawai'i was much more reasonable, and they offered me "in-state" tuition since I was applying from overseas. The tuition for one semester was less than one tenth of the tuition for a semester at Antioch, and only about a third of the cost of the University of Arizona. Additionally, the catalog from 'U.H.' bragged about the cosmopolitan nature of its student body, with students from over fifty countries and cultures. The choice became quite easy.

Bibbi got his wish to attend Lehigh, and Kris opted for Augustana. Lyn was going to Tabor College, a Mennonite school in Kansas. The distances seemed insurmountable, and after we had made our decisions and discussed them, we all felt glum. We were going to be spread out across the country, with me at one end and Bibbi at the other. We started making plans.

Plans   Our first plans dealt with our travel back to the U.S. upon graduation. The stamps Bibbi had seen in my passport struck a chord. He wanted to spend time in Europe on his way back to the States and began asking me about the places I'd been there.

"Why don't we travel together?" I asked. "We could make a grand tour of it."

Our plans developed from there. Bibbi's parents had been saving money towards his trip home, and his mission would pay the basic fare. I knew that Dad would cover my expenses, especially since I had chosen the least expensive of my college options. Kris and Lyn were kind of on their own, and were interested in making some money during the summer. A relative of Kris' had a pig farm in Denmark and had offered them a job for a month or so during the spring slaughter to help make sausages. After their month of work they would have enough money to travel the rest of the way with us.

We also agreed that we would meet up the following summer, after our first year of college, somewhere to get jobs and hang out together. Making these plans helped stave off the anxiety and despair we were feeling about leaving our sheltered existence at Kodai. The fact that they came to fruition was a bonus.

End-of-year event followed event one after another, while we continued to work on our travel plans. Our class went into overdrive planning each of the set pieces: Choosing the class song: *'Climb Every Mountain'* and practicing it; selecting our class Salutatorian: Barbie Ford (my Senior Prom date), and class Valedictorian: Ron Koepke; naming our class historians, Lyn, Bibbi and me; getting the programs for Baccalaureate and Commencement Exercises printed; having our white raw-silk graduation jackets tailored by Peter, the tailor in the Budge; and many, many other details.

Our parents began arriving. Lyn's dad, School Principal, was obviously already there. Kris' mom and dad came a month before the events. They stayed in a nearby cottage on 'Budge' Road, and Bibbi, Lyn and I were invited over a number of times to have dinner during the month. Kris' dad had been asked to give the sermon at our Baccalaureate Service, and engaged in many discussions with us about our class activities and classmates as he worked on what he was going to say. Emmy was usually there, and Kris' little brothers Karl and Johnny were often there as well, which made for a merry, but not intimate time. I did get to have several conversations with Emmy, nevertheless, which served to fan the flames of my crush on her.

Bibbi, Lyn and I started thinking about what to write for our class history. They had both been at Kodai since grade school, and there had been a lot of shenanigans during their early years, but we decided that that would make any history way too long if we were to do it any justice. We decided to concentrate only on the high school years, and they began telling me about what I had missed in ninth grade. As kind of a joke, after one discussion of how intimidated they had been by joining the upperclassmen in Wissy, I wrote the following couplet in doggerel verse:

> In the year that we were freshmen,
> Lowly freshmen, small and weak,
> Hear the upper classmen taunt us,
> Lowly freshmen, 'fraid to speak.

Bibbi and Lyn laughed, and then Bibbi said, "What a great idea! Charlie, we'll tell you what happened and you can write it all down as a poem!"

"You mean all of it?" I asked.

"Yeah, all of it," said Bibbi. "It'll be fun! You can write a couple of verses for each semester. We'll help you, and Fuzzy said she would help as well." ('Fuzzy', as in Ms. Frantz, our English teacher.)

I ended up writing fifty-four verses of similarly banal poetry, which got me an 'A' in my English class, more because of the quantity than for the quality, I'm sure. Unfortunately, it also got me the 'honor' of reading the Class History at our Commencement, which, when the day arrived, I did poorly due to the absolute terror I felt at being front and center in front of my classmates and their parents.

Besides the Class History, I had also committed to performing 'Four Strong Winds' with Sam, Stan and Dave for the Commencement program, so we were practicing and refining every evening, having been given permission to skip the last half hour of Study Hall and practice in the Wissy common room for the last week of the semester.

The wonder of all the frenetic activity and preparations was that it allowed us to forget about our impending separation and focus on the present. Along with minor details like final exams our minds were always focused on the here and now, with little time to think about times to come. Unfortunately, they also put a lot of stress on my life, and the stress caused my face to break out with a large red bump on my chin and another on the left side of my nose. These were the bane of my teenage love-life, always making me very self-conscious around girls.

Nonetheless, Bibbi and I did spend time working out the details of our trip back to the States, and, with the help of my dad, securing passage on a ship, the Italian Line SS Guglielmo Marconi, out of Bombay for the first leg and 30-day Eurail passes for the second leg. These plans postponed the final day of our companionship nicely, so that we could relegate it to the distant future.

Studebaker Lark Cruiser   My parents arrived at Kodai several days before our Sunday Baccalaureate service was scheduled and took up residence in Keith Lodge, one of the cottages for rent in the area. It was a rustic stone cottage a short walk from the school. They drove up in the Studebaker, and since I now had my Driver's license, I borrowed it to drive Bibbi and Kris around the Lake.

Our 1963 Studebaker Lark Cruiser at Keith Lodge

They were mighty impressed with the sleek interior in red leatherette and the power of the V-8 engine. I made sure to drive by the front gate of the school and around Bendy field to be seen by as many schoolmates as possible.

The next day at lunch in the cafeteria, Emmy joined our table as she sometimes did. Conversation came around to the drive I had taken Bibbi and Kris on, and I asked Emmy if she would like to go for a ride, and she said it sounded like fun.

"How about this afternoon after school?" I suggested. "We could go and be back in time for supper."

"Oh, the family is going to have supper at the cottage with my parents," said Emmy. "We usually don't eat till six thirty or so. So I guess it would be okay if my mom says I can. Come by the house after school and we'll ask her."

Kris began to act like the invitation had included him and Bibbi, but Bibbi understood my feelings about Emmy and said that he and Kris needed to study for their Calculus final (a course that I had happily not taken that semester). He must have given Kris some sort of a high sign or a kick under the table, because he changed course and agreed that he and Bibbi would not be able to join us.

My thoughts were fluttering all afternoon as we attended classes. I couldn't concentrate, and continually watched the clock, which seemed to have stuck. Eventually, though, the final bell rang and I ran down to Wissy to change into a clean shirt and put on some deodorant that I borrowed from Narain. I almost ran to Keith Lodge to beg Dad for the car again. Alas, when I got there, there was no one home. My parents must have gone out for a drive or something. Once again, I thought, my hopes to spend some time with Emmy were going to be dashed.

The cottage was locked, which wasn't the usual practice in Kodai, but par for my security-conscious dad, so I sat on the front steps to wait. I had no idea where they might have gone or when they might return. Knowing Dad, they might have gone off to some temple or shrine tucked away in the hills that he wanted to visit. They knew that I was going to come over for supper, so they would be back by then, but that would be too late. My chance to take Emmy for a drive would have vanished.

It seemed like I waited a long time, but it was before a quarter to four when I saw the Studebaker approaching. Mom and Dad were deep in some discussion they had been having, and didn't notice me sitting on the steps until they opened the doors.

"Oh, hello, Chas," said Mom. "What brings you here so early?"

"Um, I was hoping to borrow the car for a while," I said. "I told Emmy I could take her on a drive after school if her mom Okayed it."

"I don't know, Dear," said Mom. "Where are you planning to go?"

"I don't know. Maybe around the Lake or the 10-mile round; maybe out to Lake Berijam, something like that. Not far, I don't think. I don't know how long her mom will let her stay out."

"What do you think, Bert?" she asked my dad.

"I think it would be okay. He's a good driver, according to Krishnan, and he knows the roads around here," said Dad. Dad handed me the keys.

"Well, then, alright, Dear," said Mom, "but make sure you're back before dark. I'll worry about you if you're not."

"Thanks, guys," I said. "I'd better get going. I think I'm already late, but hopefully not too late!"

Forty-Mile Round   Feeling like I had wings on my feet, I slid into the driver's seat and cranked the engine. I had trouble keeping my eagerness under control while I backed and turned around, but did so as carefully as I could so as not to alarm my folks. I may have spun out a little at the edge of the driveway as I pulled out onto the paved road.

I drove past the school and down Bazaar road to the cottage Emmy's folks were staying at. I pulled the car as close to the side of the road as I could, got out, and went to knock on the front door of the cottage. Emmy answered almost at once.

She was a tall girl with straight, white-blonde hair and a generous smile with pouty lips and even white teeth. She was wearing no makeup, as usual, and her eyebrows and lashes were almost white. Her eyes were a sparkly blue, and the corners crinkled when she smiled, which she was doing now. She was dressed in a plain white blouse and dark skirt that fell to below her knees.

"Oh, I thought you had forgotten," she reproached, but she was smiling.

"No, it's just that my folks were out when I got home, so I had to wait for them. Sorry," I explained.

Emmy's mom came out of the kitchen to say hello.

"Do you have your license with you?" she asked. I nodded and pulled it out of my pocket. "Okay, good. Please drive carefully, and have Emmy back before sundown. You can stay for supper if you want. We're having pork chops."

"Gee, thanks!" I said. "I'll check in with my parents to see if it's okay with them before we come home. I'm pretty sure it will be okay with them."

Emmy Answers the Door

"See you soon, then," she said. "Emmy, behave yourself. Have fun."

Emmy grabbed a sweater off the back of a chair, and we walked out to the car. My heart was suddenly beating fast and my palms were sweaty. Emmy walked around to the driver's side and pulled on the handle. When the door opened she looked confused.

I laughed. "It's a left-hand drive car. It's made for the U.S. I guided her around to the passenger side and opened the door for her. She stood for a moment admiring the interior, and then slid into the bench seat with the barest flash of calf and knee, and smoothed her skirt over her knees as I closed her door.

"Where shall we go?" I asked.

"I don't know. What do you think?" asked Emmy.

"Why don't we start out on Upper Lake Road?" I suggested. "The view of the Lake is great from up there. Then we could head out towards the Observatory and the Ten-Mile Round. I can show you where we had to climb up the embankment from the shortcut when we were coming back from Kookal." ('…the sight of my heroic climb', I wanted her to think.)

"Sounds fine," she said, so off we went.

I drove slowly and carefully back out to Club Road and made the right turn that would take us back past the main gate of the school. I hoped that there would be some classmates of mine and of Emmy's who would see me driving her around. Sure enough, at that hour there were several groups of kids walking to the Budge who noticed us and waved, including Narain and Phil, and a couple of Emmy's sophomore classmates. I was in heaven.

We drove past the campus and onto Observatory Road, which took us around above the lake. The afternoon was clear and mild, and we had the windows cranked down. I drove in silence for a few minutes, trying to think of what to talk about. I needed to think of something that didn't sound awkward or contrived, but my mind went blank. The view down to the lake caught my eye, so I slowed down and pointed it out.

"Look at that!" I exclaimed, lamely. "The boat house is busy today."

"Yes, the lake is always packed in high season. I like it better when there are fewer people. Some of those guys don't know how to steer their punts and they run into each other," she replied.

As an icebreaker it was sort of okay. We began to talk about the places we were passing and distant vistas of Mount Perumal, and about the traffic on the road. At one point we caught a glimpse of Bear Shola, and I said something about couples going up there to neck and make out on Sunday afternoons. She said that she had gone up there a couple of times with Bibbi when she was dating him when she was a freshman, but that they had only held hands and talked. She laughed and said that Bibbi loved to talk. I agreed and said that he and I were always having deep, philosophical discussions, especially after R.E. classes with Reverend Reble.

"How come you and Bibbi broke up?" I asked her.

"I don't really know," she said. "He got really busy with homework and sports, and when we got back to school after the break, we just didn't hang out any more. And I think he started liking Carol Gibson."

I figured that there was more to the story, but that she didn't want to tell, so I left it alone. I didn't really want to talk about her old boyfriends anyway.

I bore to the right at the intersection with Upper Lake Road, keeping us on Observatory Road, rather than left which would have taken us back around to Kodai. Soon we drove by the Solar Observatory at the start of the Ten-Mile Round. A few hundred feet further on, we passed the sign marking the Kodaikanal Township limit. I picked up speed and showed off my skill at taking curves, especially the ones to the right that threw her against me. After the third or fourth one, she laughed and told me to stop it.

I pulled over at a curve in the road that gave us a view of some cliffs and a green valley. Emmy seemed nervous, probably sensing that I might be thinking about making some sort of advances, which I totally was. Not wanting to scare her off, I asked if she wanted to walk around for a bit, so we got out and walked about in the eucalyptus trees beside the road. After a few minutes, we got back in the car and continued on our way. I was a little disappointed that there had been no sign from her that she would welcome a play.

We came to the embankment that I had climbed in the rainstorm, and we stopped again. We got out and I pointed out the trail we had come on, and where the steps had washed out, and where I had climbed out onto the retaining wall. It was much less impressive than I remembered, but Emmy seemed to think it must have been quite a difficult climb. She kept her distance as we looked around.

I pointed out where the trail led back out to Poombari Road about five hundred yards away, and suggested that we should drive around to it to see how much the trail really cut off the distance. She was game, so we got back in the car and continued to where Ten-Mile Round intersected Poombari Road, and then made the sharp, hair-pin right turn. We were driving virtually a stone's throw from the road we had just been on, but in the opposite direction. I kept a careful eye on the odometer, calling out each tenth of a mile. We calculated that the five-hundred-yard shortcut had saved us a mile and two tenths when we took it on our hike.

The exercise of measuring the distance seemed to relax Emmy a little, and distracted me from my objective of getting closer to her. I asked her if we should turn back, or if we should drive around the full 40-mile round. I figured we had gone about a fifth of the way, and that it would take us about an hour to an hour-and-a-half to complete the circuit if we didn't make any stops.

"If we can make it in an hour, it would be nice to do it," said Emmy. She looked at her watch. "That would get us back to Kodai before six, and you wouldn't be driving in the dark."

"Okay," I agreed. "I'll try to keep my speed up to thirty-five. That should get us back in time, and we can stop by Keith Lodge to let my parents know I'll be at your house for supper. I've got to be back at Wissy by nine o'clock, though."

"You're not staying at Keith Lodge with your folks?" she asked.

"No, Sam, Stan and I are practicing our song for the Commencement, and I still have some more verses to write for the Class History. So I'm staying at Wissy through Friday," I said.

So we drove on, pausing briefly at the Poombari overlook to admire the rice paddies in the late afternoon light, and later at the Mannavanur view point. Each time we stopped I found that I had to hurry to keep the mile markers clicking by at a pace that would get us back to Kodai in time.

It dawned on me that I had been played. If we had opted to return and complete the Ten-Mile Round, we would have had time to stop and park for a while at Moir Point, for instance. By choosing the longer route that we would have to hurry to complete, Emmy had avoided situations that might have led to opportunities for me to try moves that would make her uncomfortable.

As we drove, we talked about our times at Kodai. I found out that she and I had much in common: Bibbi, Kris and Lyn were my best friends; Kris was her brother; she had dated Bibbi for a bit, both things that I knew; and, I learned, she had also dated Lyn, albeit secretly, when she was in eighth grade and supposedly not allowed to fraternize with high-schoolers… but since he was the principal's son, they got away with it.

Talk turned to the coming year. I told her that Bibbi and I were planning a tour of Europe on our way back to the States, and planning to meet up with Kris and Lyn at some point. She talked about working to improve her grades in her junior year so she could get into a good college, maybe even Augustana to be near Kris.

I couldn't help feeling that I was getting mixed messages. Emmy was warm and friendly. She laughed easily and seemed to be relaxed in my company. She had agreed to come out on a drive with me into the country with no chaperone. But I also felt that she was holding back, avoiding the step I had so hoped for of showing any more intimate feelings for me. My lack of experience with girls was no help. I was trying to give signals that communicated my feelings for her.

We stopped at the Mannavanur View Point, where Bibbi, Linwood, Dave and I had rested for a few minutes on our hike. I was desperate to do something to please Emmy and show her how I felt about her. We sat for a few minutes on the rock wall that bordered to road, looking down across the valley to Mannavanur Lake. Should I try to hold her hand? Should I let my knee brush against hers? She kept her hands folded in her lap and sat with her knees pointed away from me, so I did neither.

After a few minutes we stood to go back to the car. Still wanting to show my feelings, I saw some wild flowers growing at the top of a nearby rock face. They were small, white orchids that grew in abundance around Kodai. I showed off my climbing prowess by scaling the rock and picking one which I gave her with a gallant flourish. When we were ready to drive on, I opened her door for her. I told her how nice she looked in the afternoon sun. Like a stiff elbow during a slow dance, she kept deflecting my gestures with a laugh or a joke.

As we spoke about our plans for the coming year, I realized that, while she might have kind feelings towards me, she wasn't willing to invest emotionally in a short-term relationship. I would be leaving Kodai for good in about a week, and she would still be here for two more years. I understood that, as one of the most popular girls at Kodai, she was going to be there for her junior and senior proms and all the other social activities that the school afforded. Being 'attached' to a departed student would make things uncomfortable. Thus I came to terms with our relationship as good friends, as ships passing, and enjoyed the last few miles of our drive in peace. However, I carried a torch for her for many more years.

Dinner at the Ribers'   My parents agreed to allow me to have dinner at Emmy's, so long as the car was back by eight-thirty, and we made it to Emmy's house by the appointed time. Dinner at Kris and Emmy's house was a special event. Emmy's dad said grace as we all held hands around the table. I gave Emmy's hand a friendly squeeze as I let it go, and she returned it. Then her dad served a pork chop onto each plate in the stack in front of him and passed it to her mom, who added mashed potatoes and vegetables. It was then passed down the line to the last person until all at the table had their plate. No one was asked whether they wanted more or less of anything. Emmy's younger brothers, Karl and Johnny were there as well, so there were seven of us around the table.

Conversation at the table flowed easily.

"When do you head off to Denmark to make sausage?" I asked Kris.

"Emmy and I are going to travel around and stay with our uncle for a week or so, until Lyn gets there. Then he and I will work in my uncle's factory for about a month to earn some money."

"Sounds like fun!" I said, sarcastically.

"Yeah, well, wait till we get together and we have money to spend and you don't. That's when the fun will start," he replied. "How was your drive this afternoon?"

Before I could answer, Emmy said "It was nice. Charlie's a really good driver. He showed me how to shift the gear stick when he pressed on the pedal thing."

"You mean the clutch," I inserted.

"So, is he a good parker, too?" asked Karl, the eighth-grader. "There are some nice secret spots along that road that are pretty secluded, heh, heh."

"You have such a dirty mind!" Emmy exclaimed, blushing. "We went all the way 'round the 40 in about an hour and a half, so we didn't have time to do much more than drive. Even at that, we had to hurry to get back in time for supper."

After supper I thanked Emmy's mom and made my excuses, because I had to get the car back to Keith Lodge and then walk to Wissy to practice with Sam and Stan. Emmy walked me out to the car.

"Thank you for the fun drive," she said, as I pulled the car keys out of my pocket. She leaned toward me and gave me a chaste peck on the cheek. "I had a nice time."

My heart was jumping around in my chest. "Oh, wow!" I said. "Um, thank you for coming with me."

She laughed and tossed her head. She knew the effect she had on me. "I'll try to come through Hawaii on my way back to the States when I graduate in a couple of years. I'll write to you if you send me your address."

I got in the car and waved as I drove off toward Keith Lodge. It was the last time I was alone with Emmy until she stopped in Honolulu on her way back to college two years later. For the last week I was in Kodai, we attended many events at the same time, but not together; she with her family, and I with mine.

Lousy Luck   After exams were over, I was allowed to spend the nights with my folks at Keith Lodge. Johnny slept on the couch in the living room, and I was relegated to the unused servants' quarters, since the main cottage only had one bedroom that my parents occupied. Unfortunately, some birds had nested in the eaves of the servant's quarters, and I woke up Saturday morning with my head itching furiously. The nest was right above the head of the bed and had deposited bird lice in my hair during the night. I didn't know why my head itched, so I went into the house and showed Mom. She parted my hair with her fingers to look at my scalp, and let out a stifled shriek.

"Oh, dear!" she exclaimed. "You have lice! However did you get them?"

I remembered a kid in my fifth grade class in Jerusalem who had had lice, and the poor guy had come to school after a few days absence wearing a beanie on his shaved head. I didn't have a beanie.

Mother pushed me back out the door of the cottage and told me to wait for her. I heard her rush over to the kitchen sink and vigorously wash her hands.

A moment later she came out the door. "Take off your pajamas and drop them over there," she ordered, pointing to the grass beside the walkway.

Luckily, it was May, and the morning, while still a little chilly, was not that cold. I complied and stood naked on the walkway while she walked around me and inspected me all over.

"Okay," she said. "I think they're just in your hair. I'll bring a bucket of warm water. Wait here."

She came back a few minutes later with a bucket of water, a bar of soap and a bottle of vinegar. By then my teeth were beginning to chatter.

"It sure would be lousy luck if we had to shave your head!" she said

It took me a few seconds to realize that she was making a pun.

My head itched terribly, and Mother scrubbed it with vinegar and then shampoo, hoping that she could get them out so that I wouldn't have to attend graduation exercises with a shaved head. She ran a fine-toothed comb through my hair after each cycle of the process, and eventually declared that she thought she had gotten them all. Thankfully, bird lice are apparently not as tenacious as regular lice, at least on humans, so in the end I didn't have to sing 'Four Strong Winds' and read the class history with a bald head.

Last Time at Wissy After breakfast I headed over to Wissy. I entered the main gate and walked up past the chapel toward the Flag Green. I made my way through the Quad and past the Library. At the top of the stairs sown to Wissy, I looked down the uneven flight one last time. Smiling to myself, I remembered the first time I had negotiated those steps with my trunk, and how awkward the passage had been. With a laugh, I set off, skipping effortlessly down. A wave of nostalgia flooded in as I realized that this might be the last time.

Bibbi, Kris and I had arranged to meet to pack our belongings into our trunks and duffle bags and spend one last morning together in Room 11. Room 11, tucked in the corner, was the only three-man room in the dorm, and, because of its strategic location in relation to lines of sight from the house-parents, was the most sought-after room at Wissy. It was almost always occupied by seniors. We had already heard of several eleventh graders who were vying for it.

We packed up our belongings and stripped our beds. Kris had the idea of slightly loosening the mattress support straps to enhance the rickety squeakiness of the beds as a prank on whoever followed us in the room. We also left a note tucked under the strap for whoever tightened them to find. Something about not making the bed squeak so much after lights out.

Kris was in a hurry to leave, as he was going to have lunch with Maureen at her mother's cottage, and headed out as soon as we were done packing. Bibbi and I sat on the now-stripped beds reminiscing about our years together at Kodai. As we thought about it, we calculated that we had spent more time with each other in the last three years than with any other human. Many of our adventures would find their way into school legend, but most would be duplicated or exceeded by subsequent adventurers. We agreed that we had made each other's lives more difficult and more fun. We talked a lot of bull.

Final Walk   After a short while, Bibbi suggested that we take a farewell walk around the lake before lunch, so we set out by hopping the wall below the dorm, this time not caring if anyone saw us. I told Bibbi about my ride around the forty-mile round with Emmy, making it sound a little more romantic than it had actually been. I also embellished the peck on the cheek she had given me as we bade farewell after supper. He seemed duly impressed, but I later found out that he had had the story from Kris, and knew I had been slightly exaggerating some of the details.

I also told him about my brush with bird lice, which he thought was hilarious. He laughed especially hard when I told him about standing outdoors naked in the early morning chill and shivering while my mother washed my head with vinegar. He was exceptionally taken with the image of me getting up on stage to recite the class history with a shaved head.

We walked quickly and companionably around the lake, enjoying the May late morning and greeting many other Kodai-ites and parents who were out walking or paddling around in punts. We talked about our Kodai years, twelve for him and three for me. I expressed how important his welcome and guidance had been for both me and my brother Johnny when we arrived, and how it had helped us immerse quickly into Kodai life and culture.

As we talked, it became clear that our hike through Manjampatti had been an important inflection point, more for me than for him, in our time at Kodai. Our reminiscences returned again and again to the events that had happened on that trail. We marveled at the starry sky on the way to Poombari, and the views of rice paddies in the morning sun. We wondered how the old woman with the black turd was faring. We relived the pain of the descent into the valley. We laughed at Linwood's spill in the stream. Bibbi shared the fear he had experienced when he saw me lying stretched out on the trail. We ran mentally through Leech Shola. We talked about the climb up the embankment in the thunderstorm.

"When I think about it," I said, "my life at Kodai splits into two parts: before Manjampatti and after Manjampatti. Somehow it has made everything about Kodai seem much more meaningful."

"I know what you mean," said Bibbi. "That really was a great adventure, and I was glad that you were with me on it. Maybe we can come back in a few years and do it again."

"We could do it again, but, you know, it wouldn't be the same. Something about that experience was unique, I think, and even if we went exactly the same way, it wouldn't be fresh or new. I don't think you can really go back to places you've been and loved. When you do, they're different, and so are you," I stated.

We were a few minutes late for lunch, but since we had been having meals with our parents for the last few days, neither of us was feeling the constant hunger of boarding school life, so we weren't that bothered. We were the only seniors in the dining room, all the others having lunch with their families, so we sat by ourselves near the windows by the flag green.

We could have gone to eat with our families as well, but we had decided that we would have this one last meal together. Through the window, we watched the last few kids on campus walking around, some with their parents and some with their buddies or their girlfriends.

The following day, Sunday, was our Baccalaureate Service. Monday would be Commencement rehearsals and finishing details. Tuesday would be our Commencement activities, and then we would all take off, leaving Kodai for the last time. It would be hectic, and we had wanted to have one last Kodai meal together.

After finishing our meal, we sat in contented silence. Kodai was almost behind us and our trip through Europe and back to the States was ahead of us. We didn't know what challenges life would throw at us, but I felt that having conquered the climb from Manjampatti to Kookal and making in through to graduation, we were well prepared for what lay ahead.

Epilogue *The train's whistle was barely audible through the thick glass windows of the first-class carriage and over the clatter of the tracks below. Bibbi and I were stretched out on the bunk beds of our sleeper compartment talking about what we had ordered for breakfast.*

The conductor had knocked on our compartment door shortly after we pulled out of Madras. "I will presently be sending a telex ahead to Yadgir Station with breakfast orders, Sars," he announced. "Please to tell me what you will be taking."

"I would like idlis with sambar and hot chai," Bibbi answered without hesitation.

"And could I have a masala dosai, also with hot chai?" I chimed in.

"Well, Sars, please to know that we have fine Western breakfast available for our first class passengers, including eggs and ham or bacon with toasts and coffee for only ten rupees. Maybe you will be preferring such meals, isn't it?"

"Oh, no, thank you!" Bibbi exclaimed. "This may be my last chance to have idlis for a long time. How much will my idlis be?"

"I'll check for you, Sar." Turning to me he asked, "Will you be taking a Western breakfast, Sar?"

"We'll be leaving India forever in a couple of days," I told him, "and masala dosai is one of my favorite foods."

"Do they have any fruit we could get with our breakfast?" Bibbi asked.

"Of course there is orange juice, Sar," he replied

"No, thank you," said Bibbi, knowing that the juice would come from a can. "I would prefer fresh fruit if it is available."

"I will check, Sar."

"For both of us, please," I added

"Very well, Sars. I will check back shortly with your charges." The Conductor looked decidedly disappointed with our orders. "I will take your lunch requests when I bring up your breakfasts in the morning. We will be picking lunches up at Solapur Junction at midday."

He left us, shaking his head.

"Our breakfasts are prob'ly less than two rupees each," Bibbi chuckled. "He prob'ly gets a commission based on how much we order."

A week earlier I had met Bibbi at the train station in Madras. We had spent the next few days at Agnur, the American Consul General's residence, taking care of last minute preparations for our trip to the States. We got our vaccinations and World Health Card updated, and Dad made sure that the American Consulates in all our stops were informed of our itinerary.

Our first leg was twenty-four hours on a First Class Express Train to Bombay with our own sleeping compartment. We had boarded at around 8 o'clock in the evening, after a farewell supper with my parents.

A car from the consulate was to meet us at the train station in Bombay and ferry us to our hotel. Our ship, the SS Guglielmo Marconi, was leaving at three in the afternoon the next day, and would take us on the second leg of our journey to Genoa, Italy. There we would visit the Thomas Cook Travel Agency to pick up our 30-day First Class Eurailpass tickets and travel through Italy, Switzerland, France, Holland, Denmark (where we would meet up with Kris and Lyn), Austria, Germany, Belgium and England.

In London we would part ways. We had different flights back to the States, one of the few parts of our trip that we had not been able to coordinate with each other.

We all swore to keep in touch and meet up when we could, and for nearly sixty years, we did.

Dramatis Personae   (Pictures from the Year Books)

The Legacy

John Coleman

Mary Coleman

The Hikers

Bibbi

Charlie

Linwood

Dave

Some of the Boys

Lyn

Kris

Narain

Phil

Mike

Leslie

Some of the Girls

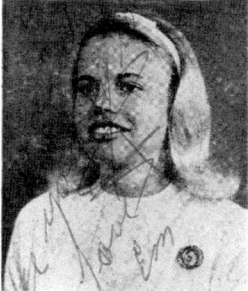
Emmy

Carolyn

Maureen

Rani

Barbie

Chellie

Cathy

Irene

Bonnie

Some of the Staff

Mr. Krause

Mr. Root

Mr. Cassady

Mr. Neufeld

Mrs. Mitchell

Mr. Reimer

Mr. Amstutz

Miss Franz

Mrs. Putz

Afterword

I wasn't planning to write a book. I had thought about writing a story about our hike to Manjampatti as a short anecdote to read at our celebration for my dear friend, Bob Coleman (Bibbi) after he died tragically from a biking accident. But the thoughts and emotions stirred up by his death kept bubbling out, made even more vivid by the forced isolation of the pandemic. I was continuously reminded of what a special and privileged period of my life I had spent in his company, and how important he was to the way I looked at life and approached the hurdles that it threw before me.

I have always felt that, in my heart and in my outlook on life, I am still that teenage boy of nearly sixty years ago. My sense of humor, my exuberance, is still as adolescent, even though I try to disguise it from the people who share my adult and professional life with me... even, to a certain extent, from my family.

One of the joys of attending Kodai School's annual reunions is that I get to revert freely to my teenage persona. The disguise comes off, the reserve is shed. I am once again the awkward, fun-loving kid I was back then, but without the shyness or the acne that used to plague me. True, I can't move around as agilely as I could. I'm growing a belly and losing my hair. But in this company, we all seem to see each other as we were. We see through the aging shells to our adolescent avatars hidden beneath. We reminisce, we share the music and the meals of bygone days, and we are rejuvenated.

These reunions provide a comfortable setting to hark back and relive old times and adventures. Often, just a comment or even a phrase is enough to resuscitate an old memory. *Blue flame, Hotel State, Watch out for the leeches, Diplomatic passport*, are phrases sure to bring back long ago experiences among my school buddies and start conversations recounting old times.

Over the years, Bibbi attended almost every annual Kodai School Reunion, which takes place over the Labor Day weekend. For many years the Reunion was held in Ohio, near Columbus, at a camp called Agape. I attended several of those Reunions, most notably the ones that occurred ten and twenty years after our class's graduation from Kodai. Bibbi was always there. When the Reunion venue shifted to Camp Kirchenwald, near Harrisburg, Pennsylvania, Bibbi attended every one, becoming the Treasurer and Bill Collector.

Between-times, Bibbi and I would often touch base with each other. When landlines and long distance charges ruled, our contacts were more sporadic and kept short. As cell phones, text messaging and email emerged, our communications became more regular and informative. He loved to call friends as he drove from his home in Sarasota to a property he was developing near Asheville, North Carolina. It was a nine or ten hour drive, so if he called, it was to pass time with you, and it was a good idea to find a comfortable chair for the duration. There were a number of us who were privileged to receive these calls.

In the year 2001, our thirty-fifth anniversary of graduation, I left my business career behind and became a school teacher, which freed up my time around the Labor Day weekend, and I began to attend regularly. Bibbi and I shared room and board when I attended and spent our time much as we had as roommates and soulmates in Kodai: talking, telling jokes, reminiscing about our adventures. We didn't always remember all the details, but together we were able to reconstruct most of the events that I retell in this book.

In 2016, our class celebrated its fiftieth anniversary, and eleven of us traveled to Kodai, spending five days at Villa Retreat at the end of Coaker's Walk, and another five touring Tamilnadu state in a private tour bus. I met up with Bibbi in Madras (Chennai), where we shared a room at the Boat Club for a night before taking the Express Train from Egmore station to Madurai. Unlike the old days, the train was air conditioned, but you could still stand in the passage between two cars and hang out the open door and watch the countryside roll by. As we did this, watching the villages and rice paddies slide by, Bibbi and I felt the intervening years slipping away.

Kodaikanal is now a messy, overpopulated and overdeveloped township. Many of the places we walked to, like Dolphin's Nose, Pillar Rocks and Silver Cascade are now tourist stops with tea stalls and tourist shops selling kitschy souvenirs, shaved ice and cotton candy. Others, like Mount Perumal, are only accessible with a special permit and accompanying guide. Permits to visit Mount Perumal were not available while we were there because of a tiger sighting in the area. The Lake, polluted by mercury from a thermometer factory in the '80's, is fenced off, and swimming is prohibited. The Boat Club is still renting punts, but you are warned not to fall in the water. In our day, it was rare to see monkeys or bison in Kodaikanal Township, but bison wander freely through the town now, and monkeys throng and beg insistently for handouts at tourist stops.

There are, however, islands amidst the chaos that remind us of how it was when we were there. The School campus is arguably the most constant of these islands, with some new buildings around the edges, but with all the old ones intact and aging well. Coaker's Walk, though now fenced and gated, and Villa Retreat, with their unobstructed views to Mount Perumal and the Plains below are another, if you overlook the brightly colored shacks and houses festooning the nearby hillsides. There are a lot more people walking through Bryant Park, but it is still a peaceful place to sit and talk. Poombari and Lake Berijam, like Mount Perumal, have been preserved by limiting access with permits and fences. The Budge has been 'updated' with 'modern conveniences' such as ATM's, a Domino's Pizza and a KFC masquerading as HFC (Hilltop Fried Chicken).

However, much of the old, entrepreneurial commerce still exists, with silversmiths manning their bellows, tea stalls and sweet shops offering refreshment, and although the Hotel State is gone, you can still find delicious and inexpensive Indian fare; but you have to look past the new gourmet restaurants for it.

These sights and sounds brought many of the tales recounted in this book back to life. Bibbi would point to a site and say "Remember?", and, of course, I did.

Bibbi and I revisited our adventures with each other many times, and reminded each other about details one or the other of us had forgotten or glossed over. As the years passed, some details faded and one adventure became confused with another. Bibbi sometimes thought that I had accompanied him on one trek or another, about which I had no recollection, and vice versa. We were sometimes at odds about who exactly had accompanied us, or what events had happened on which outing. There is undoubtedly some of that confusion included in my retelling, and I apologize in advance if I have placed someone in a situation in which they were not involved.

Details are another matter. I have taken significant license in reconstructing conversations and inserting details which I could not possibly remember as clearly as I have represented them. I have guessed at them in good faith, and presented them as fact. If anyone involved or named remembers them differently, I will happily defer to your recollection. This narrative embellishes and sets them out as I choose to remember them.

About the sketches… I am not an artist… obviously. However, as I was writing, images kept popping up in my head and I began to try to capture them with some colored pencils and a sketch pad I had acquired during my years as a teacher. A few of them turned out fairly well, so I scanned them in to my manuscript which I circulated to a few of my Kodai collaborators. All of them encouraged me to include the sketches in the published version, so I did.